IMAGES
of America

LINCOLN COUNTY
NORTH CAROLINA

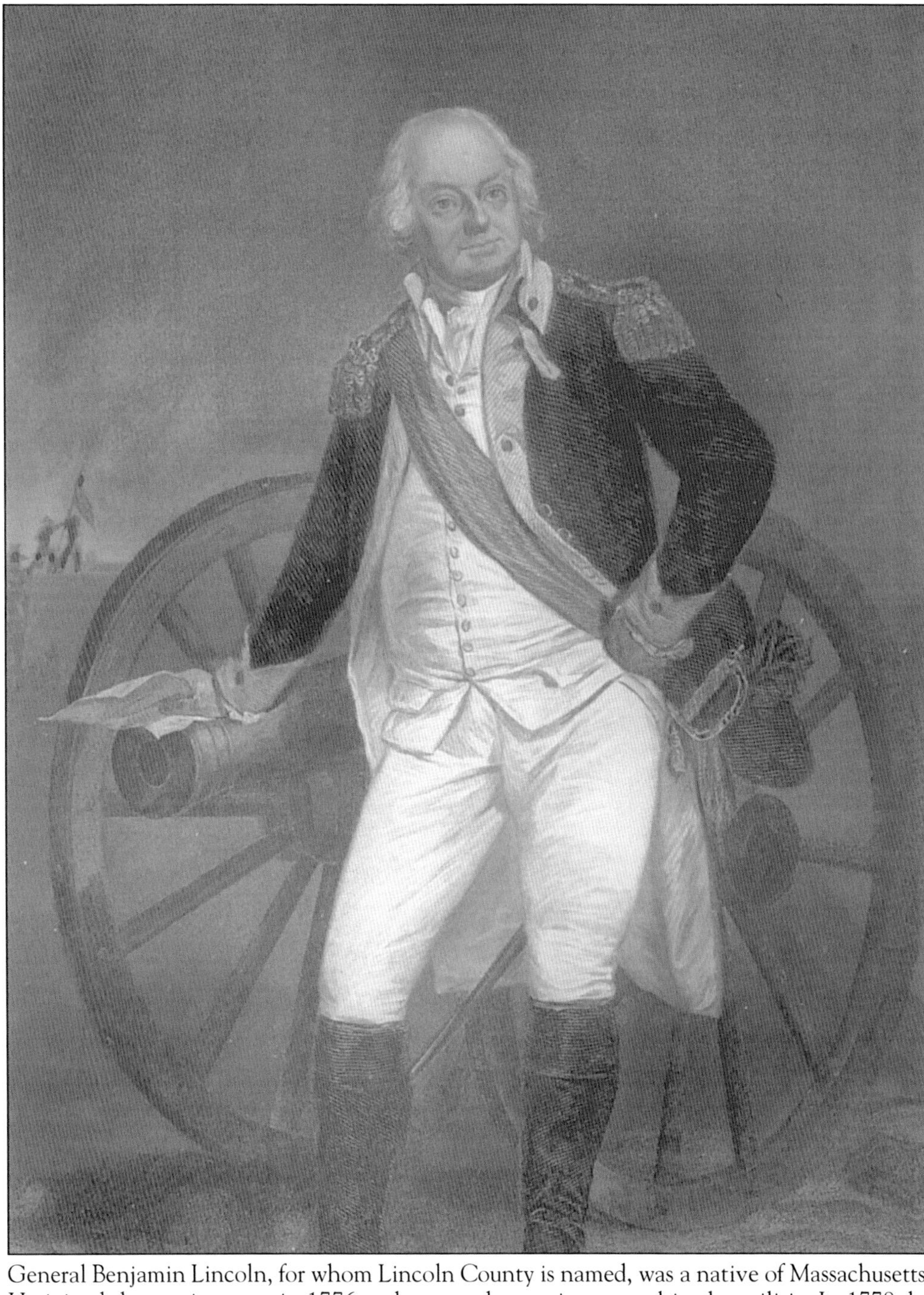

General Benjamin Lincoln, for whom Lincoln County is named, was a native of Massachusetts. He joined the patriot army in 1776 and was made a major general in the militia. In 1778, he was given chief command of the Southern Department and led the defense of Savannah and Charleston. He was in this position when Lincoln County was created in 1779. At Yorktown when the war ended, General Lincoln was selected by General George Washington to receive Cornwallis's sword. After the war ended, he served as the first national secretary of war and as lieutenant governor of Massachusetts. (Lila Friday.)

IMAGES
of America

LINCOLN COUNTY
NORTH CAROLINA

Jason Harpe
Lincoln County Historical Association

ARCADIA
PUBLISHING

ISBN 978-0-7385-0620-3

Published by Arcadia Publishing
Charleston, South Carolina

Printed in the United States of America

Library of Congress Catalog Card Number: 00-106088

For all general information contact Arcadia Publishing at:
Telephone 843-853-2070
Fax 843-853-0044
E-mail sales@arcadiapublishing.com
For customer service and orders:
Toll-Free 1-888-313-2665

Visit us on the Internet at www.arcadiapublishing.com

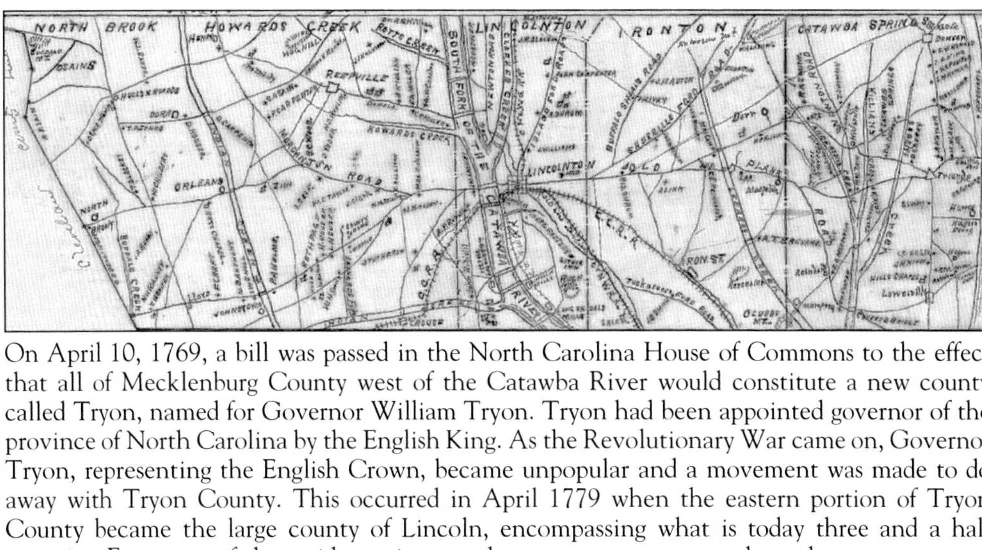

On April 10, 1769, a bill was passed in the North Carolina House of Commons to the effect that all of Mecklenburg County west of the Catawba River would constitute a new county called Tryon, named for Governor William Tryon. Tryon had been appointed governor of the province of North Carolina by the English King. As the Revolutionary War came on, Governor Tryon, representing the English Crown, became unpopular and a movement was made to do away with Tryon County. This occurred in April 1779 when the eastern portion of Tryon County became the large county of Lincoln, encompassing what is today three and a half counties. For many of the residents, it was a long way over poor roads to the county seat of Lincolnton. Often the county seat was the only trading center in a county, as well as the seat of local government. By 1840 there was considerable sentiment to divide up the county. It became a reality when Cleveland County was created from the western side of Lincoln County and the eastern side of Rutherford County in 1841. A year later, Catawba County was created out of the northern part of Lincoln County, followed by Gaston County in 1846. The divisions left for Lincoln County a strip of land 10 miles wide, about 31 miles long on the north, and some 27 miles long on the south—smaller in land area than some of the counties that had been carved from it. But the division did leave the county's 1,038 families an area rich in history and much promise for the future. (Lincoln County Museum of History.)

Contents

ACKNOWLEDGMENTS

Endeavoring to compile a complete, succinct, and comprehensive photograph history of Lincoln County with just under 230 photographs proved difficult and almost impossible. Though the Lincoln County Museum of History maintains a small collection of images, securing the intended number to represent certain sections of our story required the help of local individuals and organizations and from institutions in various parts of North Carolina. Without their interest and support in sharing the necessary material, this project would never have reached completion.

Extra special thanks to Bill Beam, Ann Dellinger, and David C. Heavner for their guidance, patience, and unwavering dedication to the preservation and promotion of Lincoln County history. Their extensive knowledge proved invaluable as I called on them for suggestions, proofreading, and objectivity throughout this entire process.

Those who so graciously loaned images and material to this publication include Martha Abernethy, Bill Beam, Elwyn and Barbara Beam, Houser Beam, Terry Brotherton, Ann Brown, Margaret Camelo, Sid Carpenter, Nelda Cashion, Josephine Childers, Mike Cline, Clara Cooper, Faye Craig, Jack and Estelle Cronland, Bobby Padgett Crowell, Frances Crowell, Jack Dellinger, Margaret Dellinger, G. Wayne Finger, Ann Ford, Allen Freeman, Lila Friday, Buddy Funderburk, Larry Gilbert, Linda Graham, Jim Hallman, Frances Hampton, Dr. James L. Haney, John Hauss, Paul Haynes, David C. Heavner, Gene Heavner, Patrick Houser, Sidney Houser, John Hoyle, Guyann Johnson, Richard Jonas, Bob Keener, Larry and Diane Leatherman, Bill and Joanna Lentz, Edward Little, Joe and Ruth Leonard, Edith Lomax, Robert Long, Jim Love, James Lutz, Reverend Mary McKey of First Presbyterian Church of Lincolnton, Leroy Magness, Ermintrude Mullen, North Carolina Cooperative Extension Service-Lincoln Chapter, Vassey Page, Avis Peeler, Eleanor Rodd Porter, Sue Ramseur, Mary Ramsey, Miriam Robinson, Betty Ross, Hunter and Ruby Rudisill, Robert Rudisill, Kristie Saine, Teresa Schwab, Jack and Ellen Shuford, Katie McIntosh Sigmon, Mercer and Peggy Simmons, Joyce Stroup, Al Tate, Mrs. Dave Warlick, Marie Whitener, and Sarah Yoder.

I also appreciate the help and cooperation from Jennifer Bean, Museum of Early Southern Decorative Arts (MESDA), Winston-Salem, NC; Stephen Massengill, North Carolina Department of Archives and History, Raleigh, NC; The North Carolina Collection, UNC Chapel Hill Library, Chapel Hill, NC; and the Southern Historical Collection, Wilson Library, UNC Chapel Hill, Chapel Hill, NC.

Lastly, I would like to thank Mark Berry for his patience and professionalism in ensuring the successful delivery of this publication.

Introduction

Lincoln County is situated in the southwestern portion of North Carolina's Piedmont region. The county's boundaries, encompassing 305 square miles, extend in the form of a long rectangle measuring 30 miles in length and 10 miles wide. Bordered by the Catawba River to the east, Cleveland County to the west, Gaston County to the south, and Catawba County to the north, Lincoln County's landscape contains a rolling terrain full of gentle streams and creeks with natural resources that enrich the area's environment and contribute to economic development.

As early as the mid-18th century, settlers from areas of Pennsylvania, Maryland, Virginia, and South Carolina, primarily of the German and Scotch-Irish persuasion, flocked to this area to take advantage of the inexpensive land and rich farmland prevalent in the Carolina backcountry. Traversing the rugged terrain of the Blue Ridge Mountains and the Staunton River Gap along the "Great Philadelphia Wagon Road," these immigrants established their settlements throughout Lincoln County. On their trip, they brought traces of their native homelands in the forms of speech, behavior, religious beliefs, art, and written and oral traditions.

The Scotch-Irish populated much of the eastern portion of present-day Lincoln County near Beatties Ford, while most Germans chose to inhabit land to the west of these settlements. These early settlers took up the task of establishing communities by building sufficient homes, churches, and schools to build a strong communal environment and a life with which to nurture the growth of their progeny.

Throughout Lincoln County's storied past, its inhabitants have endured the trials of war, economic depression, political and social upheaval, and growth and expansion. Signs of these triumphs and disasters line and dot the landscape, and they provide a lore that reflects the industrious and resilient nature of those who came before us to lay the foundation on which the county has evolved. Among this group were doctors, lawyers, farmers, preachers, professors, carpenters, masons, potters, and businessmen who maintained a level of vitality, tenacity, determination, and courage in facing the discouragements of life.

The evidence supporting the early pioneers' existence is manifested in the form of court dockets, journals, letters, memoirs, deeds, and visual images. We consult these sources for an understanding, comprehension, and appreciation of our heritage, as well as a guide by which to face many of the same adversities of life as our ancestors encountered. Whether captured by an itinerant painter or developed in a lab, these images provide a unique insight or glimpse of our past, and unlock the endless possibilities inherent in their place in time. Many times locked away in an attic, cellar, cedar chest, or deteriorating photo album, they provide some of life's fundamental truths and present a candid look at "men and women who today are tomorrow's history."

This pictorial history covers only a small portion of Lincoln County's past. It is segmented at best and contains images that span a time period from around 1790 to the 1950s. I employed a nonjudgmental selection process that entailed many hours of scrutiny and examination. Due to space limitations, only 224 photographs were accommodated from a slate of just under 500. The criterion for inclusion was based upon subject matter, location in the county, and clarity. The goal and mission of this work is not to present a comprehensive local history, which would be futile, but rather to bring into focus the need for discussion in the areas of documentation and preservation of Lincoln County's pictorial past. I began the project with the intention of challenging citizens of the county to pull out old family photographs and begin to write the names of those pictured and the stories that correspond. This publication should lay the groundwork for this process of recognition and awareness and cause the younger generation to consult with their elders to gain a better understanding of the common past we all share. As a result, we all can respect and promote the rich and time-honored history that exists in our backyard.

This book represents the Lincoln County Historical Association and Lincoln County Museum of History's dedication to fulfilling its mission of collecting, preserving, and presenting the county's past. It is my hope that the questions surrounding the identity of the individuals, buildings, and settings in this book will be answered by individuals who know and care to share important information.

Jason L. Harpe
September 2000

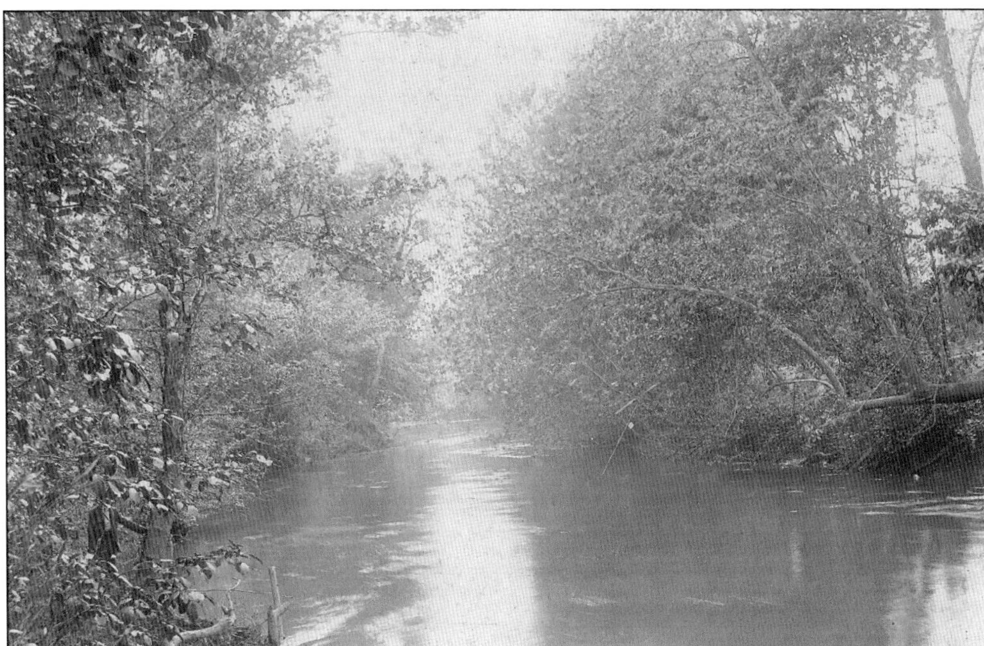

Trees provide shade from the banks of the South Fork, formed from Henry's Fork and Jacob's Fork, which runs through Lincoln County as a tributary of the Catawba River. (Lincoln County Museum of History.)

One

County Seat Lincolnton

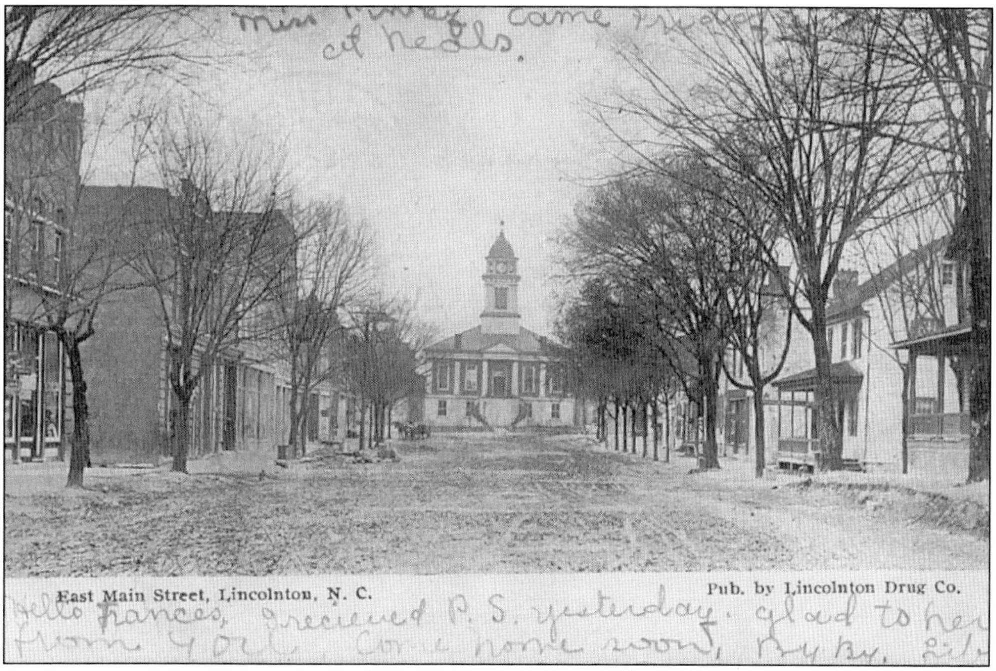

At the turn of the 20th century, the streets were unpaved but substantial buildings lined the first several blocks of East Main Street in downtown Lincolnton. There were department stores, hardware stores, and other specialty stores. By 1910, there were two banks, two railroad depots, a post office, a high school, a hospital, and churches of all major denominations. For persons needing their services, there was a good supply of lawyers and doctors. Two newspapers were published weekly. There was a host of boardinghouses and two full-service hotels. (Lincoln County Museum of History.)

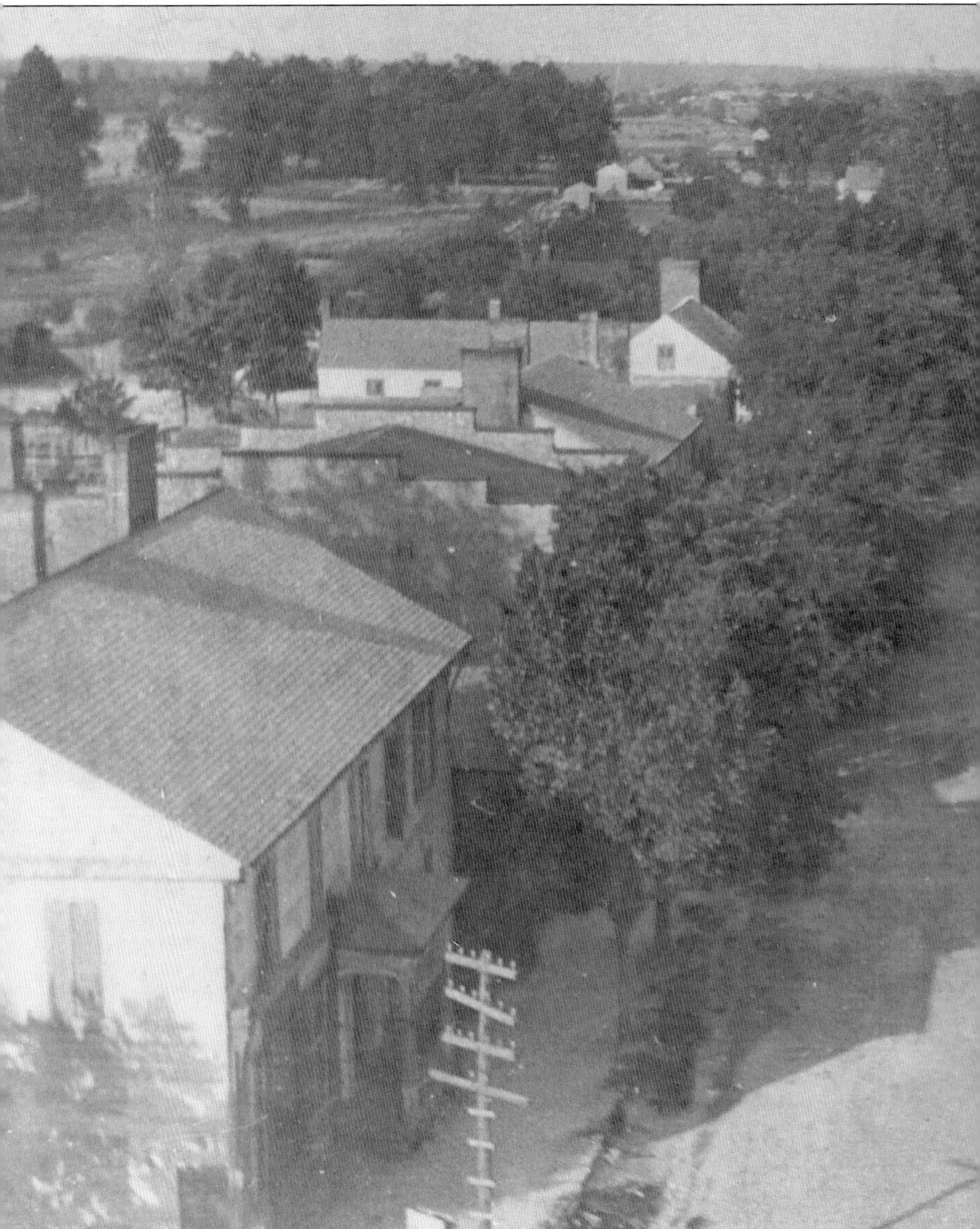

A photograph taken during the first decade of the 20th century affords an opportunity at a bird's-eye view from the courthouse up East Main Street. The large oak trees line the unpaved streets as far as can be seen. The large house situated on the left corner was owned by Captain

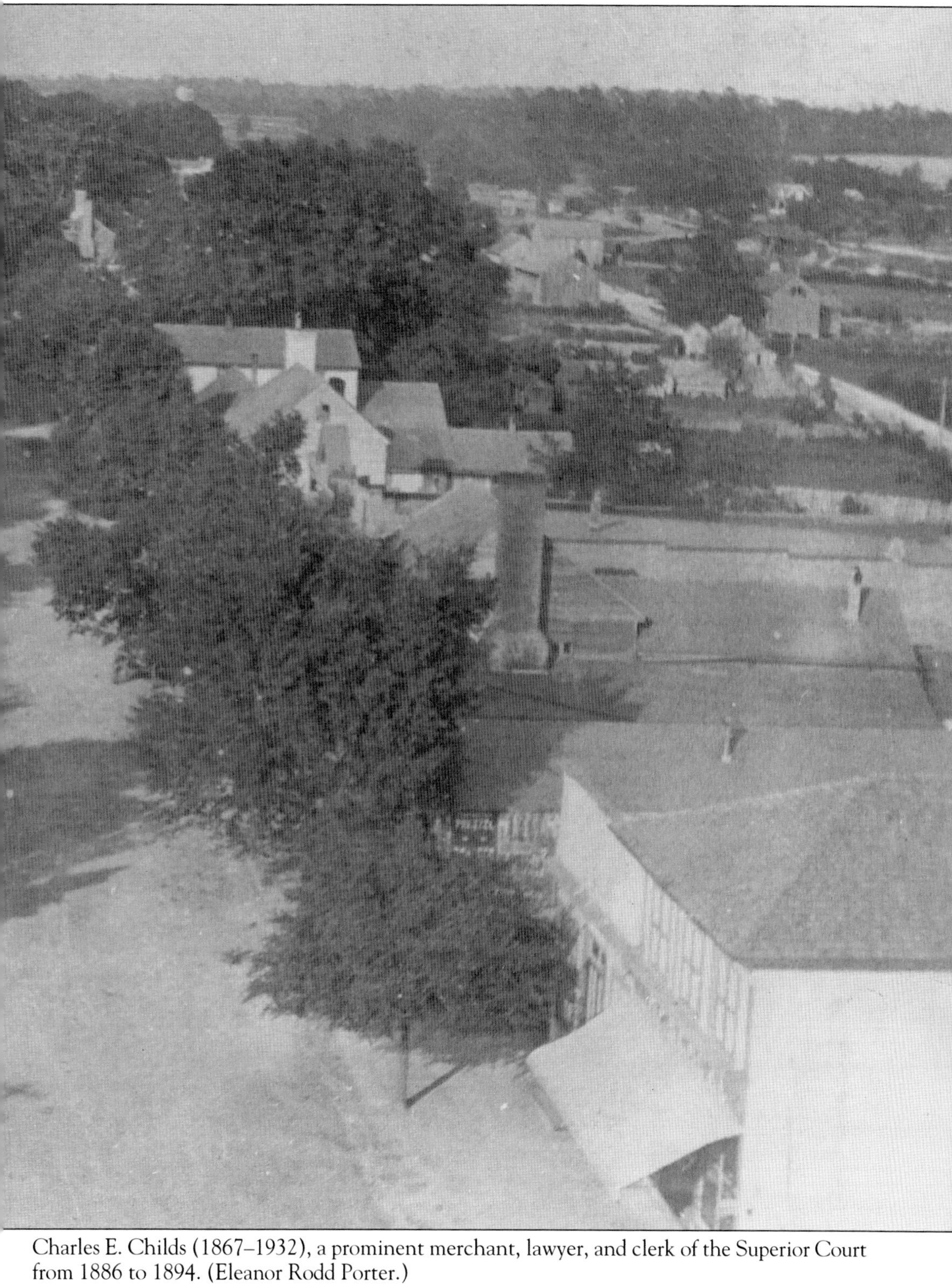

Charles E. Childs (1867–1932), a prominent merchant, lawyer, and clerk of the Superior Court from 1886 to 1894. (Eleanor Rodd Porter.)

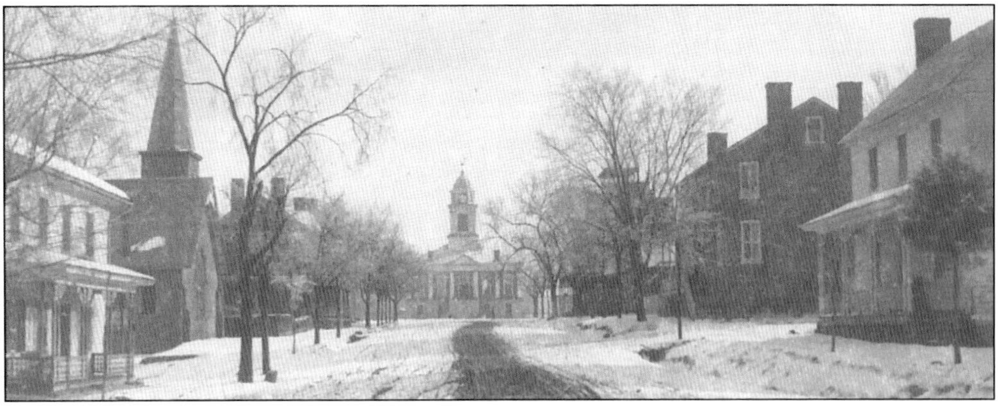

Looking east along West Main Street, Lincolnton's fourth courthouse, serving the county from 1855 until 1921, stands as the center of the county's activities. Some of the buildings that line West Main before the street was paved include (left or north side) the Dr. Brown House, later occupied by Dr. Pressley; First Presbyterian Church; David Ramsaur-Colonel John F. Phifer-Abernethy House; and the Reinhardt Building. On the right or south side visible are the Finch House, the Dr. Augustus McLean House, and the North State Hotel. Not visible are the Heavner boardinghouse and the Dr. Wise House. During the War between the States, Mary Boykin Chestnut, whose husband was a member of Jefferson Davis's Confederate cabinet, stayed at the Dr. McLean House. (Lincoln County Museum of History.)

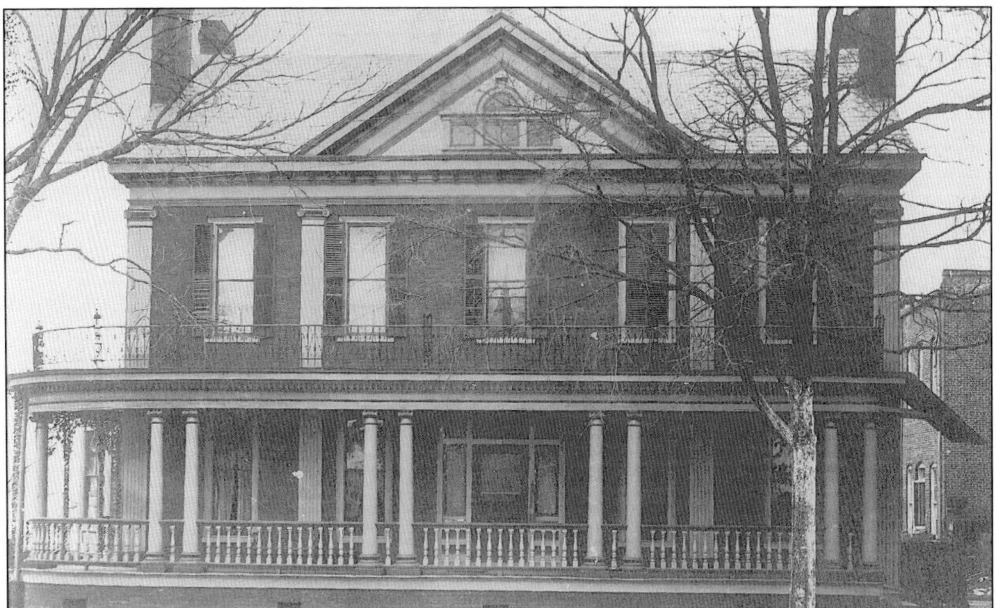

The Phifer-Abernethy house exhibits an architectural flare with its wrap-around porch, Corinthian pilasters, and denticulated triangular pediment. Built in 1820 by David Ramsour, grandson of pioneer Diedrich, the house was bought by Colonel John Fulenwider Phifer on June 8, 1842, for $4,000 from his father-in-law's estate after his marriage to David Ramsour's daughter, Elizabeth Caroline, in 1839. While occupying this house, the Phifer family mourned the death of two sons serving the Confederacy and saw Union troops under General John Palmer set up headquarters in their house in 1865. The house was razed in the 1970s for use as a park for the First Presbyterian Church. (John Hoyle.)

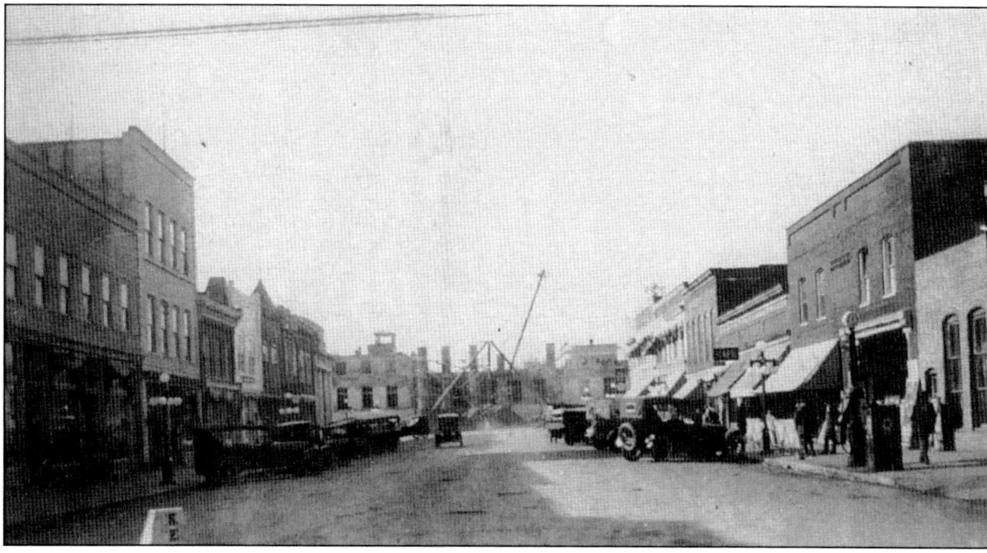

Representative Edgar Love introduced a bill to the state legislature in 1919 that directed the Lincoln County commissioners to erect a new courthouse. The old courthouse was vacated in May 1921 and torn down. It was completed in June 1923 and the first court held in it convened July 16, 1923, with Judge James L. Webb presiding. Alfred Nixon, the clerk, had prepared an interesting history of the courts and court buildings of the past which was read by his son, Joseph R. Nixon, followed by an appropriate address by Associate Justice of the Supreme Court William Alexander Hoke. (Linda Graham.)

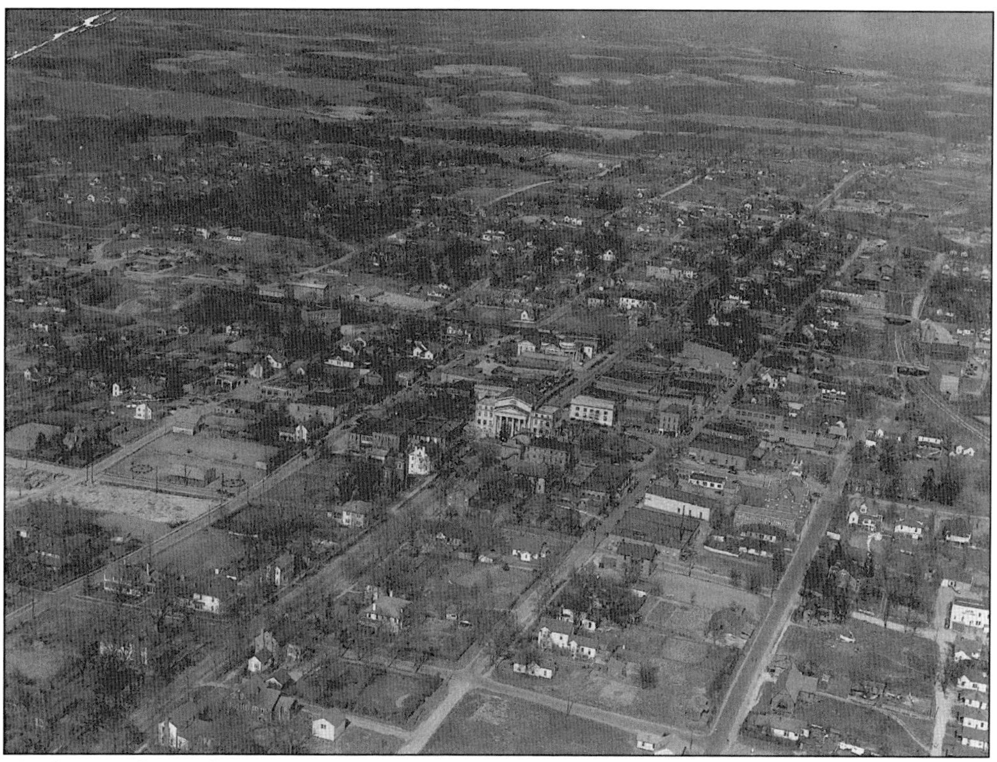

The layout of Lincolnton is visible in this aerial photograph taken in the 1940s. (Mike Cline.)

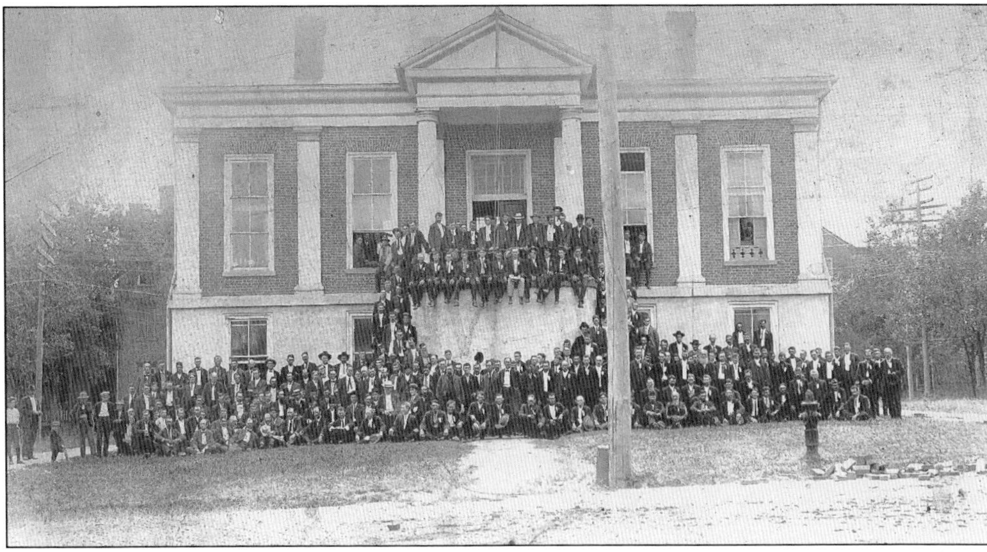

Adorning the courthouse lawn and steps, a group poses for a moment as they meet in Lincolnton for a Farmer's Day or Farmer's Institute program before the turn of the 20th century. These programs, instituted in 1885 by the North Carolina General Assembly and assigned to the Department of Agriculture, were designed to bring scientific agricultural education to local farmers. (Lincoln County Museum of History.)

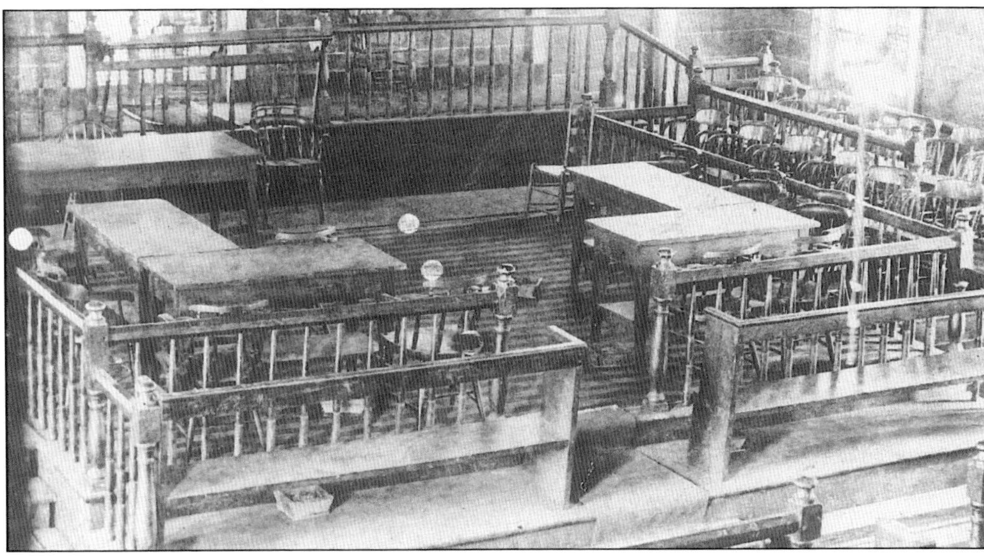

When the Town of Lincolnton was chartered in 1785, county officials were to erect a courthouse and jail on the public square. Collecting sufficient taxes to do so was a chronic problem, but by 1789 the courtsquare was graced with a two-story courthouse, although the interior remained unfinished until the mid-1790s. In 1798 a jail, stocks, and whipping post were added to the south lawn of the courtsquare. In 1809 a new brick courthouse was erected on the public square, followed in 1816 by a new brick jail, which was again erected on the south lawn of the public square. In 1848 the jail location was changed from the public square to lot #17 Southwest and a new jail was built. In 1853 work began on a new brick courthouse, again to be located on the public square. This courthouse was demolished on May 12, 1921, and was replaced by the present building.

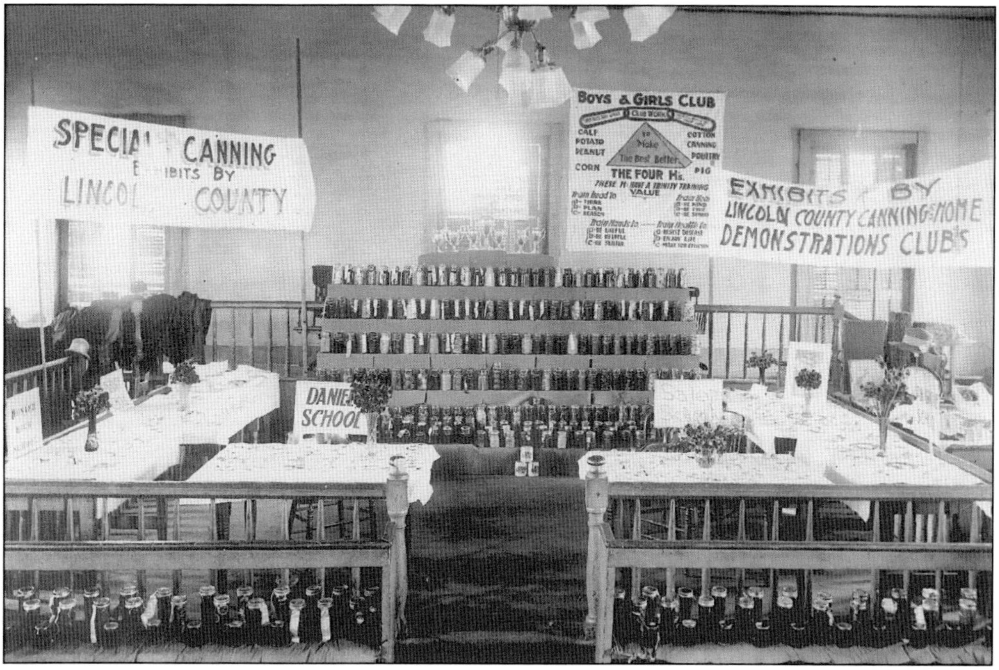

The Lincoln County Canning and Home Demonstrations Clubs in schools throughout the county contributed to this special exhibit that occupied the benches in the old Lincoln County Courthouse. The boy's club, known as the "Corn Club," began in 1909 with the appointment of a farm agent, and the girl's club started in 1912 as the "Tomato Club." The boys learned to grow corn and improve yields, while the girls learned canning techniques. (North Carolina Cooperative Extension–Lincoln Center.)

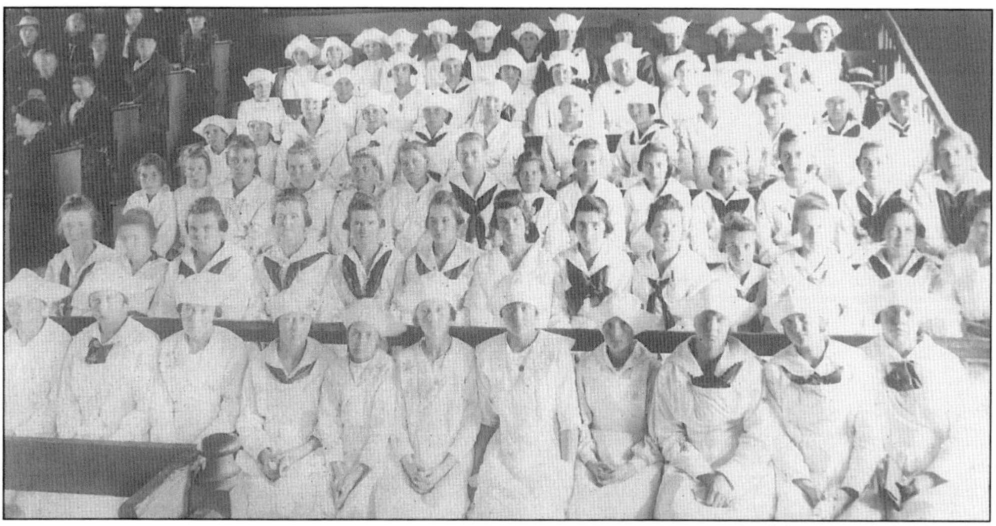

The girls of the "Tomato Club" sit in the courtroom in their 4-H uniforms as friends and family attend to view their canning exhibit. From its beginnings as the aforementioned club, the Home Extension service has used three other names: the Lincoln County Home Demonstrations Club, Lincoln County Extension Homemaker's, and its current name, the Lincoln County Extension and Community Association. (North Carolina Cooperative Extension–Lincoln Center.)

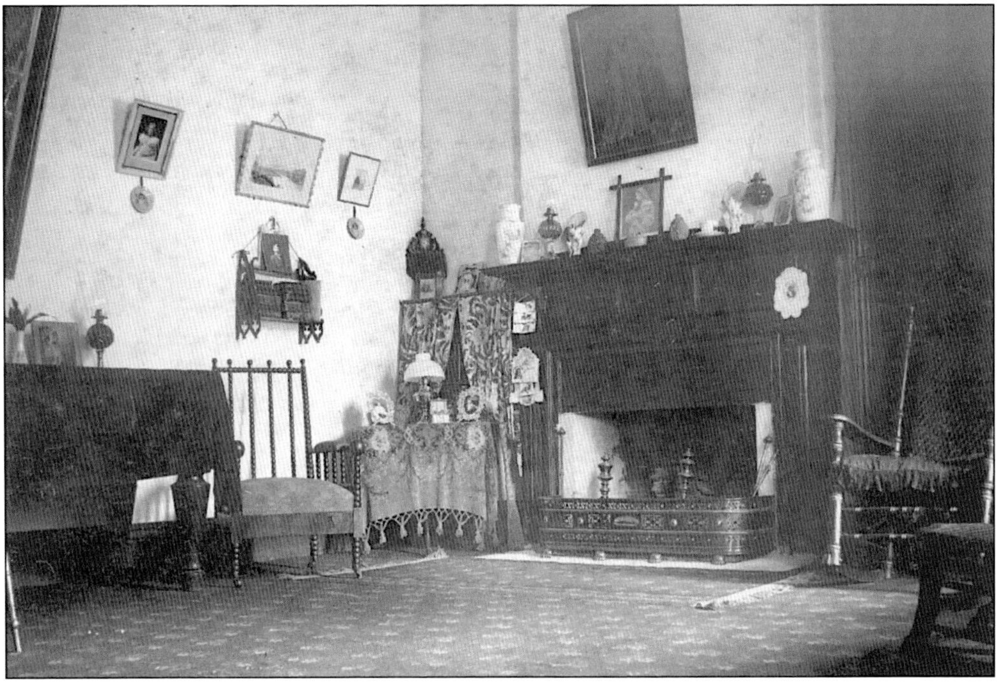

In this 1890s image, there is a quiet elegance evident in the furnishings of this parlor in the John Hoke House, which graced the northeast corner of Lincolnton's courtsquare. (Lincoln County Museum of History.)

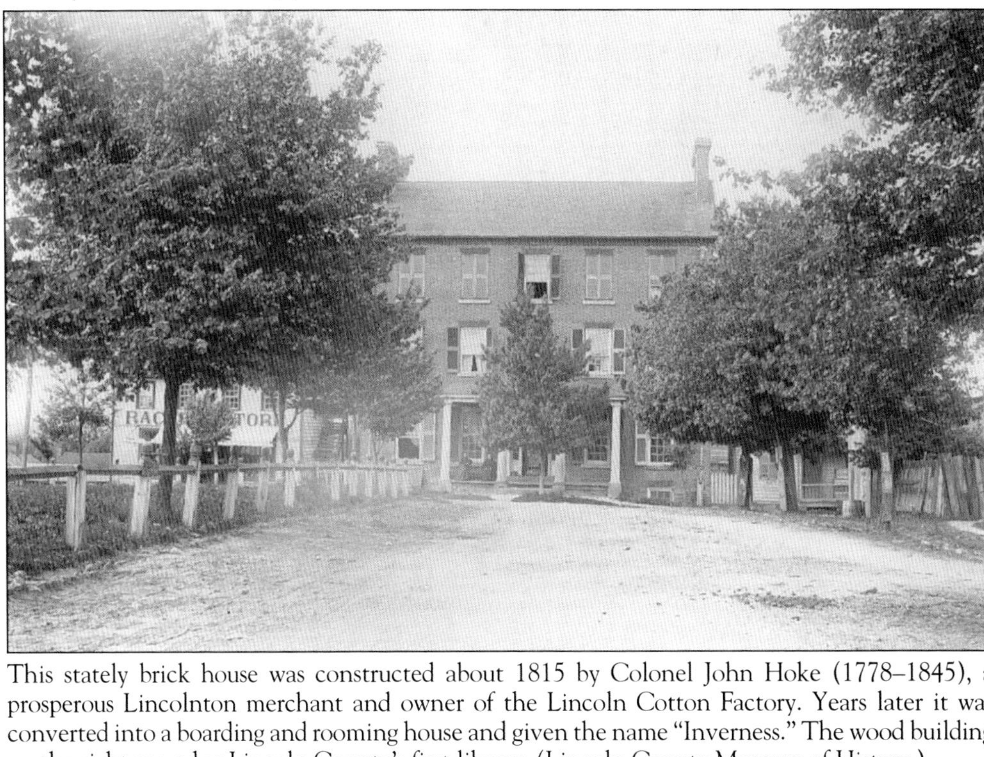

This stately brick house was constructed about 1815 by Colonel John Hoke (1778–1845), a prosperous Lincolnton merchant and owner of the Lincoln Cotton Factory. Years later it was converted into a boarding and rooming house and given the name "Inverness." The wood building on the right served as Lincoln County's first library. (Lincoln County Museum of History.)

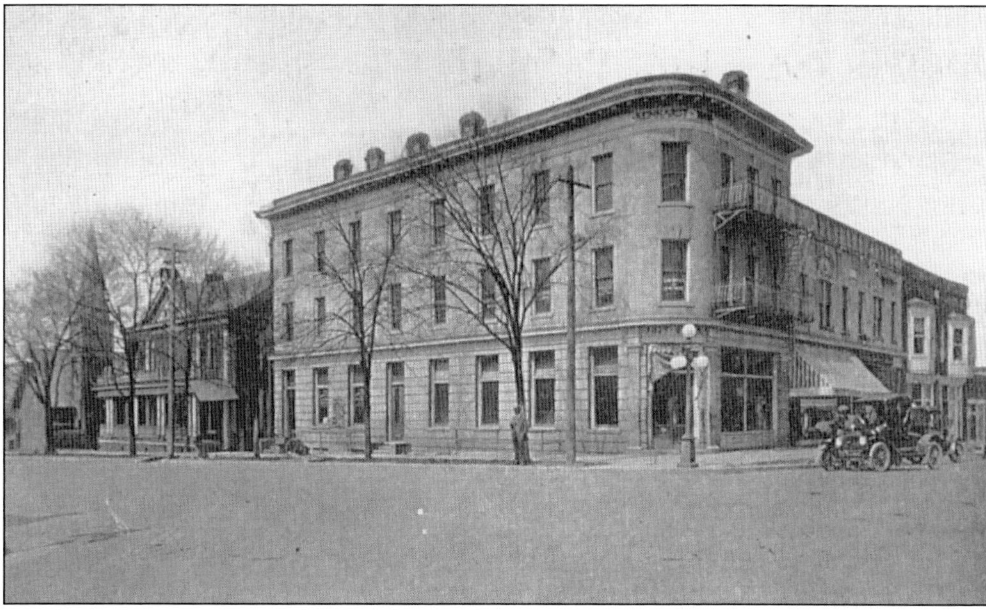

Typifying the Beaux-Arts school of design, the front section of the Reinhardt Building stands as the only example of this style in Lincoln County. Henry A. Kistler (1864–1928) built the front section for Robert S. Reinhardt (1858–1925) in 1909, with additions made during the next couple of years to extend the building down the block to meet West Sycamore Street. The Reinhardt block has been the home of the Lincolnton Post Office, Warlick and Barkley Furniture, Western Union, Hovis Grocery Co., and the *Lincoln Times*. (David C. Heavner.)

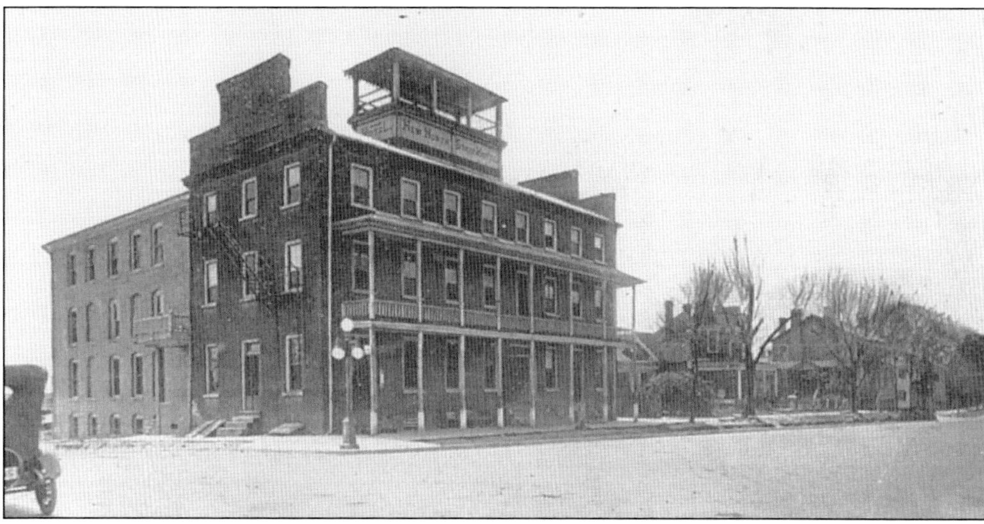

The North State Hotel, originally named the Motz Hotel, once graced the southwest corner of the courtsquare. During the turbulent years of the War between the States until 1867, Reverend Samuel Lander conducted a boarding school for girls here called the Lincolnton Seminary. Judge Theodore and Mrs. Caroline Mays Brevard succeeded Lander upon his selection for the presidency of Davenport College in Lenoir. Thomas Alva Edison checked into the hotel in 1906 along with a party of four gentlemen (his son Charles, son-in-law J.V. Miller, and two mechanics) during their trip from West Orange, New Jersey, prospecting for cobalt. (Lincoln County Museum of History.)

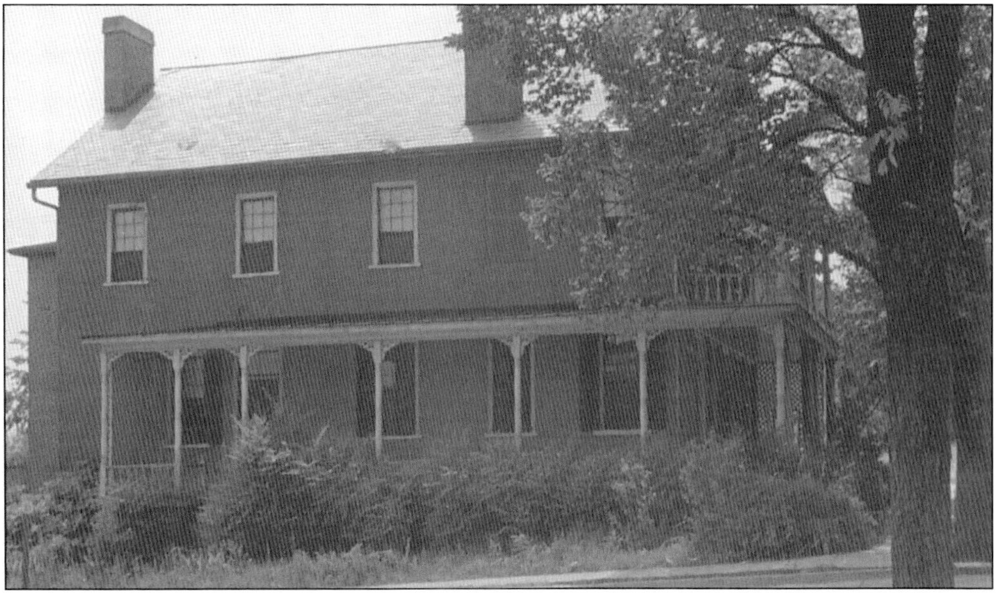

This undated photograph shows the northeast corner of a house that once stood on lot #13 in the southwest square of Lincolnton. The house was erected by Lawson Henderson as a dwelling for his son Charles Coatesworth Henderson. Lawson (1774–1843) served Lincoln County in varying capacities: sheriff, 1796–1801; clerk of County Court, 1804–1807, Superior Court clerk, 1808–1837. His son, Charles Coatesworth Henderson (1803–1870), owned a large tannery where he manufactured shoes and harnesses. He was a promoter of the old plank road, a large subscriber to stock in the old W.C.R. Railroad, and was chairman of the convention held in Lincolnton in June of 1850 favoring a plank road from Lincolnton to Charlotte. The house was razed in the 1970s, and is now used by the Emmanuel Lutheran Church as parking space. (Mrs. Dave Warlick.)

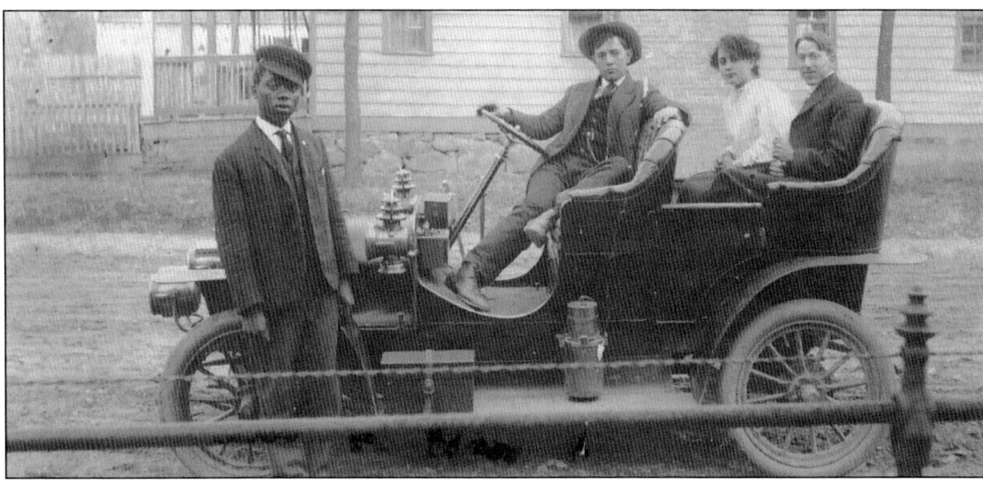

In this late-1910s photograph, Robert "Bob" Hinson lounges behind the wheel of one of Lincolnton's earliest cars while his sister, Rose Hinson Padgett, takes a back seat with an unidentified gentleman. Hinson ran Hinson's Garage in the second block of East Main Street where he sold Buicks and Pontiacs. The group is parked along South Laurel Street near the intersection with East Main Street, and the E.W. Cauble house is in view. (Bobby Padgett Crowell.)

Judge David Schenck was born in Lincolnton on March 24, 1835. He received his early education at the Pleasant Retreat Academy, along with boyhood friends Robert F. Hoke and Stephen D. Ramseur, and read law under Haywood W. Guion. He attended Pearson Law School and after graduation was licensed to practice law in County Court in 1856 and in Superior Court in 1857. On August 25, 1859, Schenck married Sallie Wilfong Ramseur, the sister of S.D. Ramseur, and the following year became the law partner of William Lander. He was elected a delegate from Lincoln County to the Constitutional Convention of 1861 to succeed Lander. In August 1874, he was elected judge of the Superior Court for the ninth judicial district (Cabarrus, Mecklenburg, Gaston, Lincoln, Cleveland, Rutherford, and Polk Counties). In 1881, he resigned the judgeship to accept the position of general counsel for the Richmond and Danville Railroad and moved to Greensboro, where he died on August 26, 1902. (Sue Ramseur.)

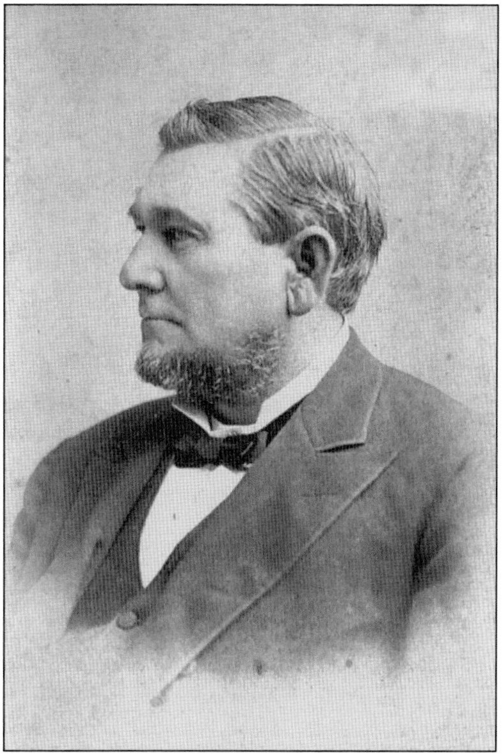

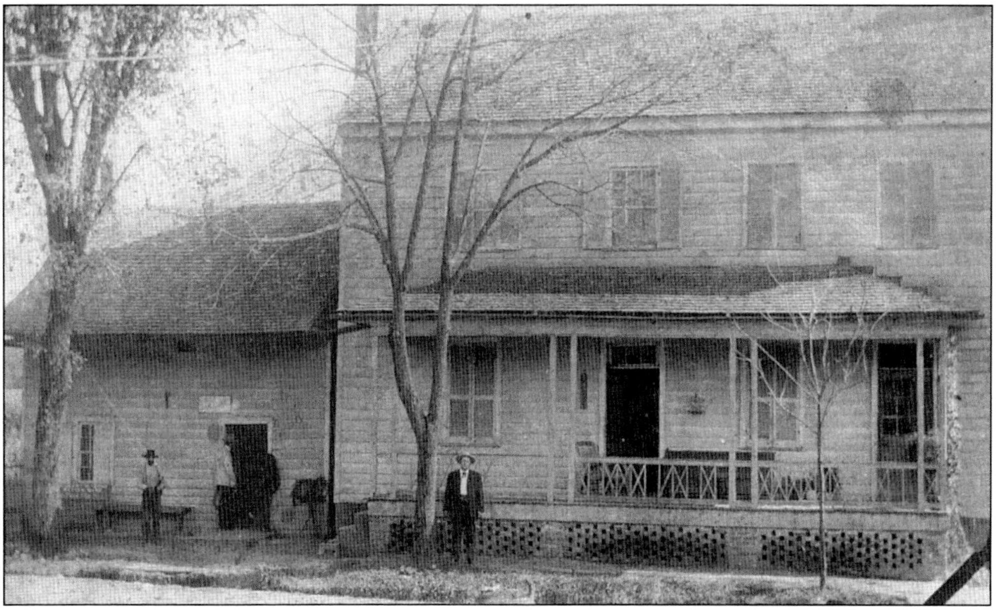

Sheriff John K. Cline stands on the front lawn of his house, built in the first quarter of the 19th century, on lot #13 in the southeast square of Lincolnton with his cobbler shop on the left. Cline served Lincoln County as sheriff (1892–1894 and 1898–1908) and as postmaster from 1914 to 1923. He purchased the house and lot in town on December 24, 1894, from Dr. Louis R. Staudenmayer for $800. In 1827, John Butts (1781–1862) resided here and ran a haberdashery in the small building beside the house. (Mike Cline.)

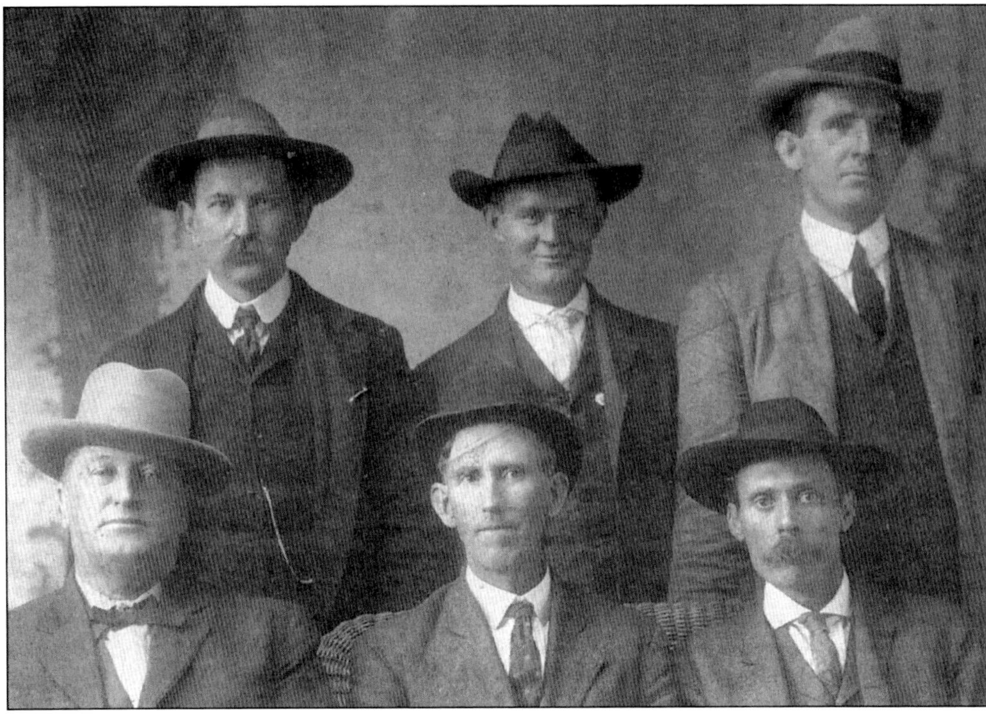

Sheriff John K. Cline, seated on the far left of the first row, and his deputies show their authority for this undated photograph. (Mike Cline.)

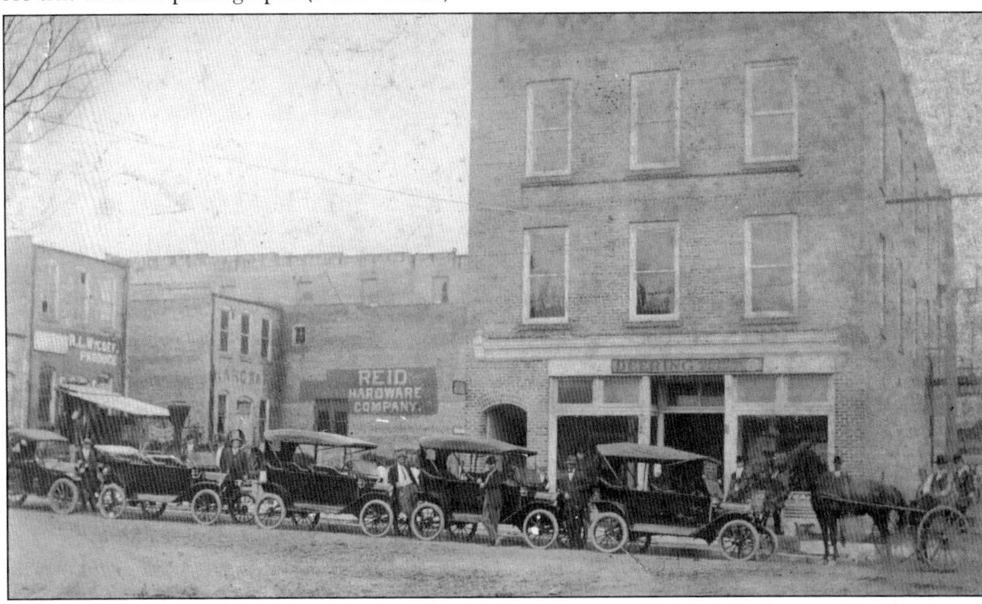

Situated on the first block in the southeast square of downtown Lincolnton, this three-story brick building bustles with activity in the early 1920s. John K. Cline, the building's owner, used the road in front of the building as a showroom for his Model T Fords. His son Guy E. Cline used a portion of the structure and bought, sold, and rented the Deering Harvesting Machines. The local Masonic order, Lincoln Lodge No. 137 A.F.&A.M., used the top two stories as a meeting hall for a number of years. (Mike Cline.)

The shade of a large oak tree casts a shadow on the southeast side of East Main Street in this photograph taken around 1900. A large sign above W.L. Lawing's clothing store advertises his "Going Out Of Business" sale: "Everything Now To Go, We Mean What We Say." Two gentlemen peek from H.E. Ramseur Hardware beyond the bank and C.E. Childs's law office. The Bank of Lincolnton, established by Captain B.F. Grigg, his son William E. Grigg, and Judge W.A. Hoke, opened on February 10, 1898, with $10,000 capital. During the early portion of the 19th century, the Michael Schenck house, the first frame house in the city of Lincolnton, stood in this block. (Mike Cline.)

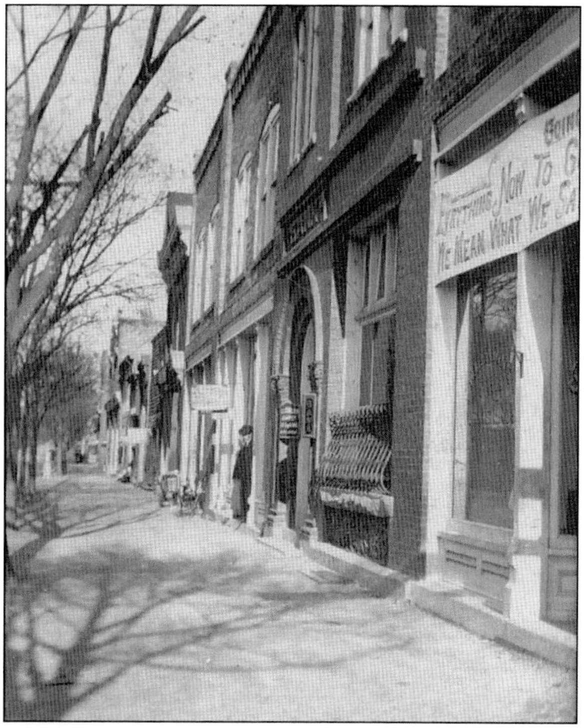

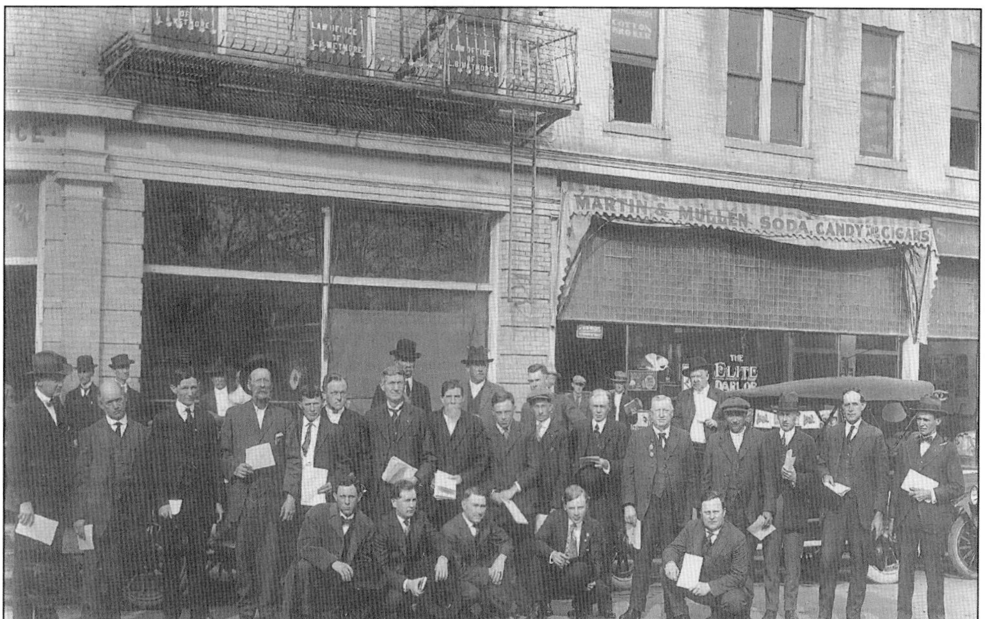

Gathered in front of the line of buildings along the northwest courtsquare, some of Lincoln County's business leaders turned out in support of the World War I fund-raising drive on June 15, 1918, the kick-off for the National War Saving Stamp Drive, conducted June 18–24, 1918. Judge J.C. Pritchard of Asheville gave an hour-long speech on the need for funds to finance the war. (Lincoln County Museum of History.)

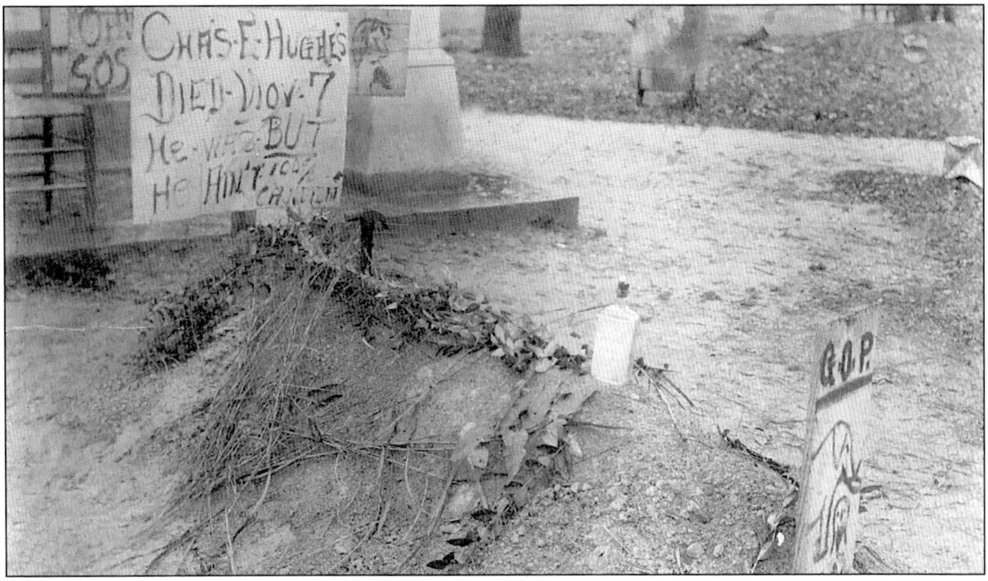

The year was 1916! The citizens of Lincolnton and Lincoln County were dealing with the tumult brought on by a number of events: war in Europe, businesses recovering from the 1914 depression, the 1916 flood, and the presidential election of 1916. This year's election pitted Woodrow Wilson, Democrat, against Charles Hughes, Republican. Wilson won by electoral votes, and the Democrats celebrated the victory with a mock burial of Charles Hughes on the courtsquare near the Confederate Monument. (David C. Heavner.)

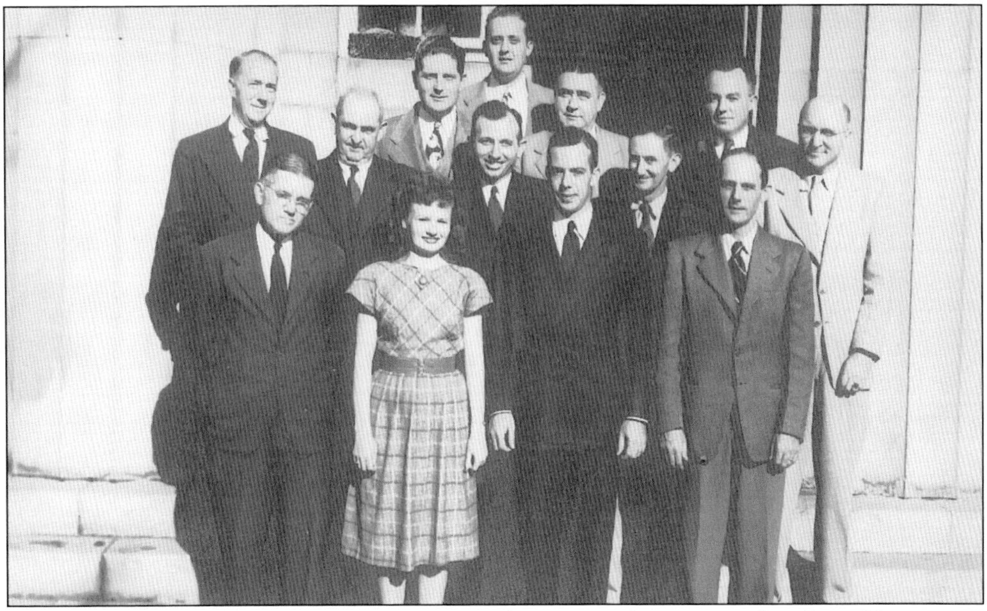

Individuals believed to be associated with Lincolnton-Lincoln County Chamber of Commerce stand on the steps of the courthouse between two of its fluted columns. They are, from left to right, as follows: (front row) Herbert Miller, unidentified, unidentified, and Henry Collins; (second row) Thorne Clark, G.L. "Shine" Goodson, Graham Morrison, and Everette Henley; (third row) B.C. Lineberger, Hubert Craig, W.C. Henderson, and Robert McNeely; (back row) Hal Hoyle Jr. (Richard Jonas.)

Son of Vardry McBee (1775–1864), Vardry Alexander McBee (April 17, 1818–February 17, 1904) was born in Lincolnton at his family's home on East Main Street and lived there his entire life. He received his primary education, as did many other young boys in the area, at the Pleasant Retreat Academy and graduated from the University of North Carolina in 1841. As a civic-minded and progressive citizen, McBee served the county three times as clerk of the Superior Court, covering a period of 14 years; represented the county in the legislature in 1861; played a major role in the construction of the old plank road from Charlotte to Lincolnton; held a position as treasurer and master of transportation for the Wilmington, Charlotte and Rutherford Railroad; and helped organize the Chester and Lenoir Railroad as director. (Lincoln County Museum of History.)

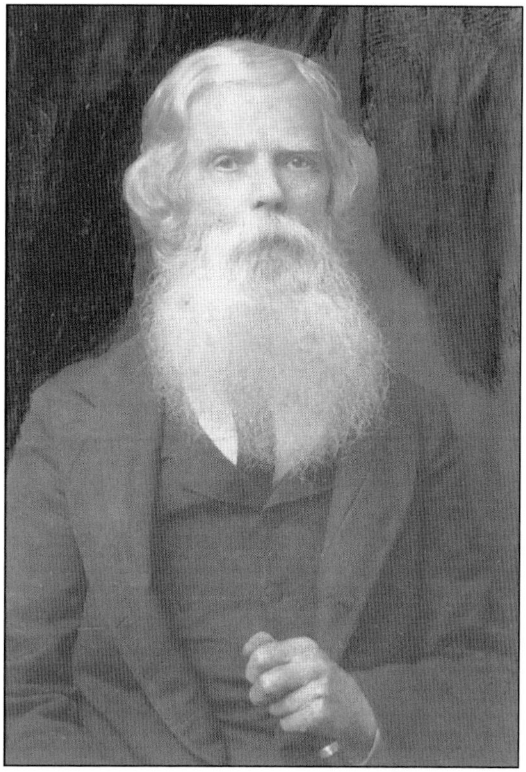

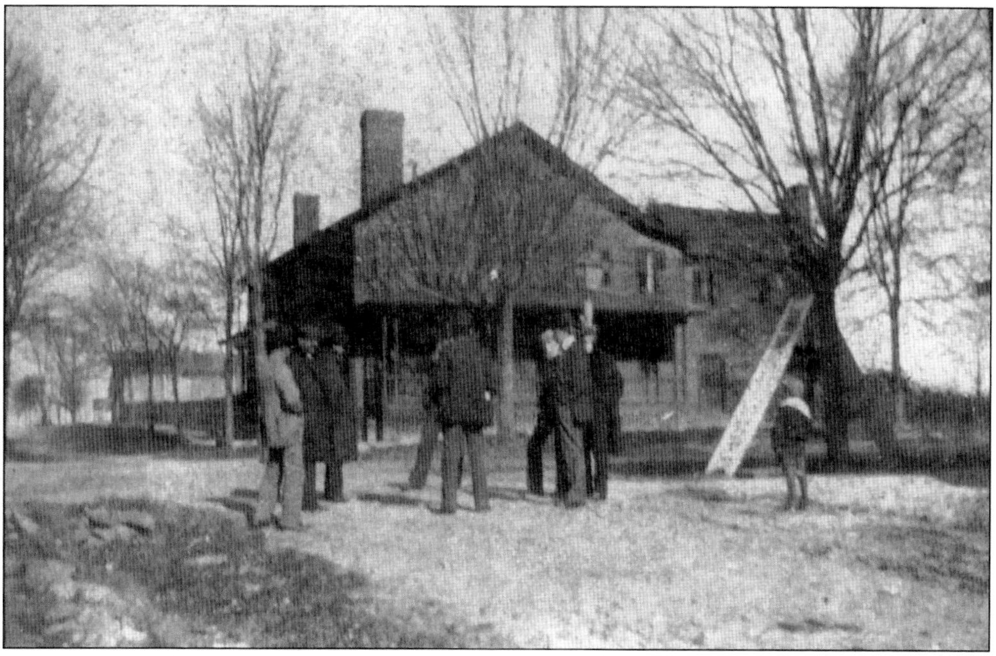

A group of gentlemen converse near East Main and Academy Streets, with Vardry Alexander McBee's house in the background. Built during the early years of the 19th century by Vardry McBee, the house was torn down in 1917 to make way for the First United Methodist Church of Lincolnton. (Mike Cline.)

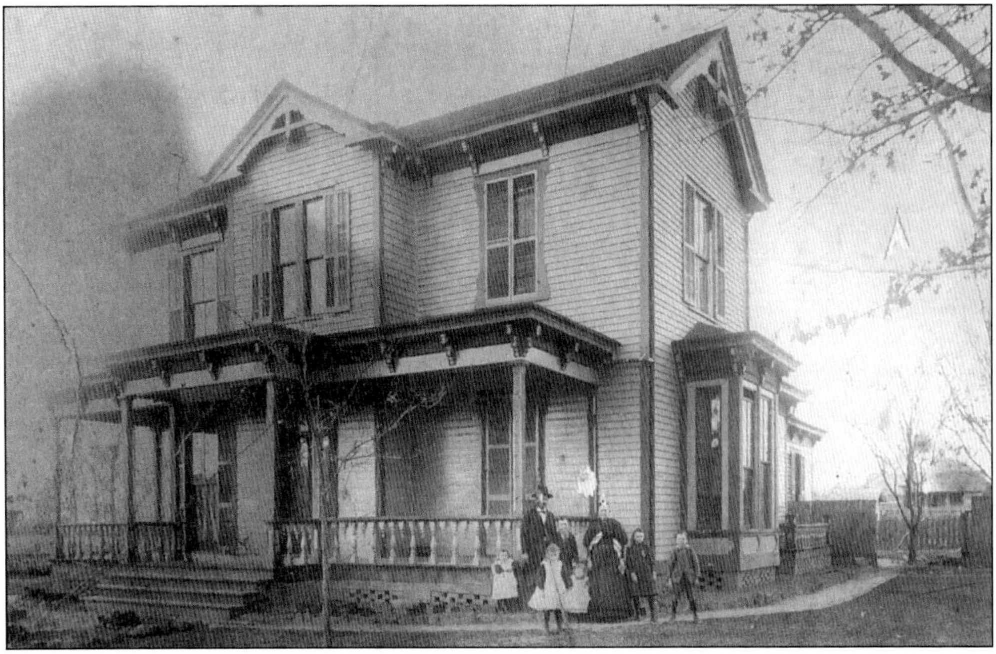

Alfred Nixon (1856–1924) served Lincoln County as an early historian; county surveyor; sheriff; superintendent of schools in the 1880s and 1890s; and clerk of Superior Court from 1898 until his death 26 years later. The Nixon House, built in 1885 on Main Street in Lincolnton, serves as a splendid backdrop for this photograph, taken in 1895. Pictured, from left to right, are Alfred Nixon, Iola Robinson Nixon, Kemp Battle Nixon (1883–1964), Lillian Rice Nixon (1885–1929), Joseph Robert Nixon (1887–1966), Annie Alberta Nixon (1889–1975), Bonnie Robinson Nixon, and Myra Nixon. (Mercer and Peggy Simmons.)

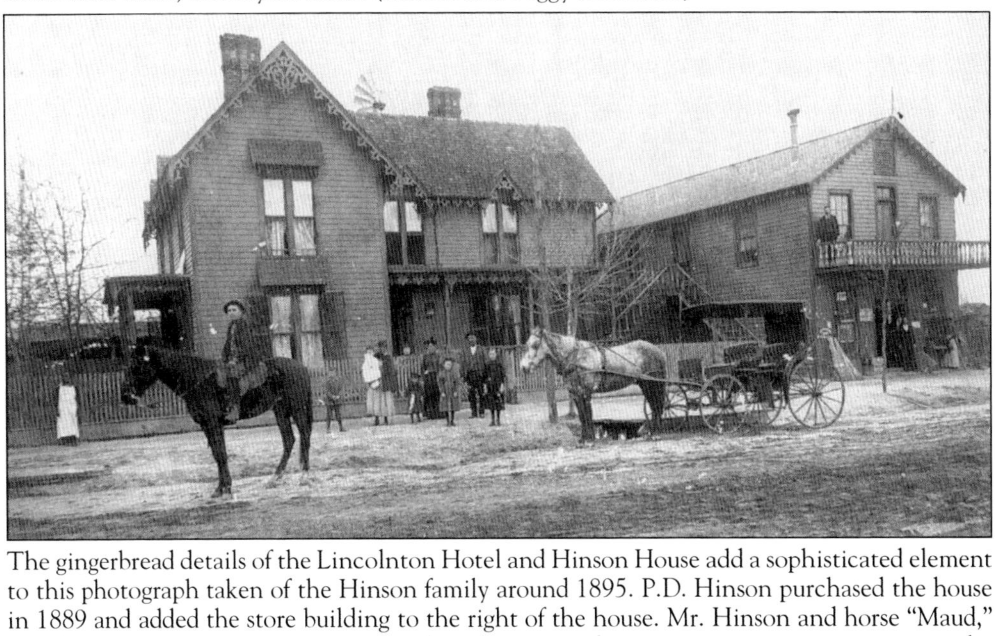

The gingerbread details of the Lincolnton Hotel and Hinson House add a sophisticated element to this photograph taken of the Hinson family around 1895. P.D. Hinson purchased the house in 1889 and added the store building to the right of the house. Mr. Hinson and horse "Maud," seen here attached to the surrey, served as the town's first jitney, meeting passengers at the depot to drive them to their destination. (Bobby Padgett Crowell.)

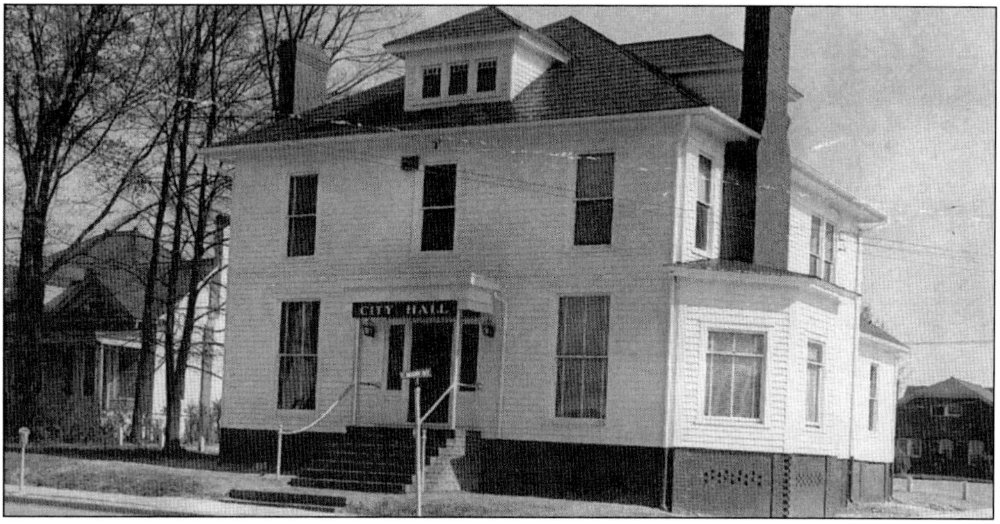

This building functioned as the home of Captain C.E. Childs until his death in 1932. Childs served as a clerk of court from 1886 until 1894, when he was licensed to practice law. From 1950 until December 14, 1970, the building at the corner of East Main and South Poplar Streets served as Lincolnton's City Hall. The new city hall welcomed in the new city offices on the anniversary of the incorporation of Lincolnton—December 14, 1785. (Allen Freeman.)

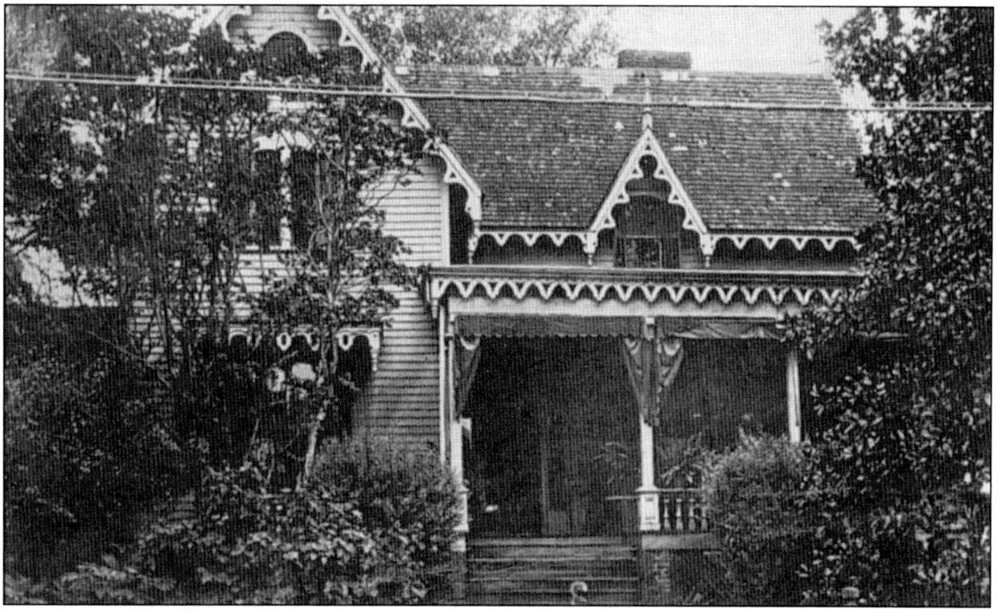

Dr. Elam Caldwell, Lincolnton physician, had this house built in the 1840s after his marriage to Elizabeth Motz. In 1877, Beverly C. Cobb (1848–1900) purchased the property from the estate of Dr. Caldwell. Cobb, a leading Lincolnton merchant, served the county as a lawyer, a politician who represented Lincoln County in the the state's General Assembly from 1877 to 1879, and mayor in 1889. During the time of Cobb's occupancy, the house was altered and Gothic Revival features were added. In 1900, after Cobb's death, Edgar Love (1869–1920), textile manufacturer, purchased the house. Love served as mayor of Lincolnton (1907–1908 and 1915–1918) and served in the General Assembly (1916 and 1918). The house sits at East Congress Street in Lincolnton. (Jim Love.)

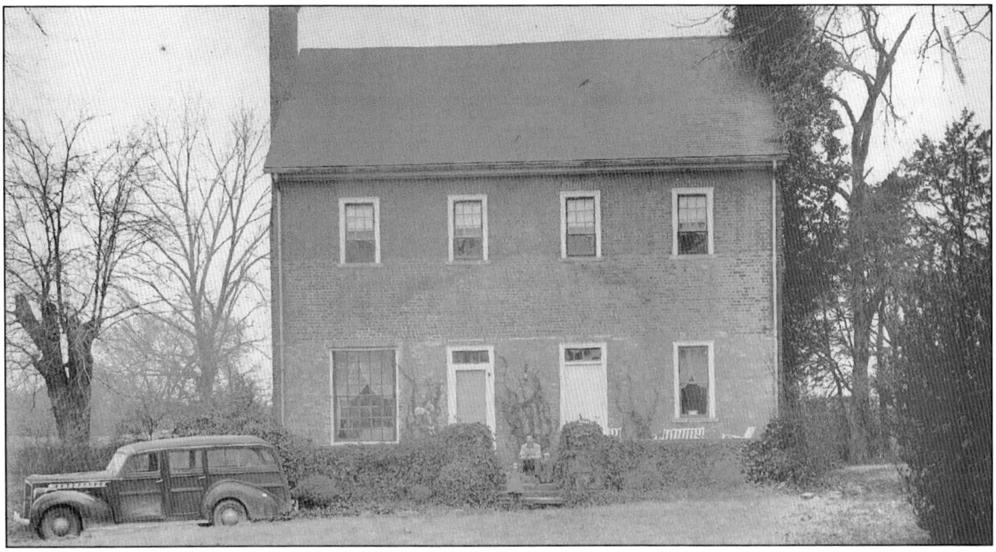

As one of three extant 18th-century residences in the county, this Federal-style plantation is situated just west of Lincolnton. Believed to have been completed in 1798 just after the marriage of Lawson Henderson to Elizabeth Caruth, "Woodside" is laid out in a Quaker plan arrangement with an exterior of Flemish bond brickwork. Henderson, a wealthy planter, served the county in various capacities throughout his life. Two of his sons, Charles Coatesworth and James Pickney, were born at this house. James (1808–1858) became the first governor of Texas in 1846 and served as a senator from this state from 1857 to 1858. The property is listed on the National Register of Historic Places. (Sue Ramseur.)

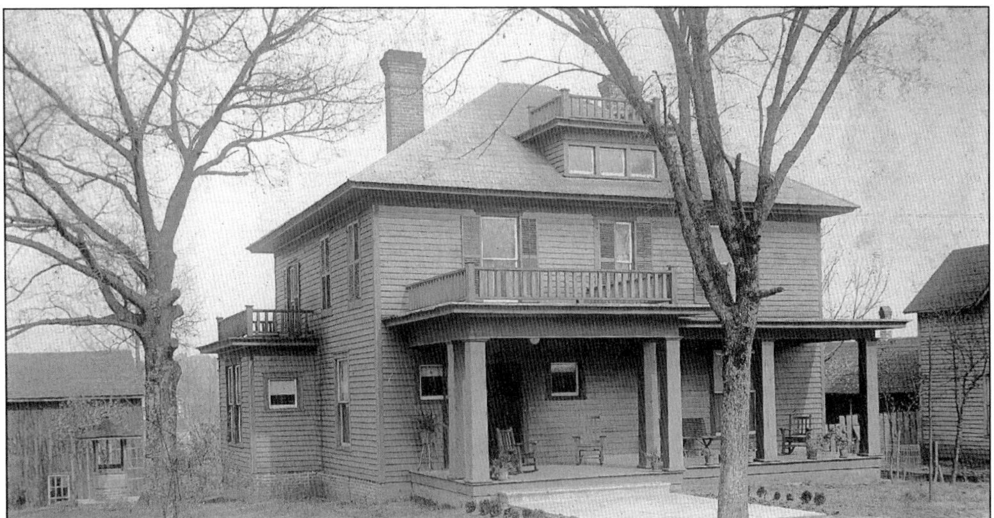

With two walnut Mission-style rockers resting on the front porch, the James House sits in solitude at the intersection of South Laurel and East Church Streets in Lincolnton. The workshop of Edgar James stands behind the house. James was a well-known cabinetmaker in Lincoln County throughout his life. Both his father, Augustus P., and his brother, William, made furniture, particularly of walnut. Eva James, daughter of Edgar and assistant postmistress, lived in the house for many years and entertained many guests. She hosted a dinner in May 1909 for the Lincolnton Graded School's graduating class. (Clara Cooper.)

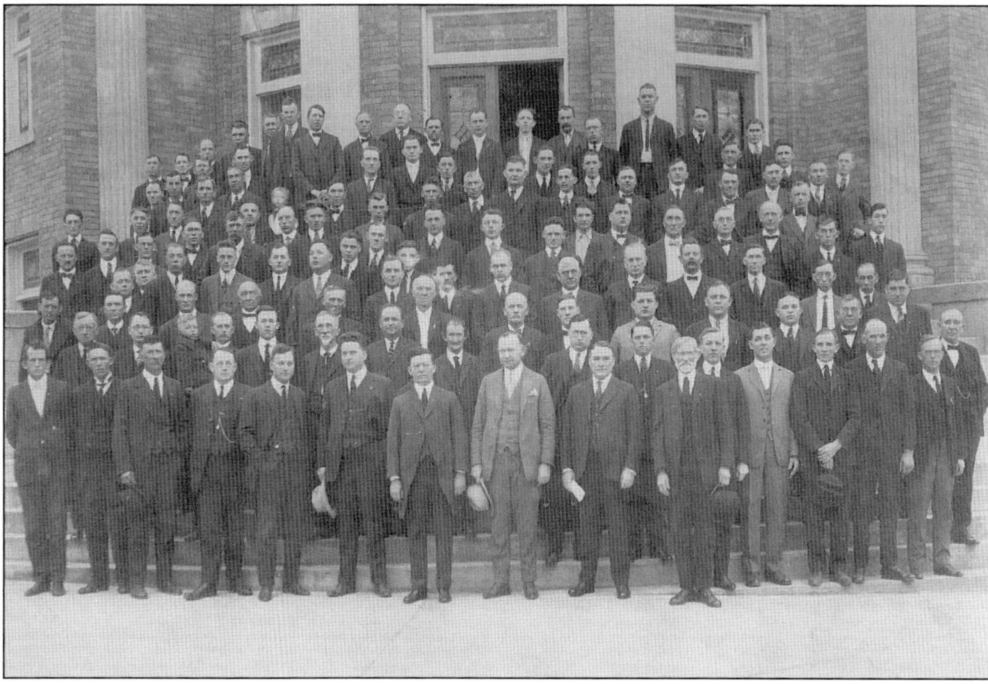

The men of the First United Methodist Church of Lincolnton block the front steps of the church for a photograph taken in the 1920s. (Richard Jonas.)

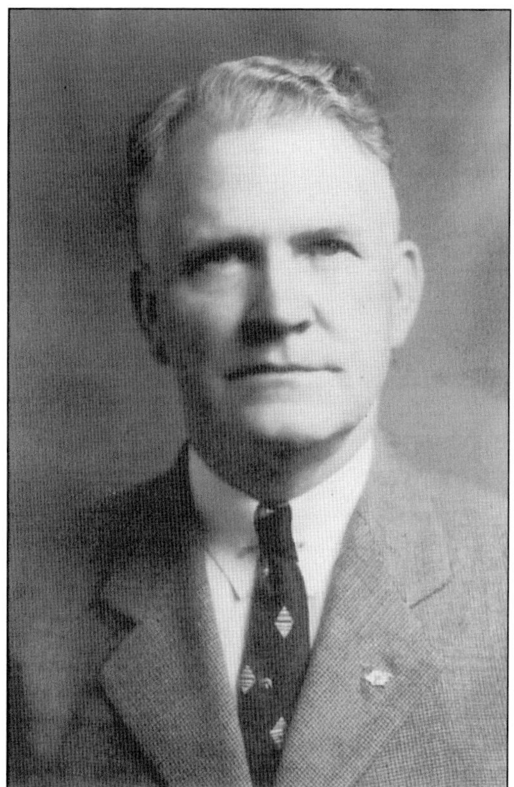

Drs. Jesse F. Gamble and John Reeves Gamble (pictured here) established the Gamble Clinic, Inc. on East Main Street in Lincolnton in June 1930. The hospital was reorganized under the Duke Endowment on April 1, 1933, and incorporated as Reeves Hospital with Dr. John Reeves Gamble as superintendent. An addition was made to the building in 1934, making it a 25-bed hospital. (Jack and Ellen Shuford.)

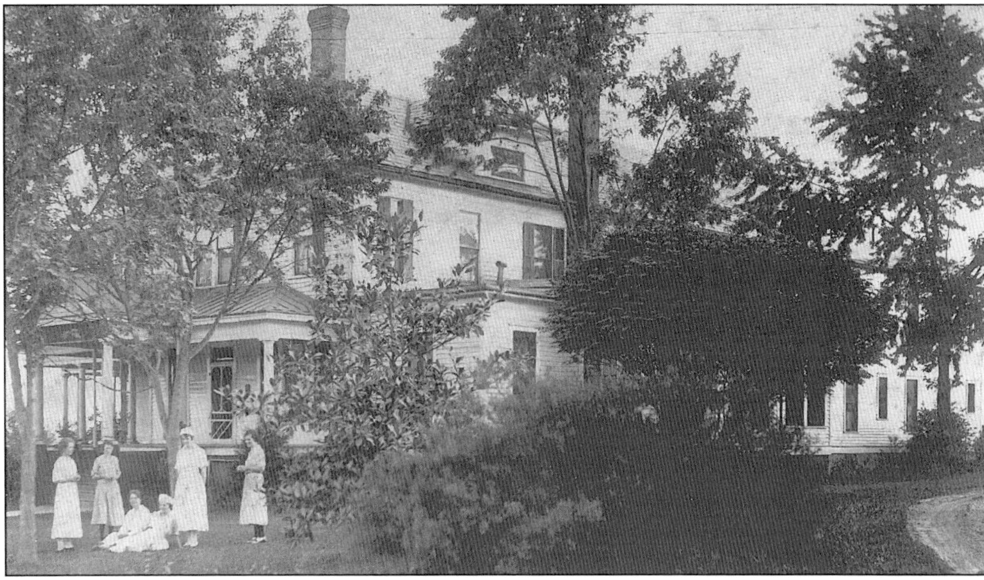

A group of nurses relaxes on the lawn of Lincoln Hospital during the first decade of the 20th century. Founded by Dr. Lester A. Crowell Sr. and Dr. R.W. Petrie, the hospital opened for patients on March 11, 1907, with 12 beds, and was the sixth general hospital to operate in North Carolina (others were in Raleigh, Washington, Salisbury, Charlotte, and Asheville). In 1936, the hospital was incorporated and the name was changed to Gordon Crowell Memorial Hospital to honor the memory of Dr. Gordon Bryan Crowell, Dr. Crowell's son, who died in 1926 at the young age of 30. (Gordon and Frances Crowell.)

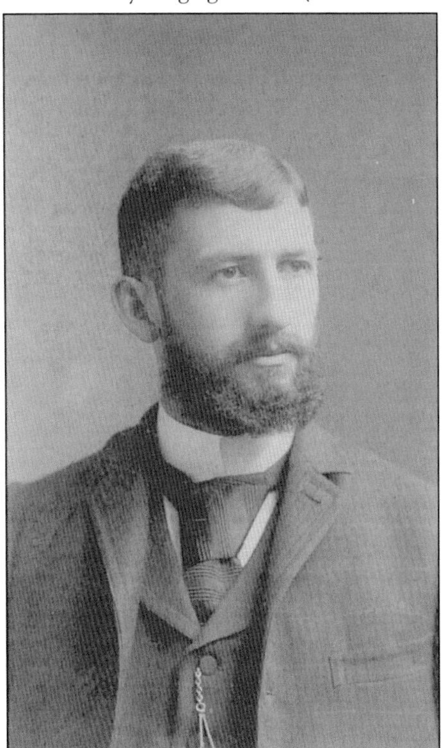

Dr. Lester A. Crowell was born October 17, 1867, near Reepsville in western Lincoln County. He attended county schools until 1886, when he entered high school at Dallas, North Carolina. After high school, he attended Baltimore Medical College (now part of the University of Maryland) in the fall of 1889. He returned to Lincolnton the following spring and practiced and read medicine under his father, Dr. Eli Crowell, until the fall of 1891. He received his degree of medical doctor in April 1892. He returned to Lincolnton as a doctor, practiced medicine near the home of his father, and later moved to Lincolnton. He was active in numerous organizations relating to the medical profession, including the Lincoln County Medical Society as secretary and president; the Catawba Valley Medical Society as its first president; the North Carolina Medical Society as president, 1930; the Tri-State Society of the Carolinas and Virginia; the American Medical Society; the Southeastern Surgical Congress and the American College of Surgeons; and the Western Hospital for the Insane of North Carolina at Morganton as director. (Gordon and Frances Crowell.)

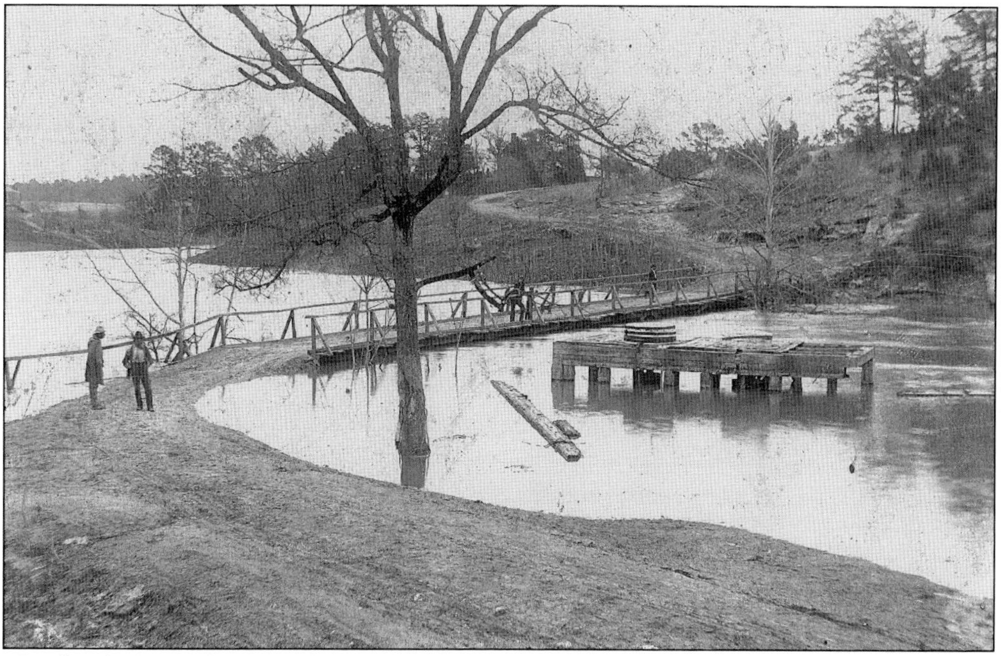

The flood of 1898 leaves onlookers in awe as they peer over the remains of Ramsour's Mill. Deidrich Ramsour built the mill on the west side of Clark's Creek around 1770. He died in 1780 and his son Jacob was operating the mill at the time of the famous June 20, 1780 Battle of Ramsour's Mill. (Lincoln County Museum of History.)

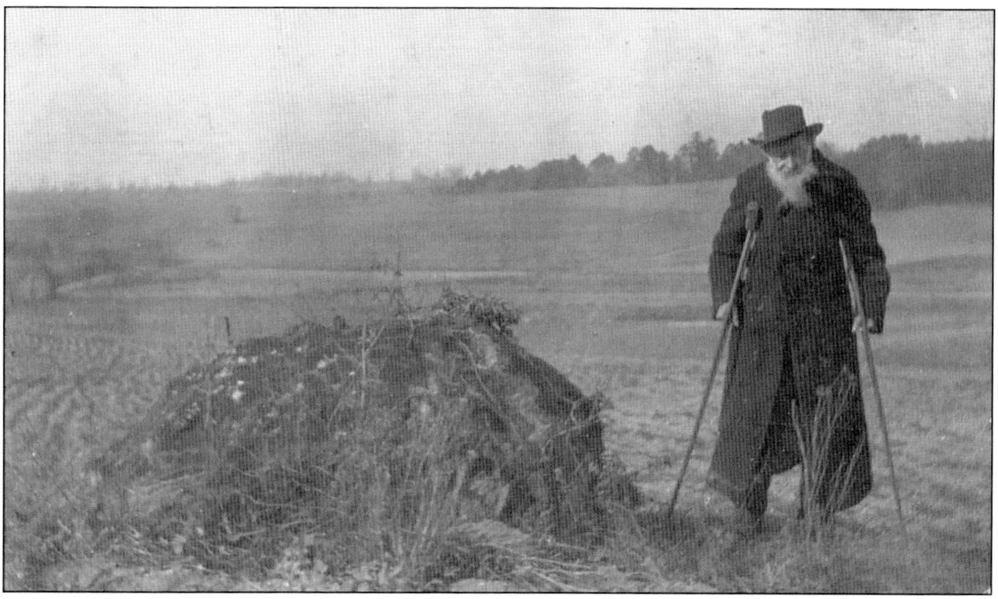

An elderly Wallace Reinhardt, son of Michael Reinhardt and grandson of Christian Reinhardt (family pioneer), stands beside the rock commonly referred to as Tarleton's Tea Table at the site of the Battle of Ramsour's Mill. The Daughters of the American Revolution had the rock moved from this site to the courthouse lawn. Reinhardt served as clerk of Superior Court from 1874 to 1880 and lived for many years on the ancestral land of his grandfather, where the Revolutionary battle commenced on June 20, 1780. (Sue Ramseur.)

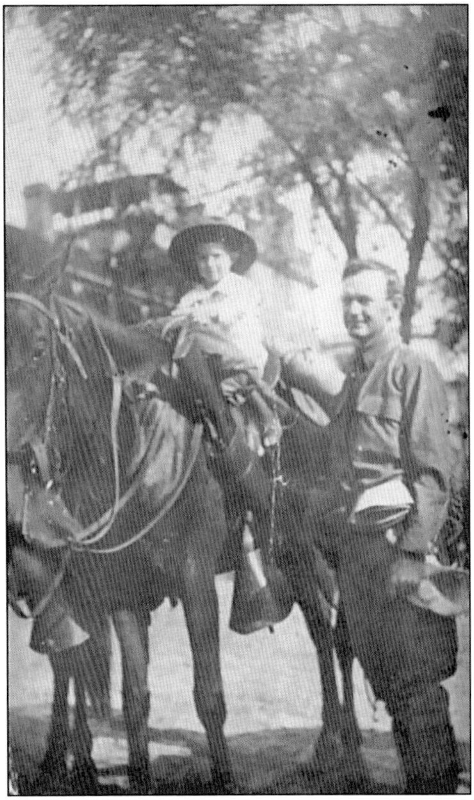

Jack Shuford climbs on Kemp Nixon's cavalry horse for a photograph in the 1910s. (Jack and Ellen Shuford.)

From June 21 to July 14, 1956, the Lincoln County Historical Association sponsored *Thunder over Carolina*, a theatrical performance of the Battle of Ramsour's Mill. Mrs. Gladys Childs, originator of the idea for the drama and who helped plan and organize the play, called upon Charles W. Loveland to write the score. The group in this photograph from 1956 represents the Christian Reinhardt family: D.H. Mauney Jr. as Christian; Mrs. Doris Weddington as Betsy; Keith Turner as Christian Jr.; John Oscar Shuford III as Michael; and William Lawrence Shuford as John. (Jack and Ellen Shuford.)

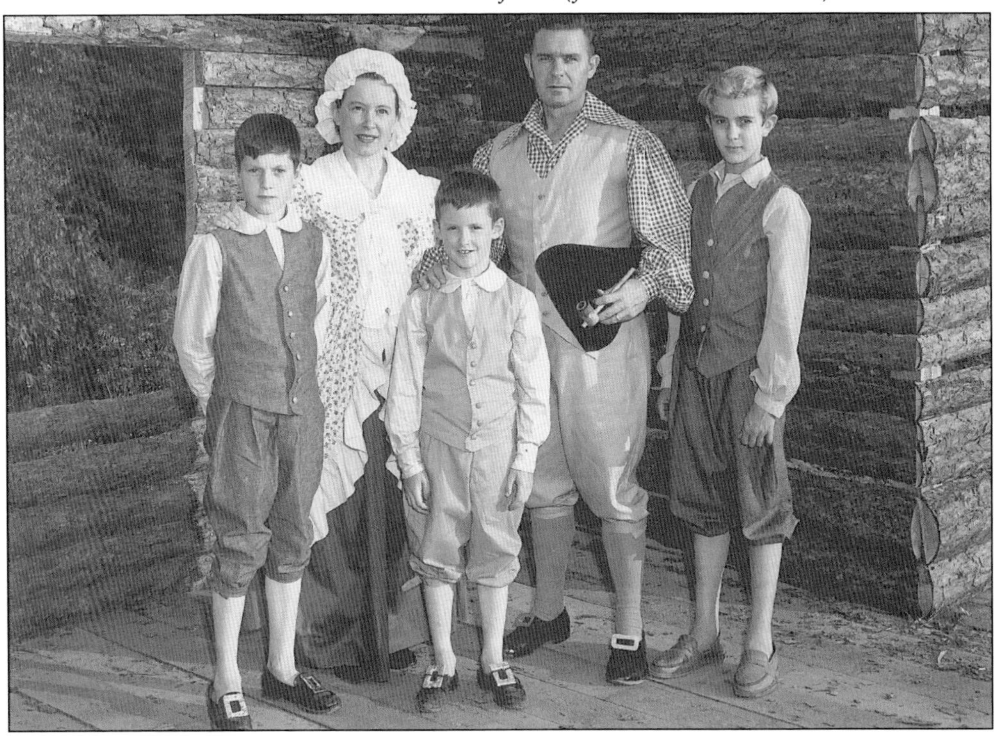

Tench Lander uses the bucket of his mail carrier to sit for this photograph taken beside the Reinhardt Building, the eighth post office location. Lander delivered mail in Lincolnton from the two railroad depots, C.&N.W. and Seaboard Airline, to the post office. The post office moved into this location in 1913 and remained there until the construction of the present post office in 1937. (Leroy Magness.)

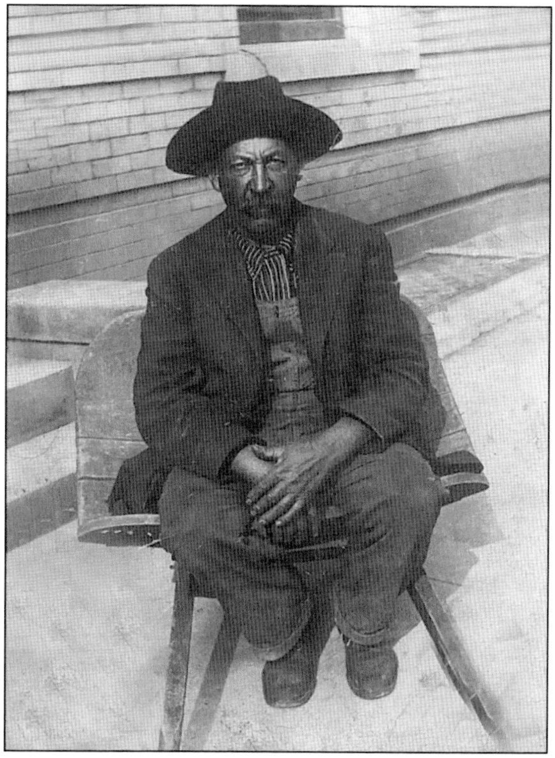

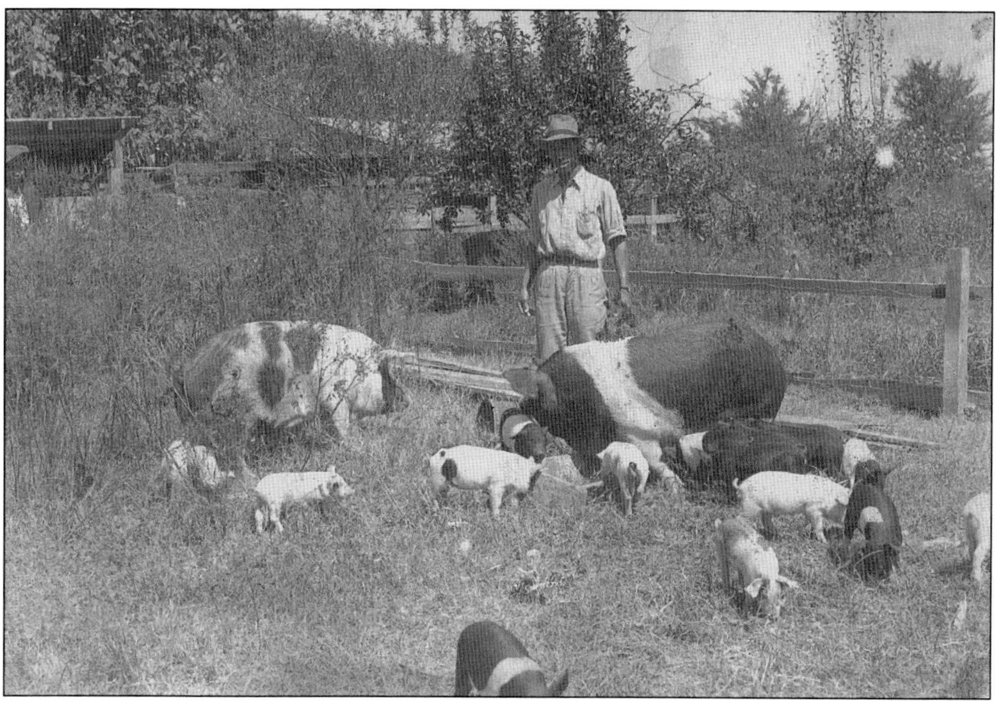

Out in the field right off of Main Street in Lincolnton during the 1940s, Leroy Magness performs the necessary chores involved with raising pigs. Mr. Magness raised and sold pigs while working at Gamble Hospital as an orderly for 16 years. (Leroy Magness.)

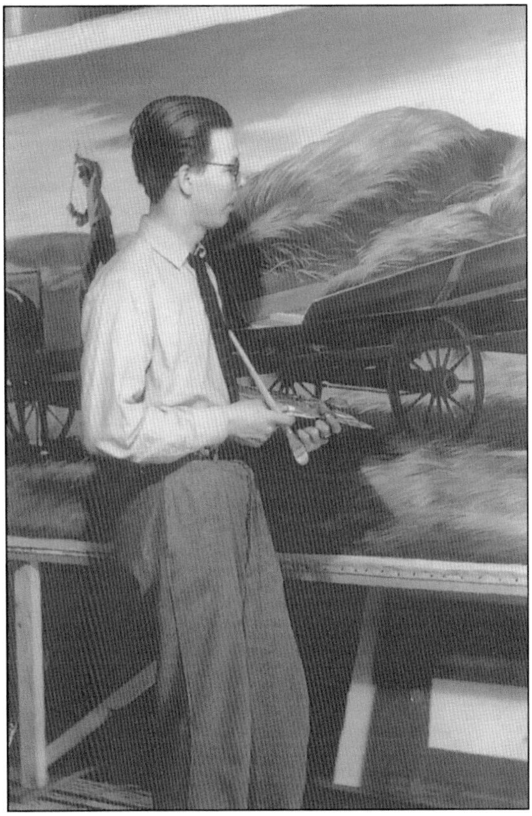

Richard Herman Jansen, native of Wisconsin, is photographed in his artist's studio in Milwaukee with brush in hand in front of a mural titled *Threshing Grain*. Jansen painted the mural, 14 feet wide by 4.5 feet high with a total approximate area of 63-square feet, with a medium of oil on canvas. In 1938, the mural was completed and installed in the Lincolnton Post Office. Jansen was paid $610 for the Lincolnton mural in three installments: $200 upon approval of preliminary sketches, $150 when the mural was one-half completed, and $260 upon completion, installation, and approval. Jansen painted the mural as an employee of the Treasury Department's Section of Painting and Sculpture, later the Section of Fine Arts. This program was established by the federal government to produce art for ordinary citizens, provide needed employment, and create a cohesiveness among communities to endure the hardships of the Great Depression. (Lincoln County Museum of History.)

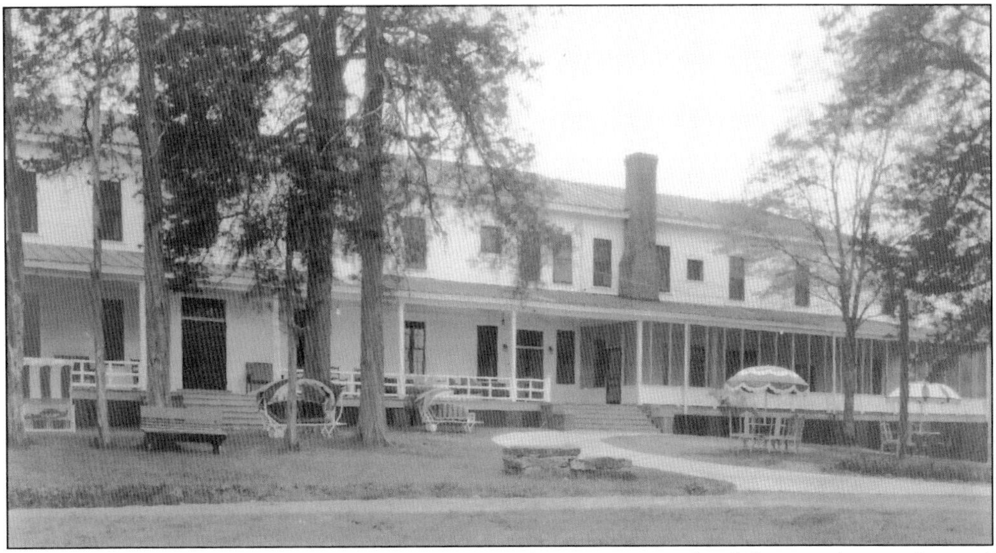

The Lincoln Lithia Inn, a two-story building with 46 rooms and a full veranda, was located at the Lithia Springs, where mineral water and the fine hotel drew crowds seeking relaxation and better health. Major Henry W. Burton was the first to develop the spring. Later owners included Major General Robert F. Hoke, Daniel E. Rhyne, J.A. Abernethy Jr., and Marcus Boyd III. In later years, Lincolnton High School and other organizations held banquets and awards ceremonies in its lavish banquet hall before it was razed in 1940. (John Hoyle.)

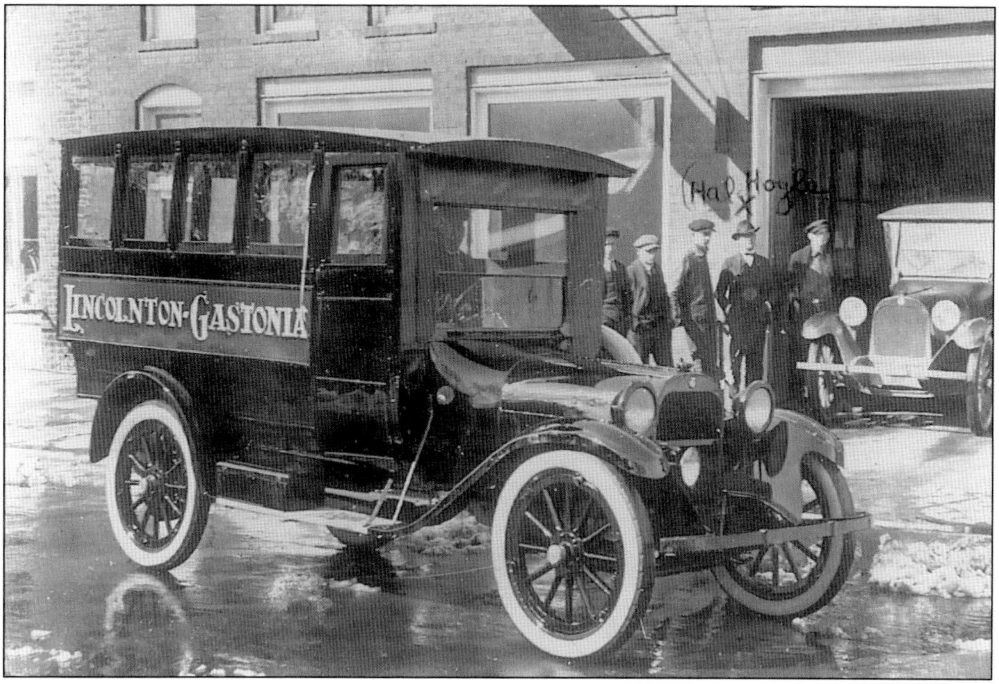

In 1919, E.A. Huffstetler purchased a Dodge from the Hoyle Motor Company of Lincolnton, a Dodge Brothers dealer at the time. Mark H. Hoyle, his son W. Fitzhugh Hoyle, and M.H. Hoyle's nephew Hal Hoyle Sr., had just opened this new business in a new building they had constructed where Broome-Early Furniture was located. The car's body was custom built by Bolick Brother of Conover, and the motor and chassis were manufactured by Dodge. Mr. Huffstetler and sons operated their Lincolnton-Gastonia bus service years before selling to another bus line company. (John Hoyle.)

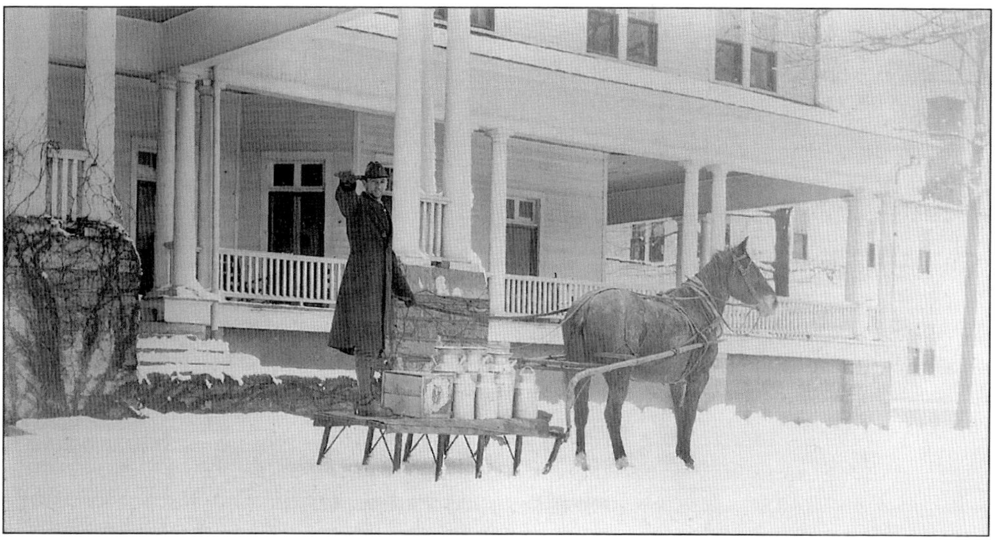

On February 20, 1924, an unidentified man salutes the camera as he stands amidst large containers of milk, either for pick-up or delivery, and holding the reins to his sleigh on the snowy grounds in front of the building that once served as the Fassifern "Miss Kate Shipp" School. (Lincoln County Museum of History.)

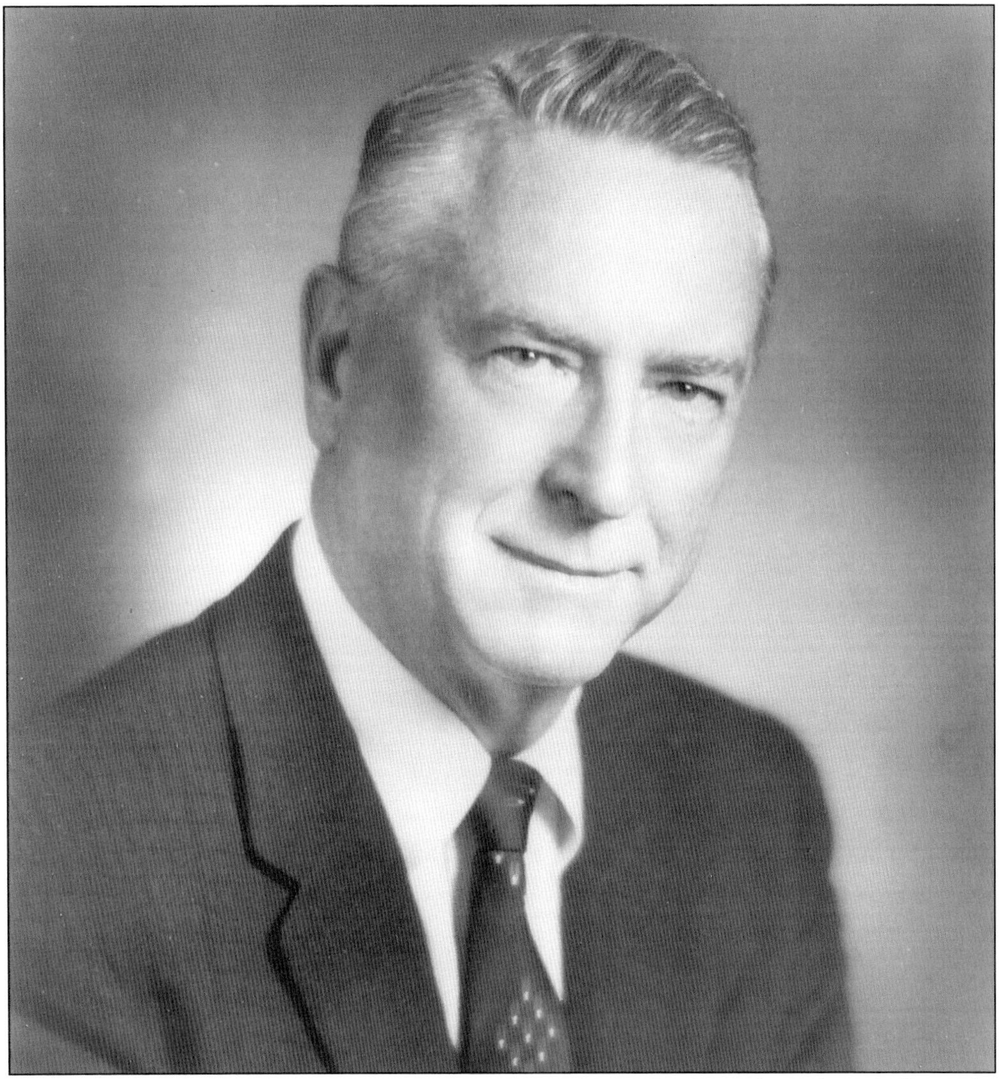

Charles Raper Jonas attended Lincoln County public schools and graduated from the University of North Carolina at Chapel Hill in 1925 with an A.B. Degree and in 1927 from UNC Law School. In 1952, he was elected to Congress from the tenth North Carolina District. His congressional achievements include being president of the 83rd Club during his first year in Congress, being elected to a committee on appropriations during his first term, and being chairman of the Republican Task Force on Budget, 1965–1966. He served as the senior Republican member of the appropriations subcommittee that handled budget requests for the Department of Housing and Urban Development, the Space Agency, the Veterans Administration, the General Services Administration, the National Science Foundation, the Federal Aviation Agency, and the regulatory agencies such as the CAB, ICC, S & EC, FPC, CSC, and GAO. He also served as president of the North Carolina Bar Association in 1946, a member of Board of Law Examiners in 1947, president of the Lincolnton Rotary Club, president of the Lincolnton Executives Club, director of the Lincolnton-Lincoln County Chamber of Commerce, director of the alumni association of the UNC-Chapel Hill, as a member of North Carolina District of Columbia and America, and as a member of the official board of the First United Methodist Church, Lincolnton. (Richard Jonas.)

Two

Industry and Business

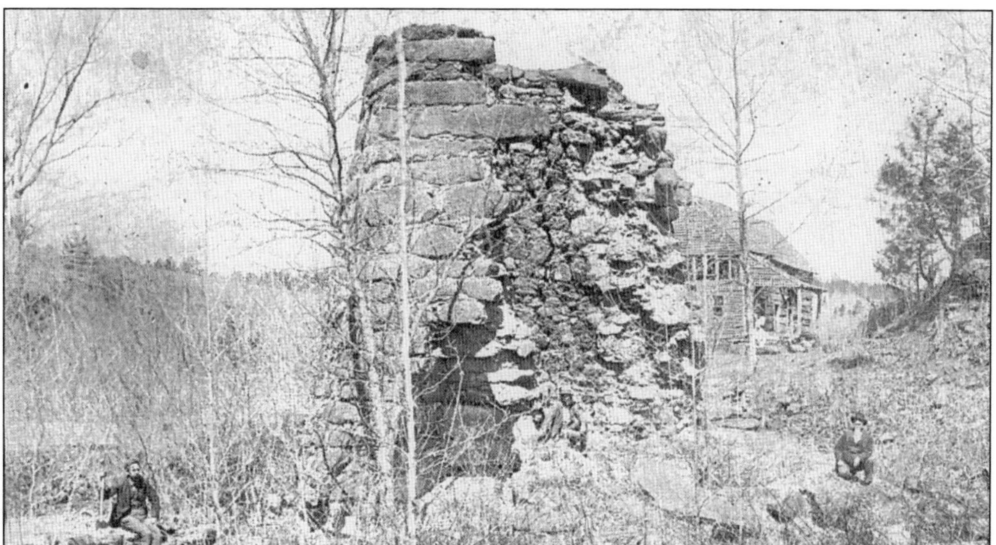

The historic remains of Vesuvius Furnace provide a reminder of Lincoln County's first industry in this photograph from the late 19th century. Peter Forney, Alexander Brevard, General Joseph Graham, and John Davidson formed a copartnership in the late 1780s or early 1790s to establish Vesuvius Furnace in eastern Lincoln County. The partners were motivated to build the furnace in 1790 by an act of the North Carolina General Assembly in 1788. The act directed the granting of large amounts of free land to persons who successfully established iron works and produced bar and pig iron. (Lincoln County Museum of History.)

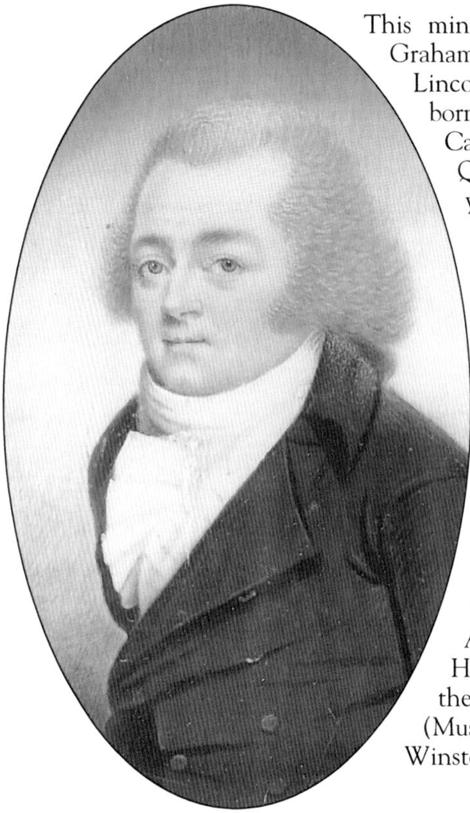

This miniature watercolor on ivory of General Joseph Graham, *c.* 1790–1800, holds a stately visage of one of Lincoln County's most productive sons. Graham was born in Pennsylvania in 1759 and came to North Carolina at the age of seven and was educated at Queens Museum in Charlotte. As the turbulent years of the American Revolution neared, he volunteered in May of 1778 in the 4th Regiment of North Carolina Troops under Colonel Alexander Lytle. He served as sergeant, adjutant, captain, and major, and was in command in 15 engagements. He was chosen as the first sheriff of Mecklenburg County and later represented this county in the state senate from 1788 to 1794. He began producing raw pig iron and cast-iron implements at Vesuvius Furnace in Lincoln County in 1790 and built his frame house in 1792. In 1814, as councilor of state, he was commissioned by Governor Hawkins as colonel of the North Carolina Volunteers to suppress the Creek Indians in Alabama. After the victory at the Battle of Horse Shoe, he was commissioned general of the state militia. General Graham died in 1830. (Museum of Early Southern Decorative Arts, Winston-Salem, NC.)

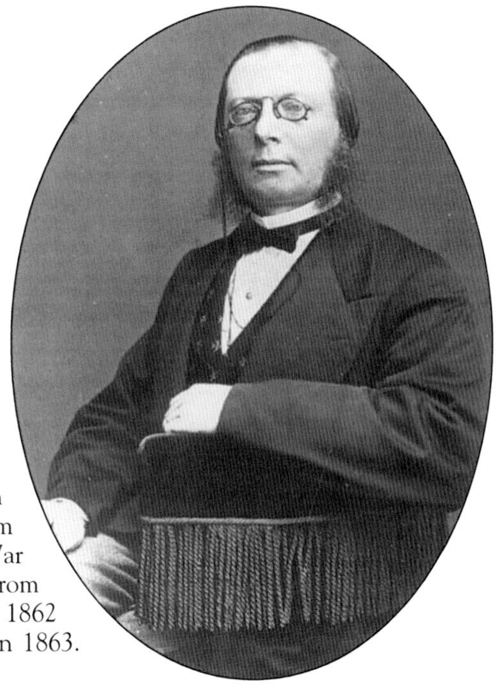

C.J. (Charles Jakob) Hammarskold was born on June 2, 1833, in Skultuna, province of Vaectmanland, in Sweden. He graduated from high school in 1849 and joined his family in immigrating to America. Hammarskold owned and operated the Spring Hill Forge in eastern Lincoln County and served as postmaster from 1853 to 1860. He served as a colonel in the War between the States during the first two years from Lincoln County. He worked as a merchant in 1862 and 1863 before returning home to Sweden in 1863. (Al Tate.)

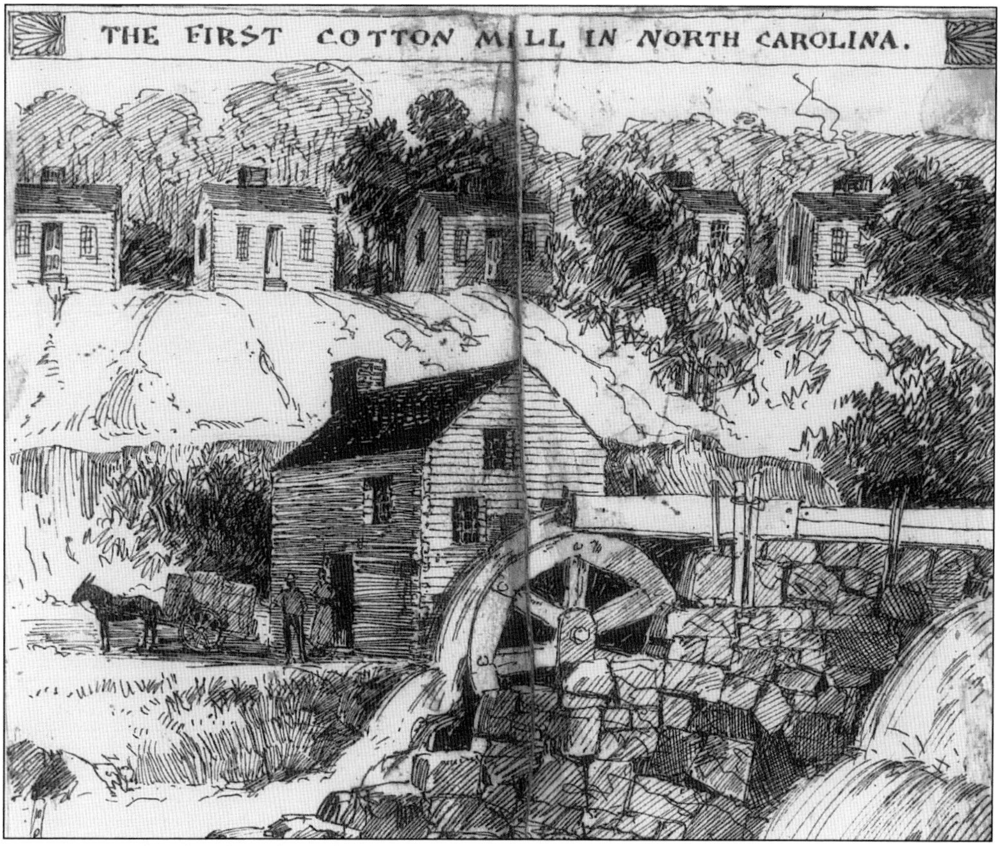

In 1816, Michael Schenck and Absolom Warlick constructed the first cotton mill operated south of the Potomac River. The mill was located about 1.5 miles east of Lincolnton near the McDaniel Spring, just north of where U.S. 321 intersects with East Main Street. David Schenck, grandson of Michael Schenck, sketched his rendition of the mill from memory. (North Carolina Collection, UNC Chapel Hill Library, Chapel Hill, NC.)

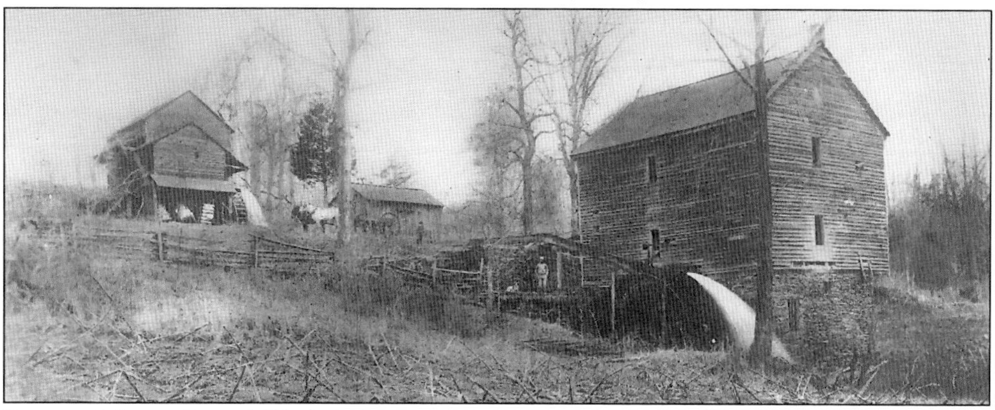

Pioneer Johann Daniel Warlick began construction of a gristmill in what is now western Lincoln County in 1750, according to a date cut on the door sill after the basement walls had been laid. The other mill (at left) was originally built with a water-powered turning lathe for making household furniture; it was later adapted to cotton ginning with a press. (Hunter and Ruby Rudisill.)

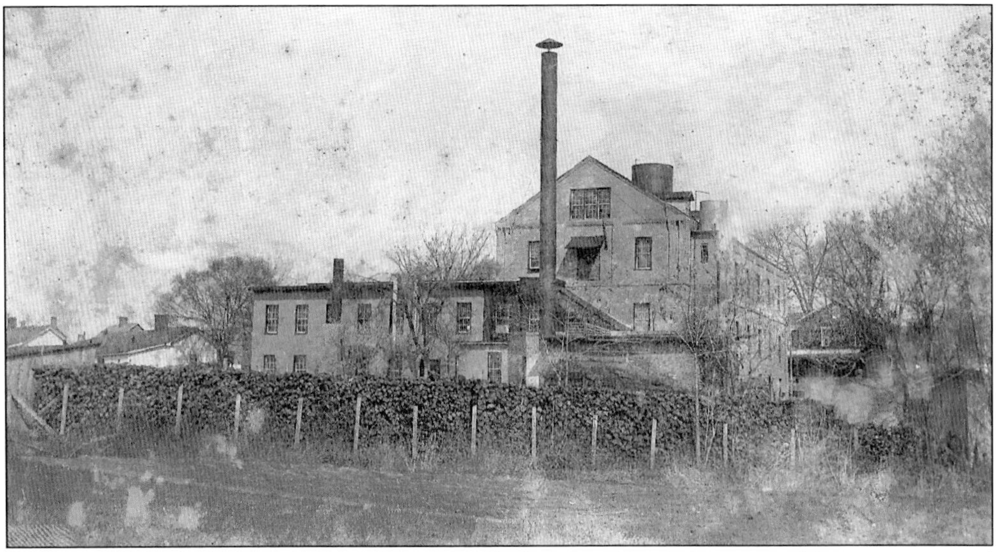

Serving as Lincoln County's third cotton mill, the Elm Grove Cotton Mill was constructed around 1850 by Andrew Motz, E.S. Barrett, and others on the South Fork River immediately above its confluence with Clark's Creek. At its inception, the mill carried the name Laurel Hill Cotton Factory with the firm name E.S. Barrett and Co. About 1858, Colonel John F. Phifer and Colonel R.W. Allison (of Concord) purchased the property and operated it under the name of Ivy Shoals until the death of Colonel Phifer in 1884. It was continued for awhile by George L. Phifer until taken over by R.S. Reinhardt, Stephen Smith, and others in the late 1800s and called the Elm Grove Cotton Mill. (Mike Cline.)

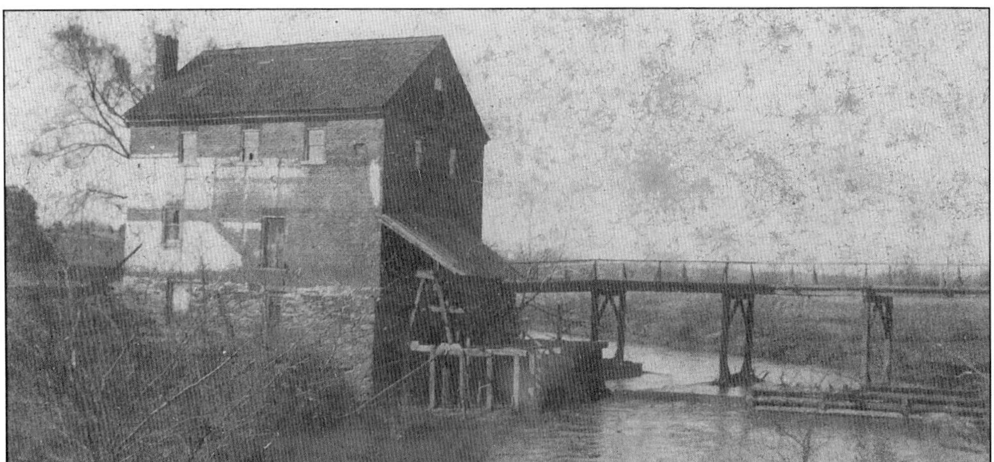

Situated on the South Fork of the Catawba River, this gristmill was built and operated by William Slade 1 mile west of Lincolnton. On December 4, 1848, Andrew Motz of the firm of Motz, Barrett & Company, proprietors of the Ivy Shoals Cotton Mill on the South Fork River at Clark's Creek, purchased from William Slade a tract of land containing 2 acres with a special right-of-way over the lands of Slade for $300. In this transaction, Slade stipulates that Motz is forbidden from building or establishing a gristmill or sawmill on the property opposite Slade's mill, for which Motz owns. On the night of March 7, 1851, Andrew Motz drowned while crossing the bridge at Slade's Mill on this way home. This undated photograph was taken after the removal of the dam. (Mike Cline.)

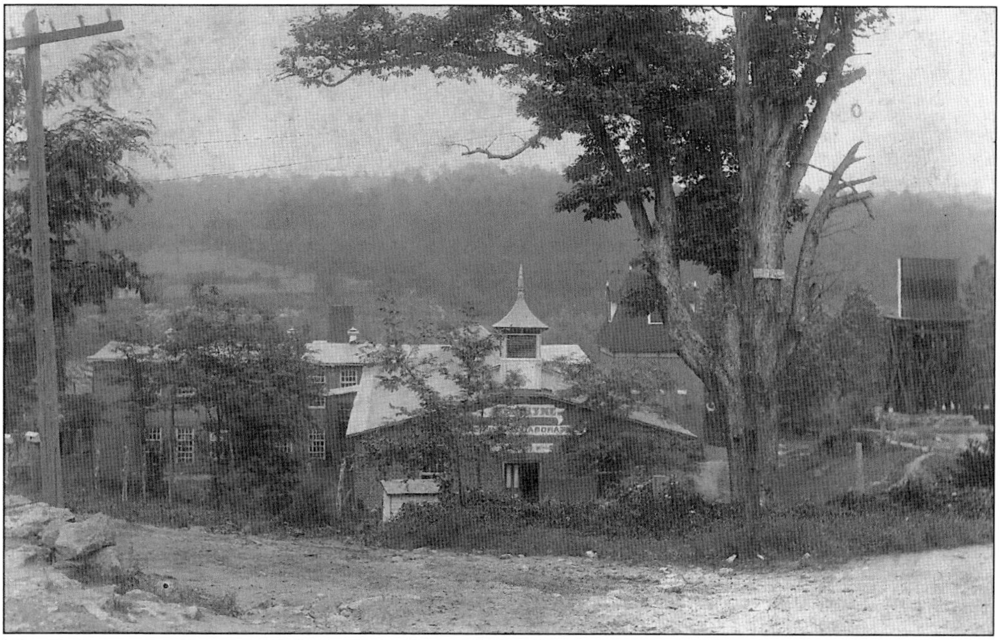

The Laboratory Cotton Mill, built by Daniel E. Rhyne and J.A. Abernethy about 1887, rests on a bend of the South Fork River. The river had been used to power mills since the 1810s. During the War between the States, this site was also used as a laboratory for the production of medicines by the Confederacy. The first cotton mill operated in the South, the Schenck-Warlick Mill, was relocated in 1818 to this site to take advantage of the greater waterpower of the South Fork. (Edward Little.)

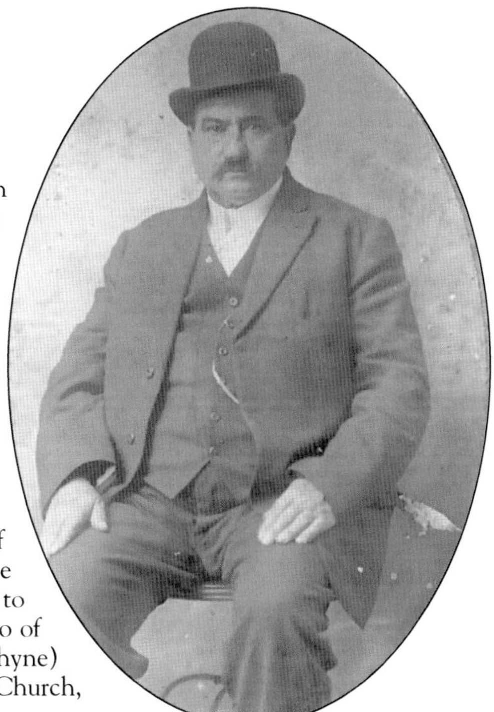

Daniel Efird Rhyne, born near Mt. Holly in Gaston County in 1852, moved to Lincoln County about 1887. Within two decades his textile interests in Lincoln County alone included the Laboratory Cotton Mill, the Lincoln Cotton Mill, the Daniel Cotton Mill, the Wampum and Indian Creek Mills, and the Rhodes-Rhyne Weaving Company. He was vice-president of the Chronicle, Imperial, Majestic, and National Mills, Belmont; director of the Commercial National Bank and the Merchants and Farmers National Bank of Charlotte; and director of the First National Bank of Lincolnton. Rhyne is remembered for his philanthropic gifts to many charitable and religious organizations, two of which include Lenoir College (later Lenoir-Rhyne) in Hickory and the Emmanuel Lutheran Church, Lincolnton. (Ermintrude Mullen.)

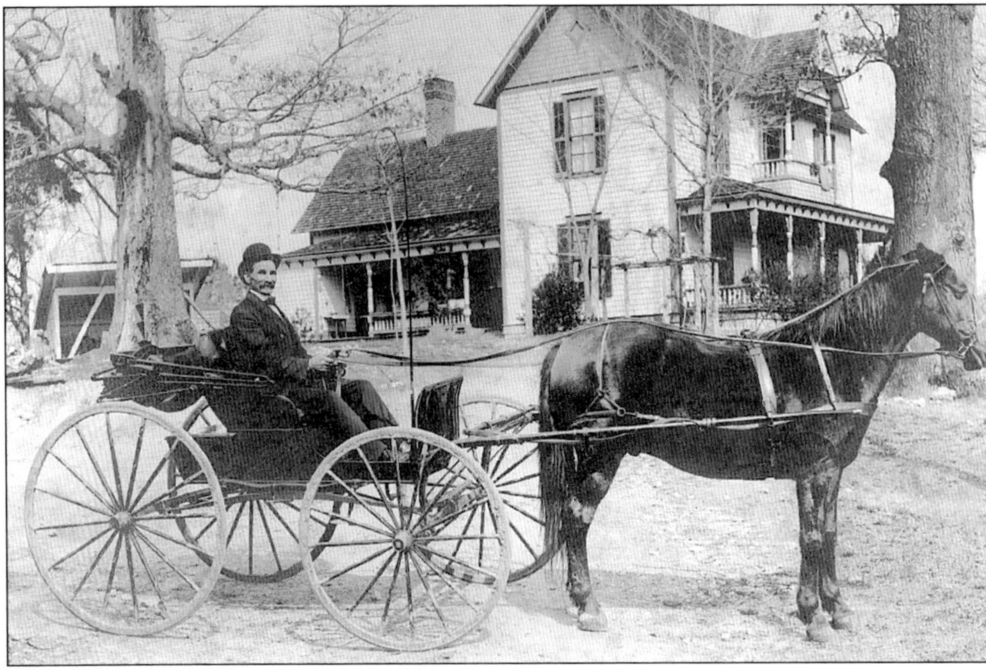

Laban Jonathan Rhyne sits up in his buggy with reins in hand, a smile, and his derby hat during the latter years of the 19th century for this photograph taken near the Laboratory Mill in Lincolnton with his home in the background. Hired by his brother D.E. Rhyne to run the company store at the mill, Laban moved his family from their home on the Moses Rhyne estate in Mt. Holly to Lincolnton around 1898. Laban and wife, Ellen Lentz Rhyne, moved into his brother's house in 1900 as he relocated to the old Francis Hoke house, built in 1844, which stood nearby. (Ermintrude Mullen.)

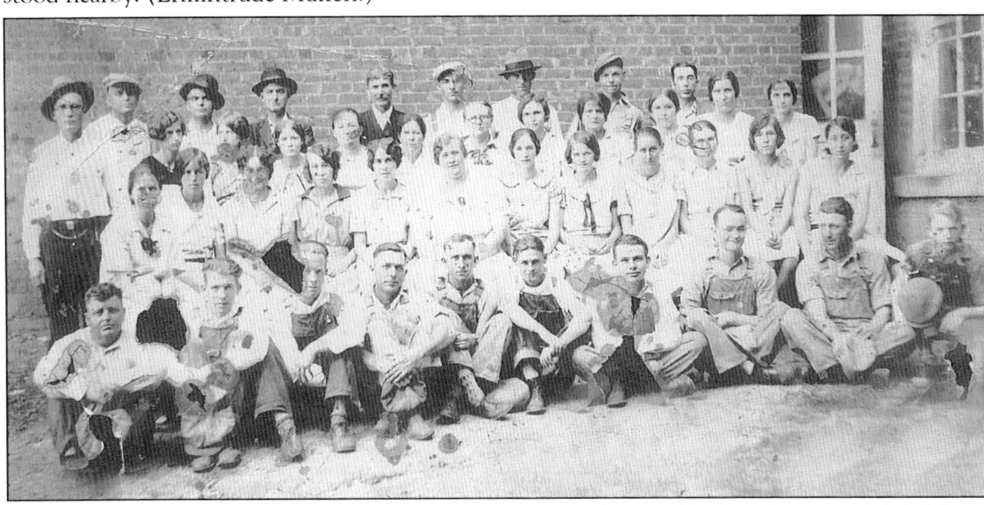

The Daniel Cotton Mill was built by Daniel E. Rhyne, Edgar and Robert Love, and A.M. Price about 1898, and was named for Rhyne. The mill produced a fine spun yarn from combed Sea Island cotton. Located on Grier Street near the Massapog Mill and Seth Lumber Co., it was operated as Arrow Mills in the 1920s. Then it was known as the Carter Mill before being purchased by Burlington. It closed in 1985. Pictured are the workers from the Daniel Cotton Mill after the turn of the century. (Jack Dellinger.)

E.O. "Lendo" Jennings rests in front of a large bale of cotton at the Seaboard Airline Railway on South Flint Street in this undated photograph. Jennings came to Lincolnton from Philadelphia and married Josie Hinson. The Jennings lived on the east side of South Laurel Street in the middle of the block during the 1920s, before moving to Philadelphia. While in Lincolnton, he was associated with the textile industry in Ranlo, Gaston County. (Bobby Padgett Crowell.)

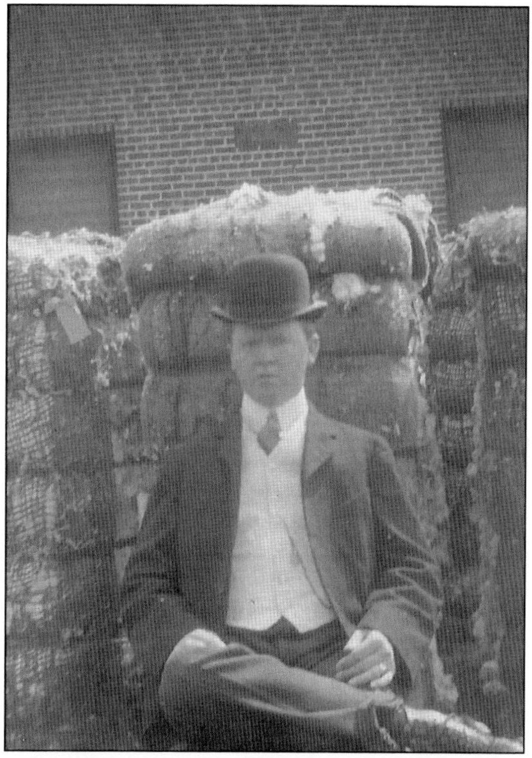

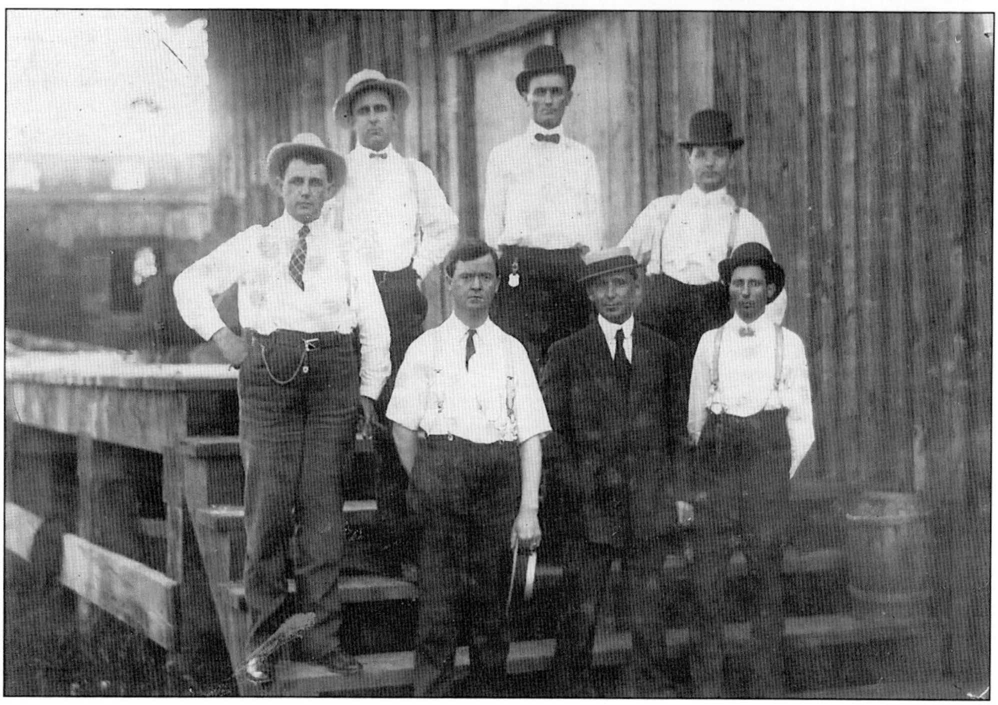

Staff members of the C.&N.W. Railway station stand on the steps of the depot. E.O. "Lendo" Jennings, the first gentleman on the first row, and J.S. Armstrong, above Jennings on the left, are the only identified individuals in the group. (Bobby Padgett Crowell.)

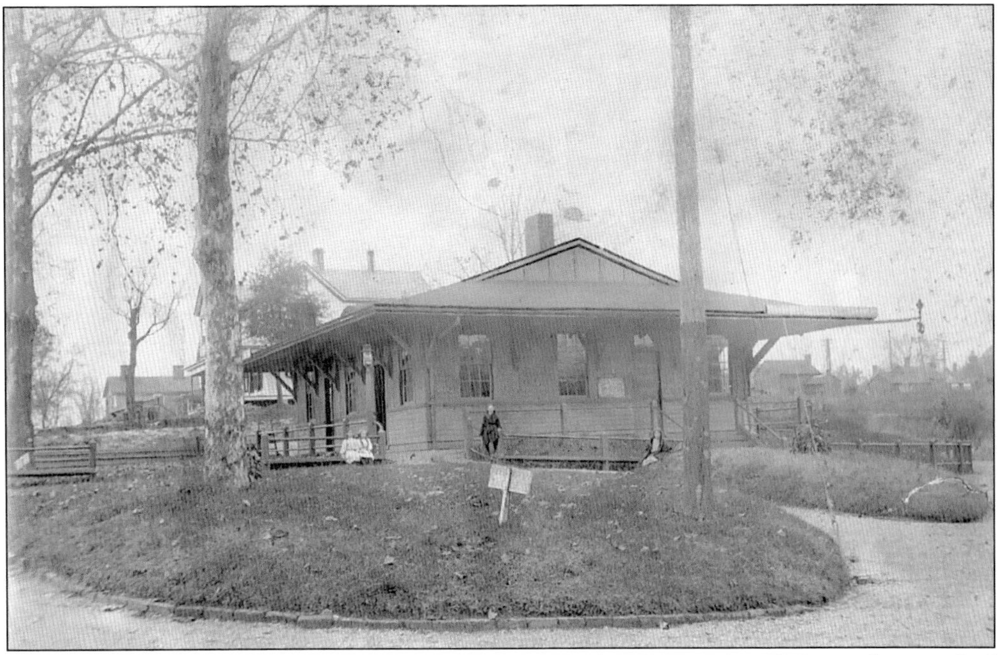

Originally run as the Chester & Lenoir Narrow Gauge Railroad in 1880, and changed to standard gauge in 1897, the C.&N.W. (Carolina and Northwestern) railroad and station ran south across Main Street in Lincolnton. Two young people pose for this turn-of-the-20th-century photograph on the porch of the depot with the sign in the foreground restricting anyone from stepping on the grass. (Ermintrude Mullen.)

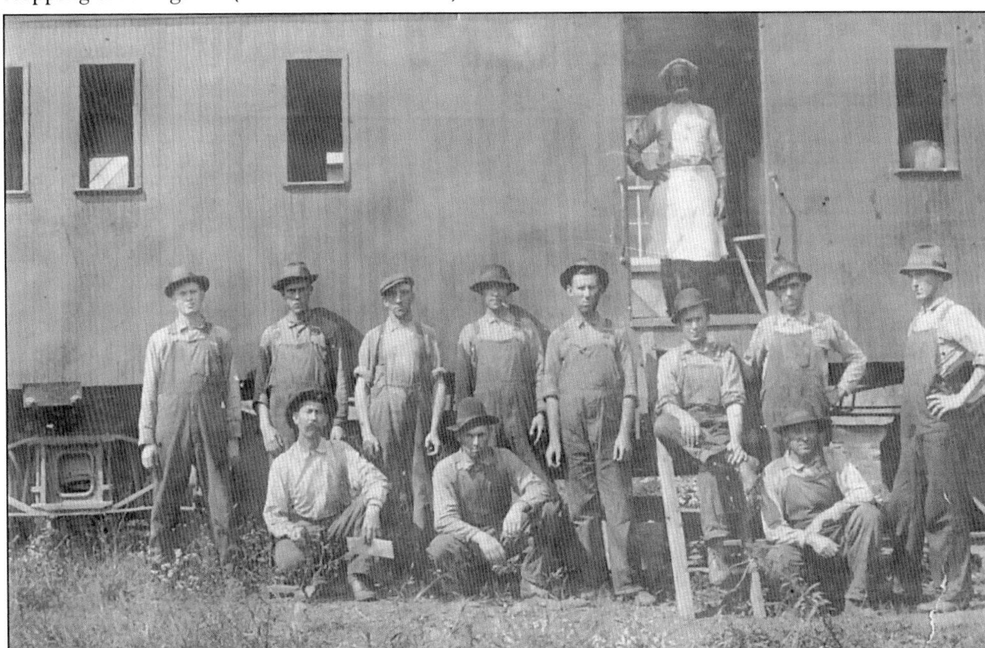

A cook with a white moustache and apron steps out from behind the wall of the car to have his image captured as part of the crew from the C.&N.W. Railway. (Nelda Cashion.)

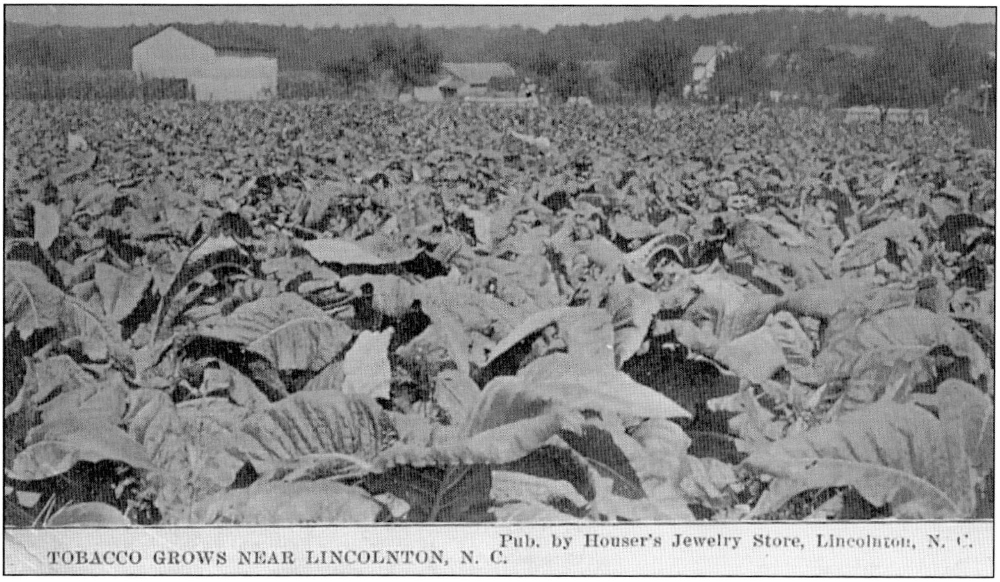

After 1880, the tobacco industry, along with textiles and furniture, developed quickly, causing many state residents to believe that tobacco provided the primary means to prosperity. By the 1880s, North Carolina's farmers had managed to equal or surpass pre-war quantities of cotton, oats, corn, and tobacco. Despite the industrial changes to the nation and to the county, from commercial to transportation improvements, Lincoln County sustained an agriculture-based economy during the late 19th century. (Linda Graham.)

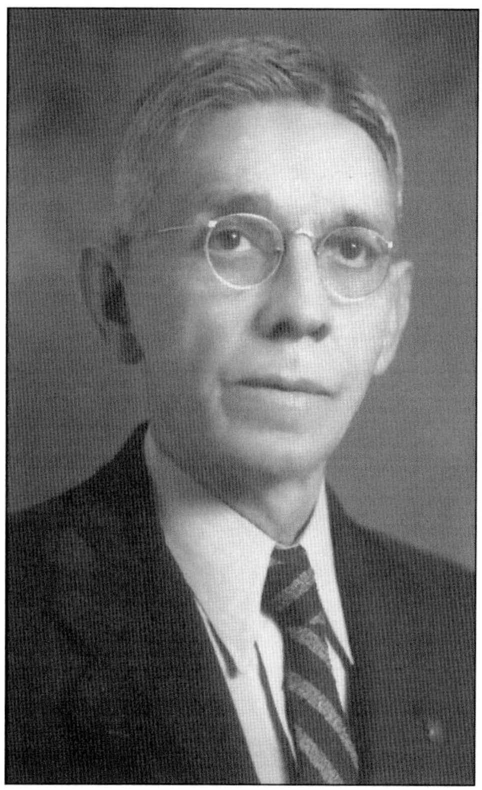

Harry Page was the owner of the Eureka Machine Shop & Foundry in Lincolnton, where he created images and objects both from patterns and the creativeness of his mind. He worked for the betterment of education by serving as a member of the Lincoln County school board for 20 years, several of which he was the board chairman. As a young man, he participated in the Spanish-American War, serving in Cuba, and later captained Lincolnton's Home Guard during World War I. Serving in this capacity, he carried his company to Charlotte to assist in quelling the streetcar riots and strike. He was director of the Lincolnton Building & Loan Association; a 32nd degree Scottish Rite Mason; a Pythian; Sunday school superintendent of St. Luke's Episcopal Church; teacher of the Men's Bible Class; adjutant of the State Department during the Eubert Lyerly administration as North Carolina Department Commander of Spanish-American War Veterans; scoutmaster for local scout troops; and was Worshipful Master of Lincoln Lodge No. 137 A.F.&A.M. during his fraternal life. (Vassey Page.)

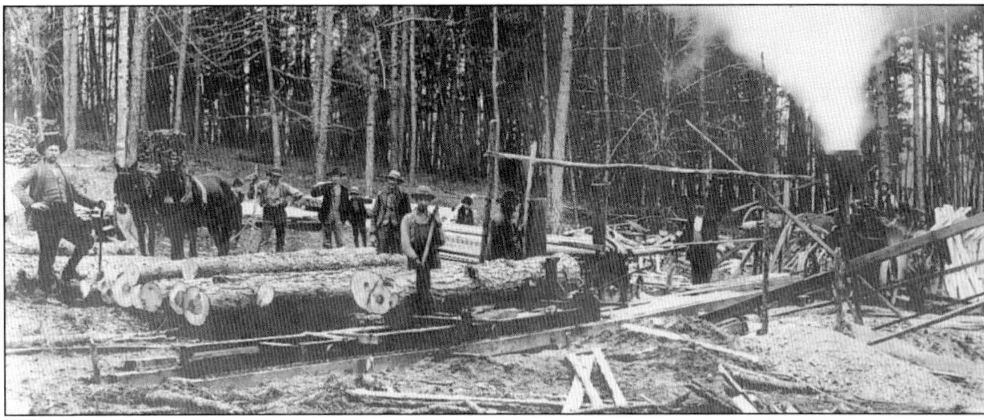

While steam bellows from the engine, the men and mules take a break from the labor-intensive duties of running a sawmill. The mules were responsible for dragging logs from the surrounding woods. The large logs rest on a carriage that runs along the track to a circular saw. The steam engine powered the circular saw. A chain conveyor, visible on the right, pulls the sawdust away from the blade. Water had to be carried to the site for the steam engine. (Jim Hallman.)

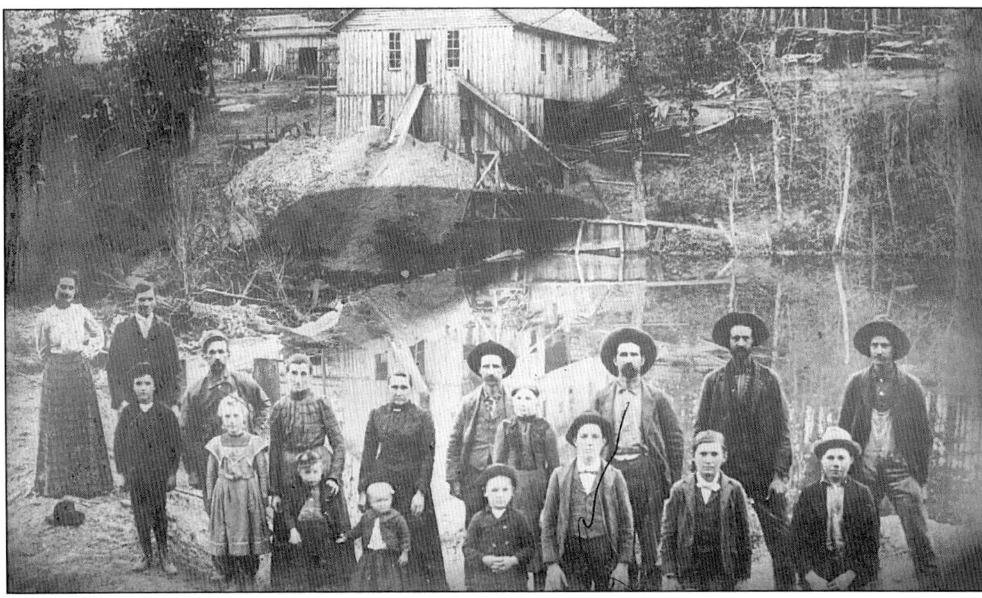

The Beam Sawmill was located near the present bridge that crosses Indian Creek on Cedar Grove Lutheran Church Road, Vale, in western Lincoln County. At the time of this c. 1900 photograph, Dave Beam and his brother George ran the Indian Creek Door and Sash Company out of the upper story. The sawmill carriage is pictured in the lower portion of the building. The members of the family, shown here from left to right, are as follows: (front row) Luther Clyde Beam (1892–1989), Josephine Maude Beam (1890–1975), James Edward Beam (1897–?), Carl Floyd Beam (1899–1962), Roy Lee "Bub" Beam (1894–1986), James Lester Beam (1887–?), George Cletus "Clete" Beam (1889–1960), and William Franklin Beam; (back row) Cora Louella Beam Jonas (1878–1961), John Frank Beam (1885–1954), John Boston Beam (1857–1918), Dora Massagee Beam (1857–1927), Margaret "Maggie" Wehunt Beam (1867–1935), David "Dave" James Beam (1861–1947), Mattie Beam Harding (1884–1959), George Lee Beam (1863–1951), Charles Lee Davis (1866–1967), and Will Thomas Davis (1873–1952). (Bill Beam.)

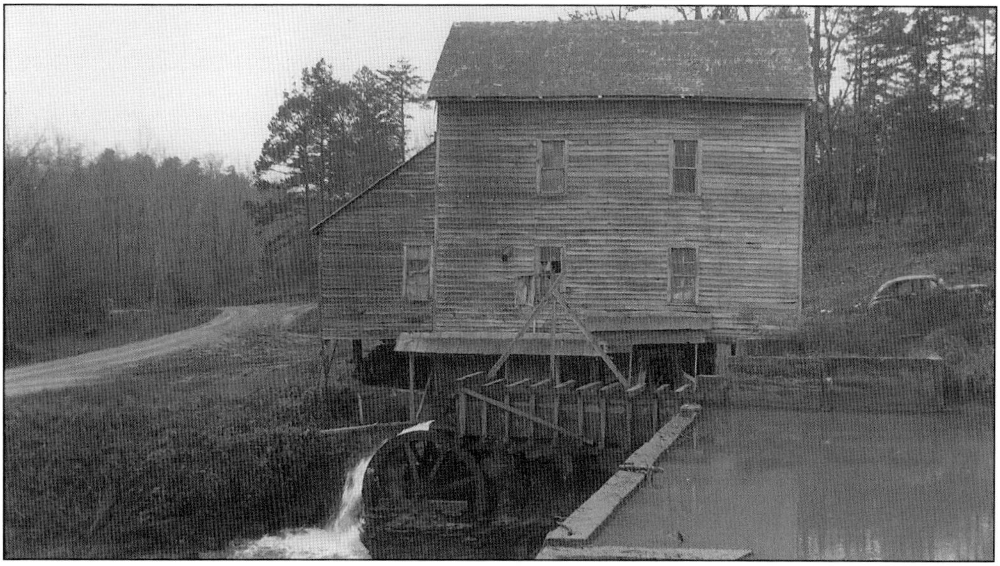

The Howard's Creek Milling Company built the Howard's Creek Mill in 1898 to serve the farming community at Howard's Creek, western Lincoln County, as there was no other functioning mill in this part of the county. The company built the mill on land carved from the Mosteller homestead. Members of the company included David J. Beam, director and builder; Charles A. Leonard, president; John E. Hoover; Cephas Cole Hoover; Thomas Monroe Hoover; and E.I. Mosteller, secretary and treasurer. (Dr. James L. Haney.)

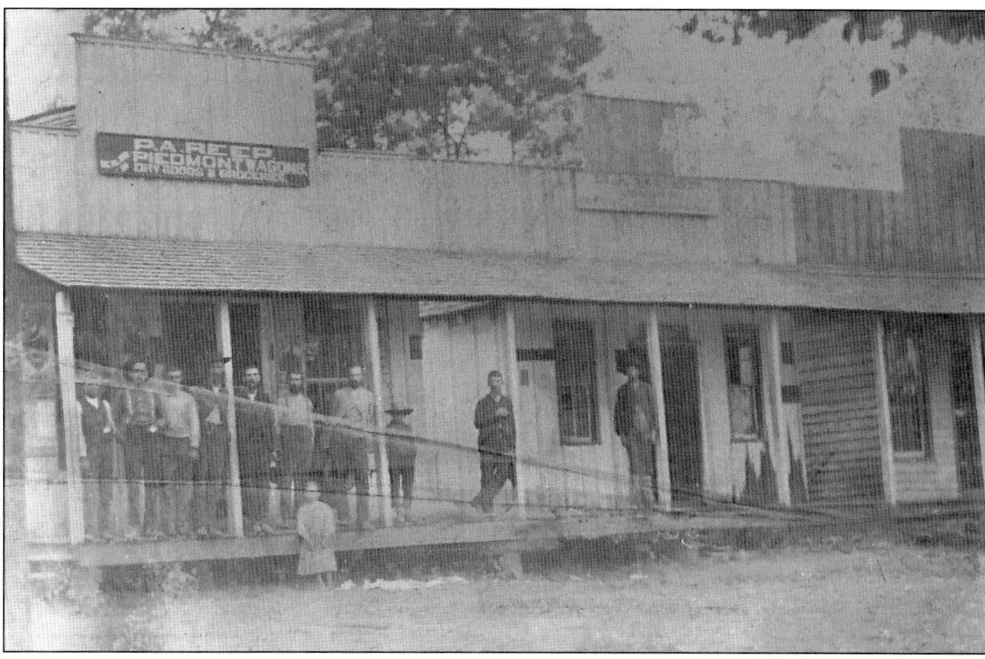

Phillip Adolphus Reep (June 20, 1847–September 13, 1904) and customers stand on the porch of the Reep store in this late-19th-century photograph. Reep ran the dry good, hardware, grocery store, and was a dealer in Piedmont Wagons in the area called Pleasant Hill in western Lincoln County before the name of the community changed to Reepsville in his honor. He was appointed postmaster of the Reepsville Post Office on April 28, 1884. (Josephine Childers.)

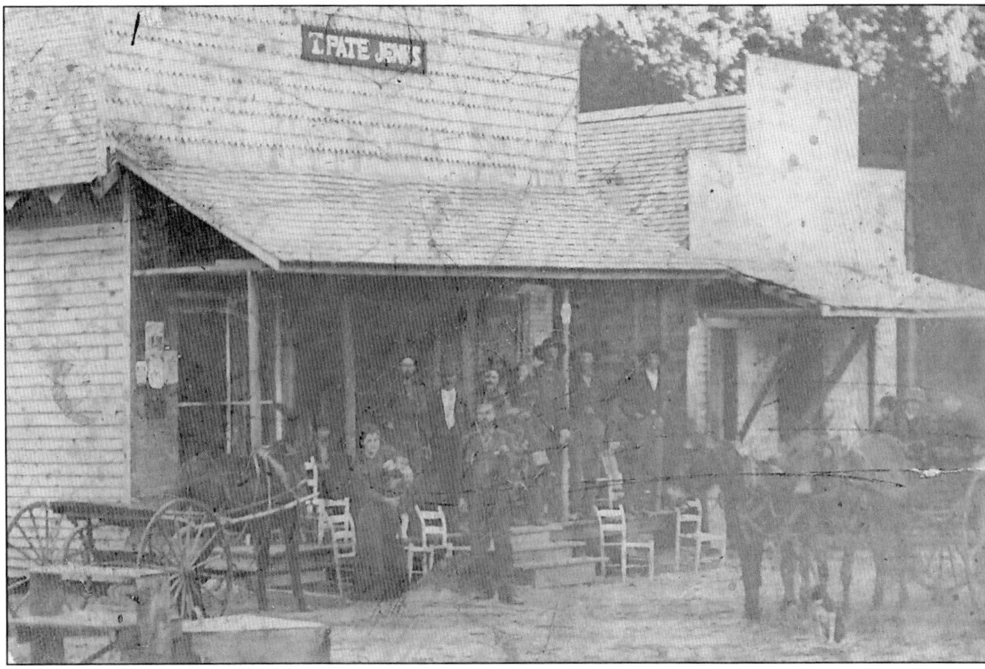

A large group of people from western Lincoln County opts to stand during this photograph from the beginning of the 20th century. Thomas Peyton "Pate" Jenks (1861–1945) and his wife, Laura Lee Bess Jenks (1865–1899), lived in the community and sold a variety of items to families throughout the county. (Guyann Johnson.)

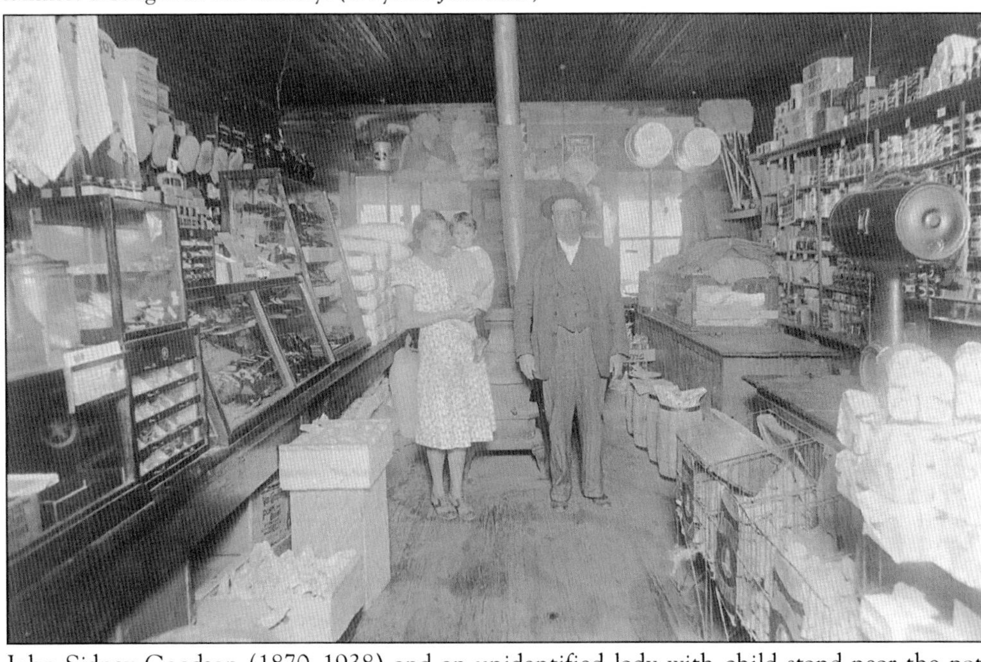

John Sidney Goodson (1870–1938) and an unidentified lady with child stand near the pot-bellied stove in Goodson's store for this photograph taken in the 1920s. The store, typical of general stores from this era, was located just east of Lincolnton on North Carolina Highway 150 facing the Boger and Crawford Mills in Boger City. (Lincoln County Museum of History.)

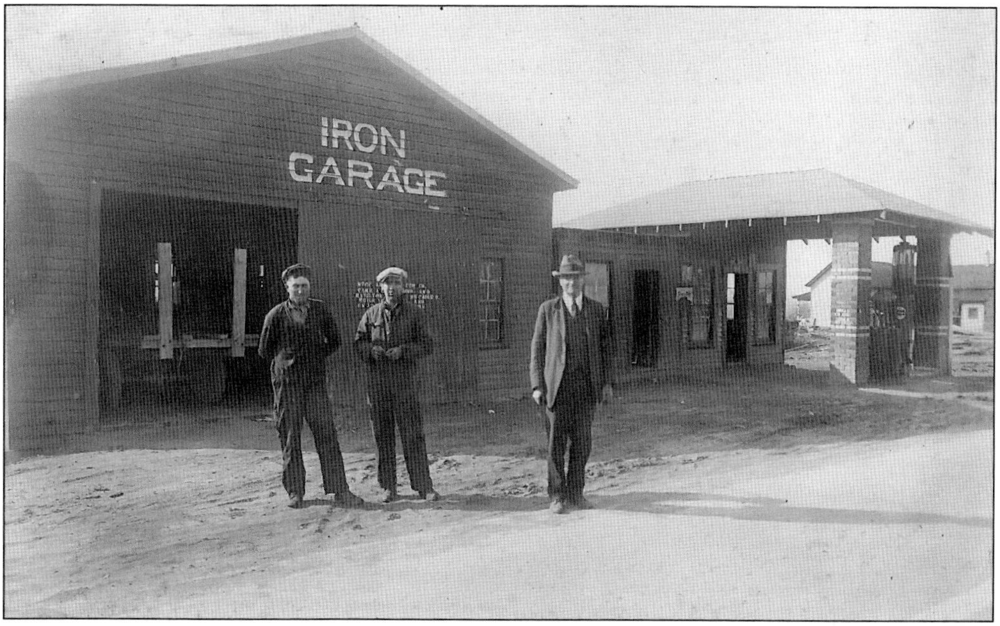

Along the southside of Highway 27, 4 miles east of Lincolnton, the Iron Garage and filling station await the call from customers in this 1926 photograph. The men standing out front, from left to right, are Earl Lawing, mechanic; Blythe Murphy "Dick" Cronland, garage operator; and John Ephrian "Eph" Cronland, service station operator. To the far right is the home of "Eph" Cronland. During the years of its operations, the garage serviced Lincoln County's maintenance trucks. (Bill and Joanna Lentz.)

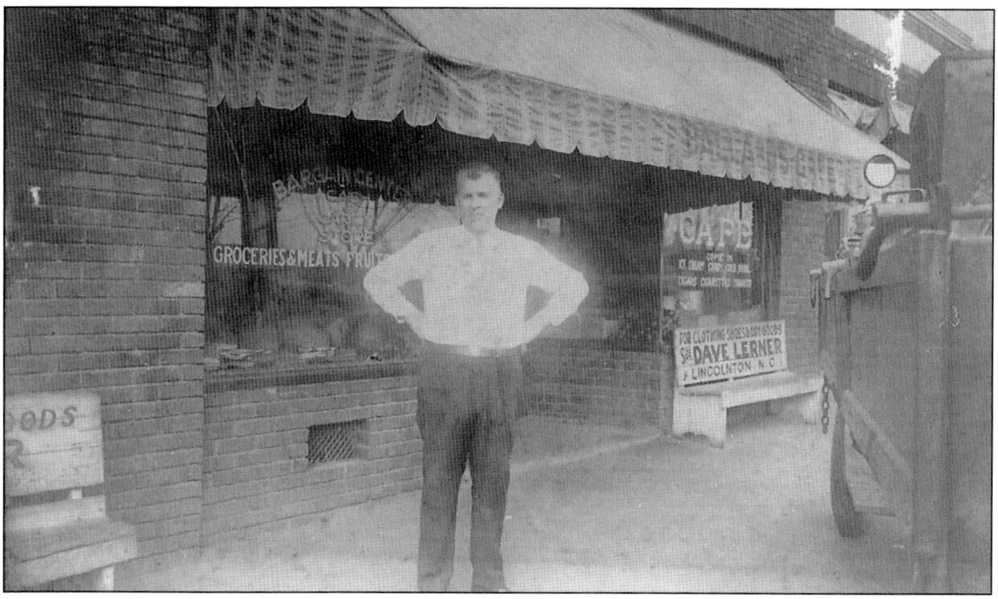

E.T. Ballard stands out in front of his cash-and-carry store after completing his usual task of sweeping off the driveway. The store fit into a long line of stores east of Mr. Ballard's house in Boger City, across from the Boger and Crawford Mills. Fred, one of his sons, ran a café in the same block and ran a lunch wagon with his son E.T. at the B and C Mills. Mr. Ballard operated his store from the late 1920s until the early 1950s. (Lincoln County Museum of History.)

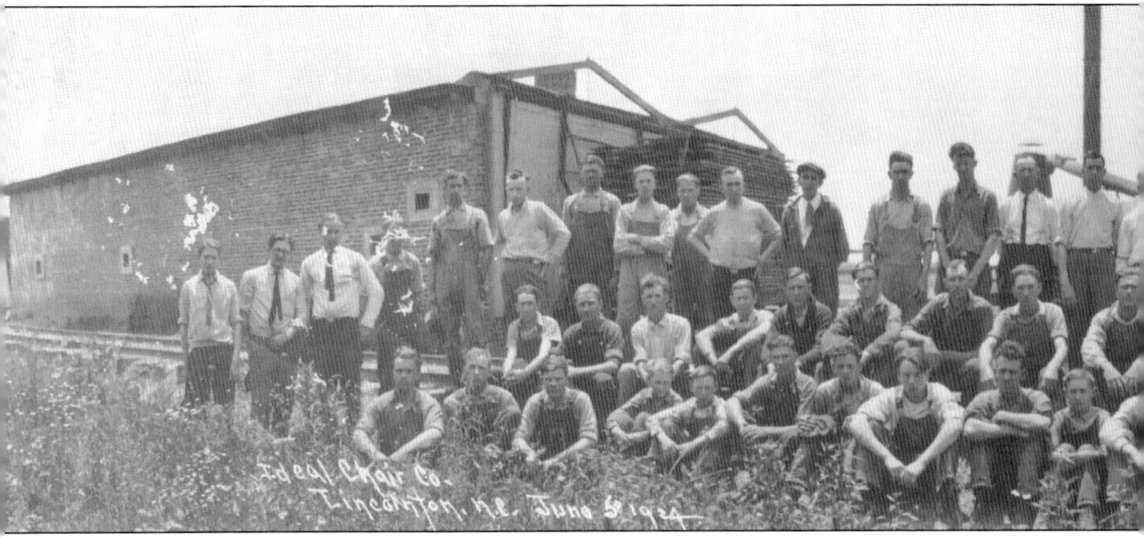

In 1922, Arthur, Nathan, and Mark Zimtbaum of Brooklyn, New York, purchased a large tract of land at the junction of North Academy and East Cherry Streets in Lincolnton for the purpose of building a chair factory. On this site, the Zimtbaums erected several wooden buildings—a manufacturing plant, boiler room, warehouse, and office. In the early years, Arthur headed the plant. Nathan made several visits from New York to the plant and later Mark came from the

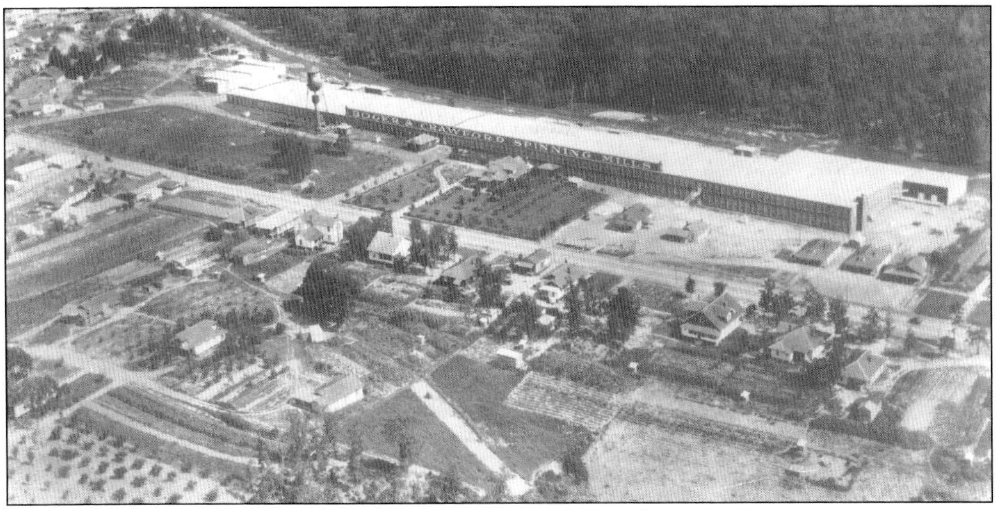

As part of the growth in textiles in Lincoln County during the early 20th century, two textile manufacturers from Philadelphia built a spinning plant between Goodsonville and Lincolnton. Robert Boger, who maintained a home in Goodsonville and supervised the mill's operations, and Mr. Crawford, a figure known only as the partner who remained in Philadelphia, opened the mill in 1919. As the years of the Depression drastically reduced the production at other area mills, Boger and Crawford operated at full production and kept wages at or above the area's average. In 1937 there were 800 employees; by the mid-1900s the number had risen to more than 1,000. The citizens in the area took notice of the mill's effectiveness in prompting improvements, and petitioned the U.S Postal Service to change the name of their town from Goodsonville to Boger City. This photograph shows the mill after two expansions in 1928 and 1938 and brought on the designation of Plants No. 1, 2, 3, and 4. After the 1964 sale of the mill to J.P. Stevens, a weaving operation was added. (John Hauss.)

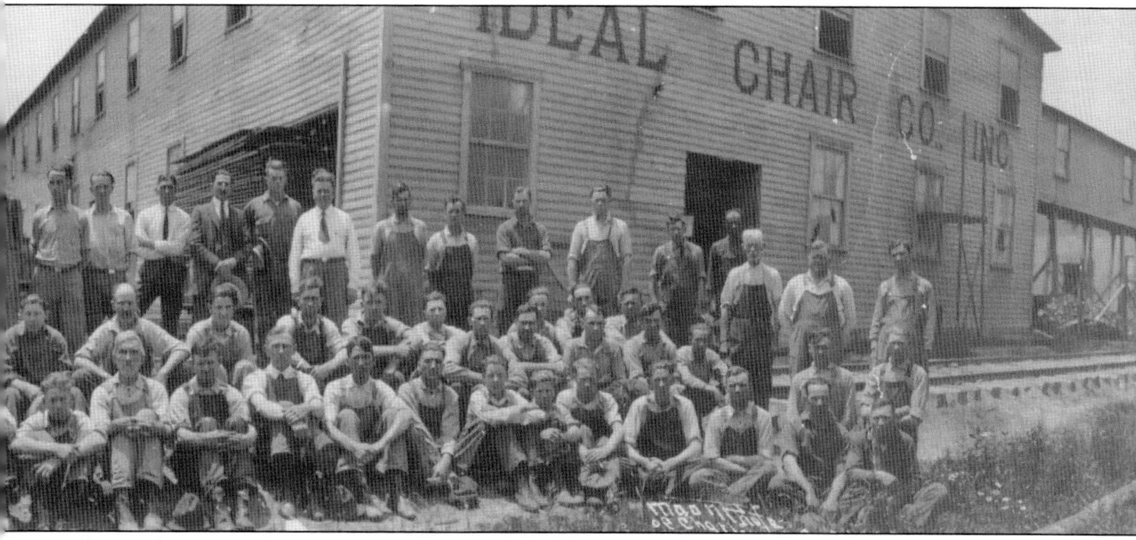

northern plant to oversee the company alongside Randolph Zimtbaum. Mildred McLean was hired to run the office, and was later assisted by Frances Buff. Joseph Long of Thomasville, Jake Schrum, and Ernest Kiger were hired as foremen to operate the plant. The employees of the Ideal Chair Company take a break along the railroad for this panoramic photograph that spans the length of their operation on June 5, 1924. (Robert Long.)

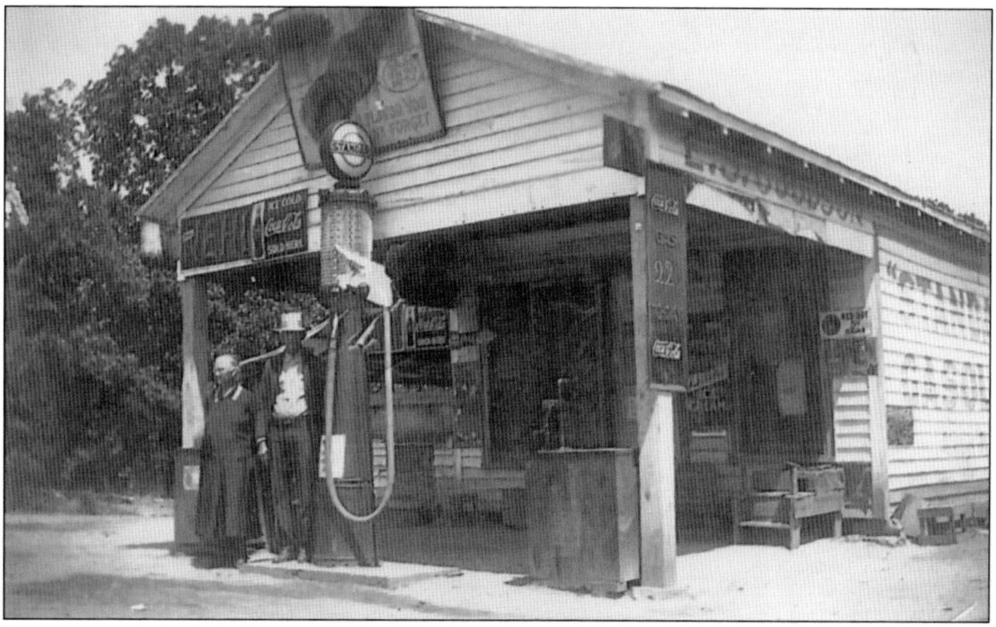

Dovie and E.J. "Jinks" Goodson ran a filling station in the Denver community of eastern Lincoln County across from the Rock Springs Campground until the 1960s. During the camp meeting, people would cross the road to buy a cold drink or a snack. Goodson built his shoeshine stand under the shed at the right of the picture to service the members of the camp meetings who needed a good "spit shine." (Terry Brotherton.)

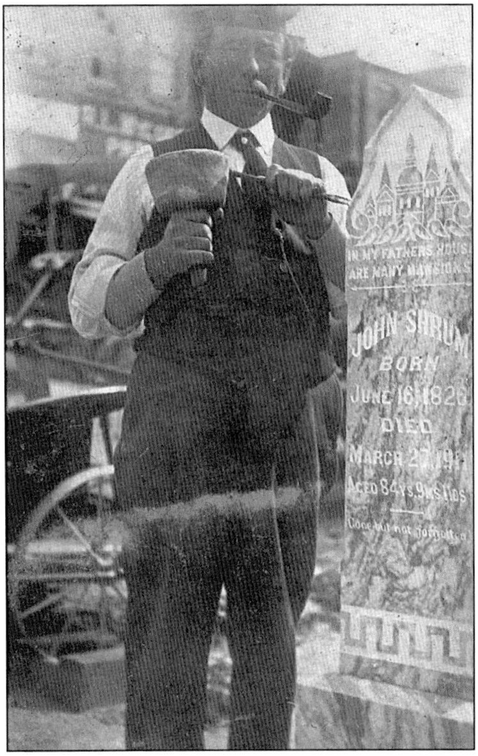

John T. McLean (1866–1922), one of Lincolnton's early stonecutters and funerary artists, stands with maul and chisel beside one of his elaborately carved monuments for a customer, John Schrum. His first marble yard occupied a vacant lot on the southeast side of the courtsquare in downtown Lincolnton. As his second shop, he used a small building on the westside of his two-story log home at 510 East Main Street. McLean served the city of Lincolnton as mayor from 1903 to 1904. (Lincoln County Museum of History.)

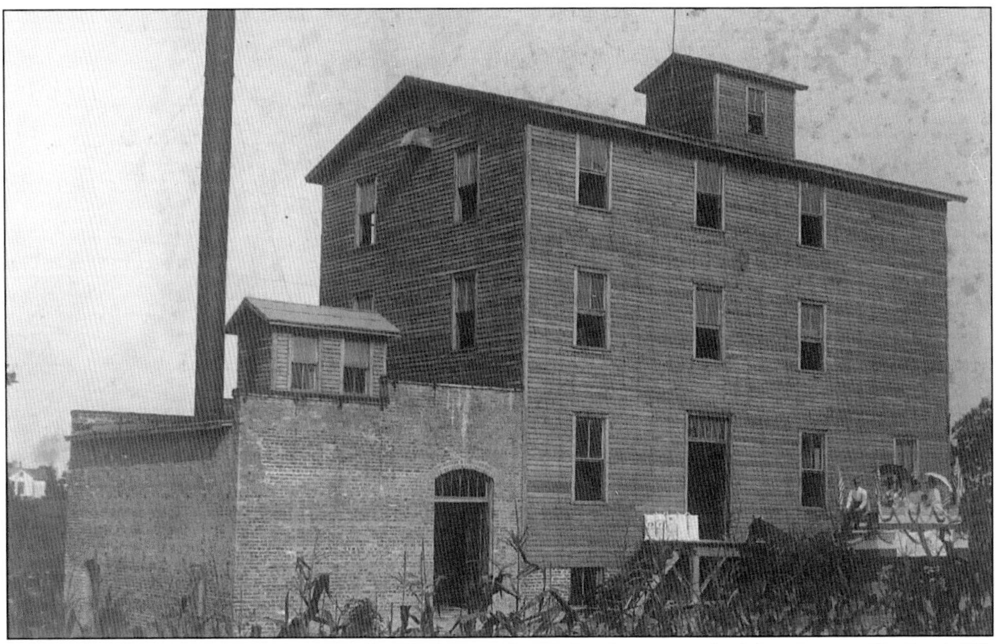

A parade float sits ready for a Fourth of July parade in the foreground of the Banner Roller Mill. Constructed in 1908–1909 by T.J. Ramseur and his sons, R.J., J.J., and George, the mill used a coal-fired steam engine, located in the smaller building at the left, as a power source until replaced by a diesel engine and electricity. It was operated as a flour and corn mill until about 1960, and then as a feed mill until 1977. (Lincoln County Museum of History.)

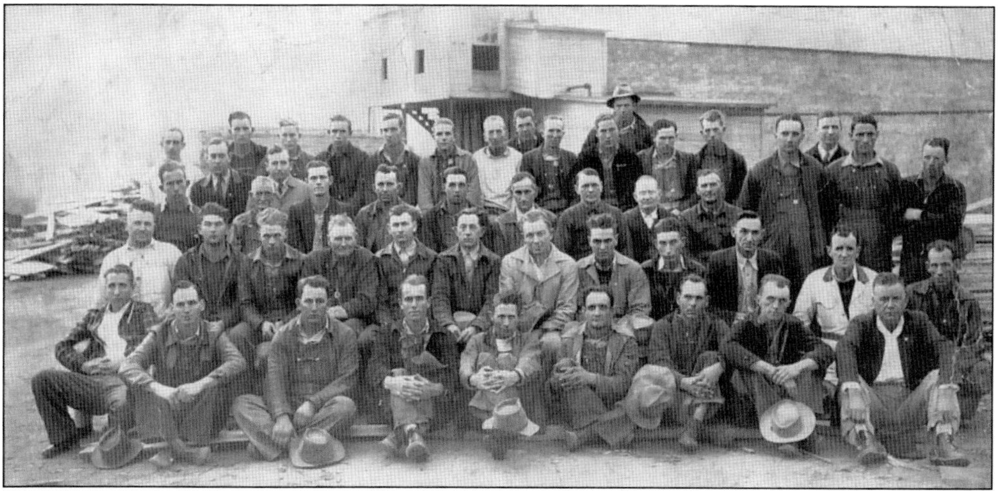

Midgett Lumber Company, started in 1924, and another lumber company that started in 1915 near Park Elementary School in Lincolnton merged to form the Seth Lumber Company in 1930. The first stockholders of this newly formed company, named for Michael Seth Beam, included John M. Beam, C.T. Hauss, and Luther Clyde Beam. Employees of the Seth Lumber Company take a break on makeshift wood risers for a photograph with the company's building as a backdrop. Seth Lumber Company closed its doors in the 1980s, and the location now at 128 Motz Avenue is the site of the Public Works and Utilities Department for the City of Lincolnton. (Elwyn and Barbara Beam.)

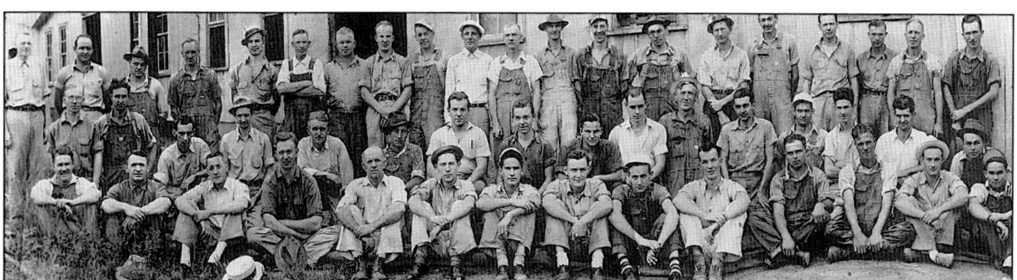

The opportunity to break from work caused some of Cochrane Furniture's finest to crack a smile in August 1931. John Cochrane, the founder, worked with Wade Manufacturing Company, manufacturer of drugstore and museum cabinets and cases, before starting in the furniture business. John's sons, Arnold, Theo, Ralph, and Paul, were employed in the business. (Lincoln County Museum of History.)

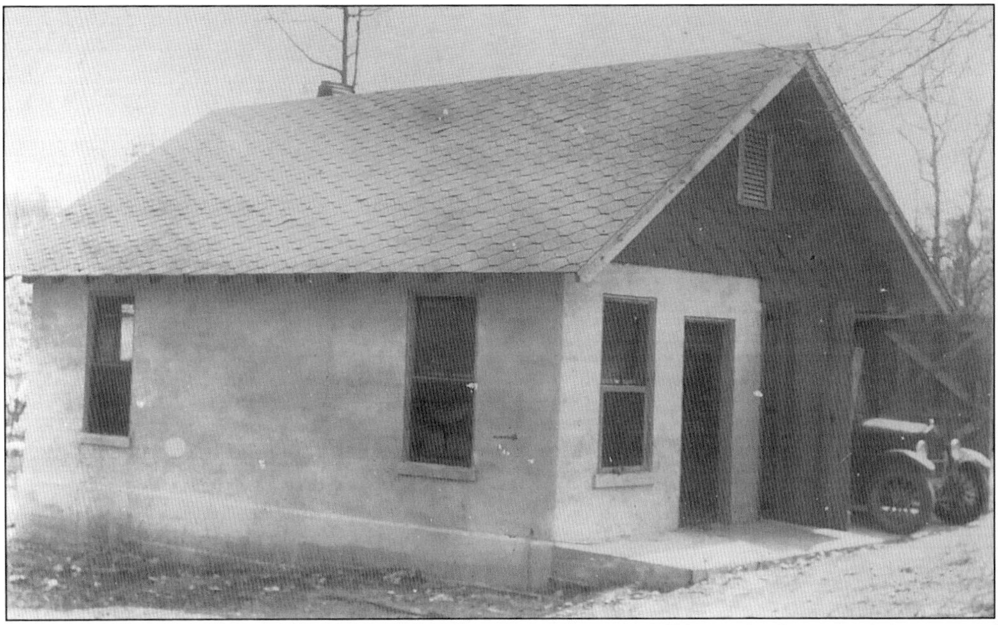

An early Ford from the 1920s is parked in the Haynes Dairy milkbarn, built around the turn of the 20th century, awaiting another day of deliveries through Lincoln and neighboring counties. Harbin Haynes started Haynes Dairy in 1914, purchasing the truck from Hoyle Motor Co. in Lincolnton in 1928. (Paul Haynes.)

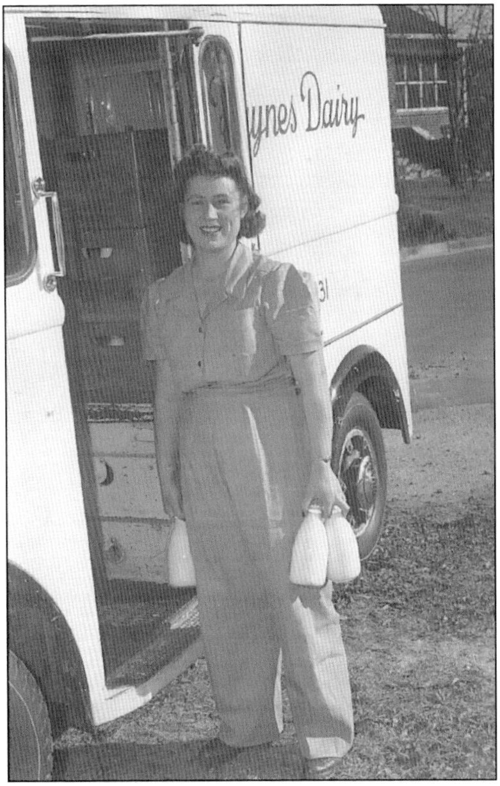

Mrs. Margaret Dellinger, Lincoln County's female milkman, handles a number of milk bottles about 1943 en route to another delivery for Haynes Dairy. Margaret's father, Harbin Haynes, was the founder of the dairy. Her deliveries, starting while still a high school student, kept her mainly in the city limits of Lincolnton. During the turbulent years of World War II, Margaret filled in on the deliveries while the young men employed at the dairy were off at war. (Ann Brown.)

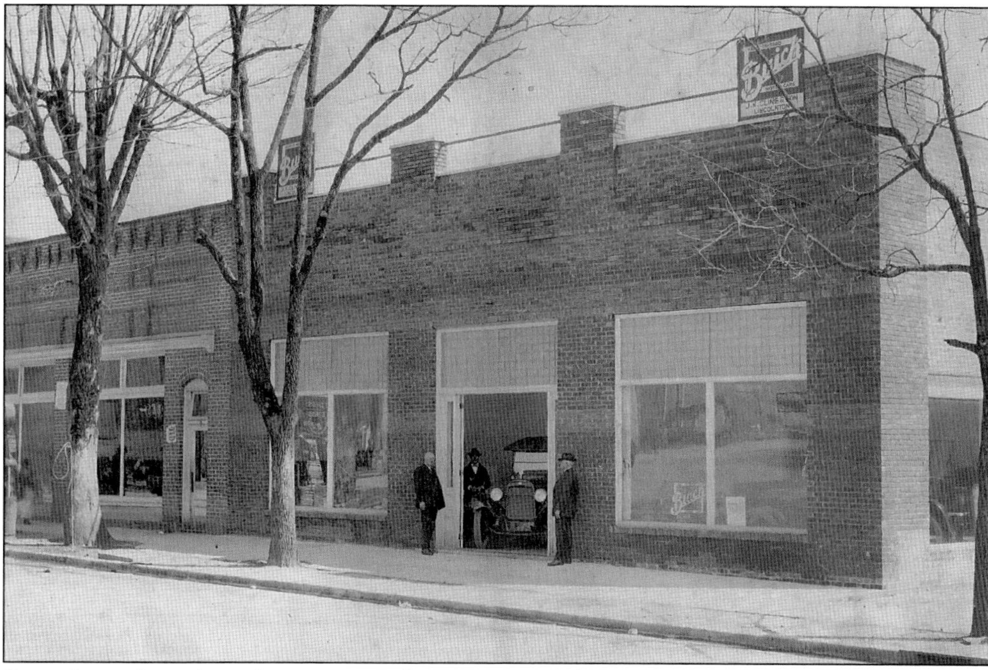

Seen above, Lincolnton's courtsquare has seen many changes since the first 100 lots were laid off in 1785. The streets all over the county and in town remained dirt, with horse and buggy tracks marking the land until East Main Street was paved with asphalt in 1921. The first county road to be paved was U.S. 321, north of Lincolnton, in 1924, followed by the section south of Lincolnton in 1925, N.C. 27 east of Lincolnton in 1925, N.C. 150 toward Cherryville in 1926, N.C. 27 west of Lincolnton in 1930, and N.C. 150 toward Mooresville in 1934. Situated on the southeast corner of the courtsquare, Guy E. Cline's Buick dealership stands as a large operation in this photograph taken in the 1930s. Originally located in the larger three-story building to the east, Guy E. Cline purchased a portion of the property in 1916 and the rest in 1928 from his father, John K. Cline (seen below). Both Guy and his father, John, sit in the showroom of the dealership with a classic Buick awaiting a look from a customer. Bank of America now occupies this corner. (Mike Cline.)

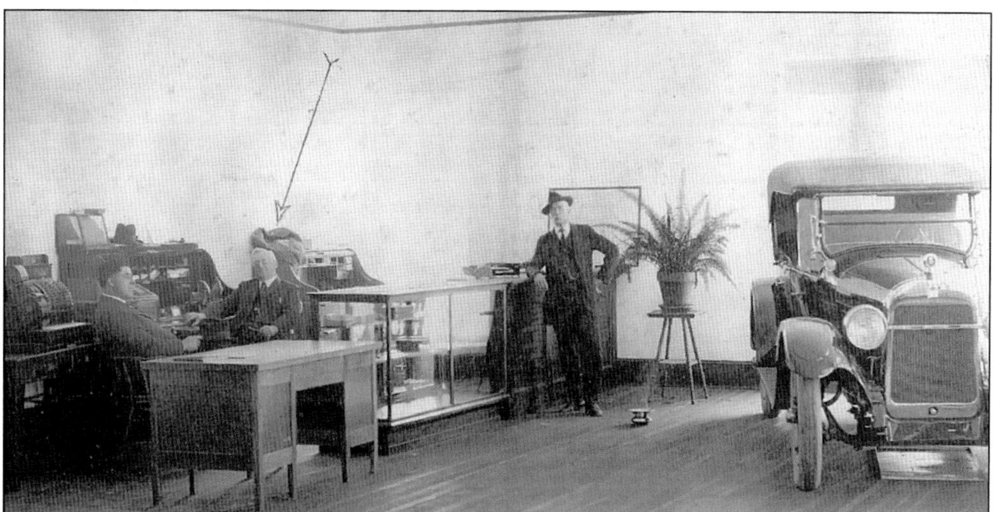

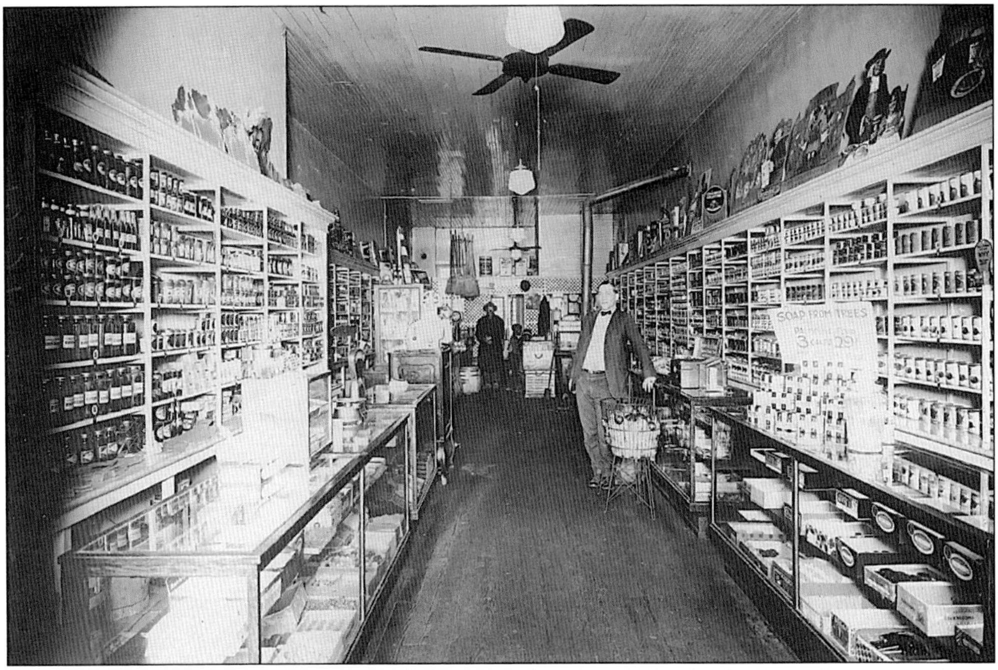

Surrounded by shelves and counters full of merchandise, M.L. Little, Lincolnton merchant, stands ready for customers in this photograph taken around 1915. The Lincoln Store was located in the first block of East Main Street in downtown Lincolnton. Little hired local high school boys to make deliveries to customers during the Depression. At one time, Little ran a variety shop in the basement of the store. (Ermintrude Mullen.)

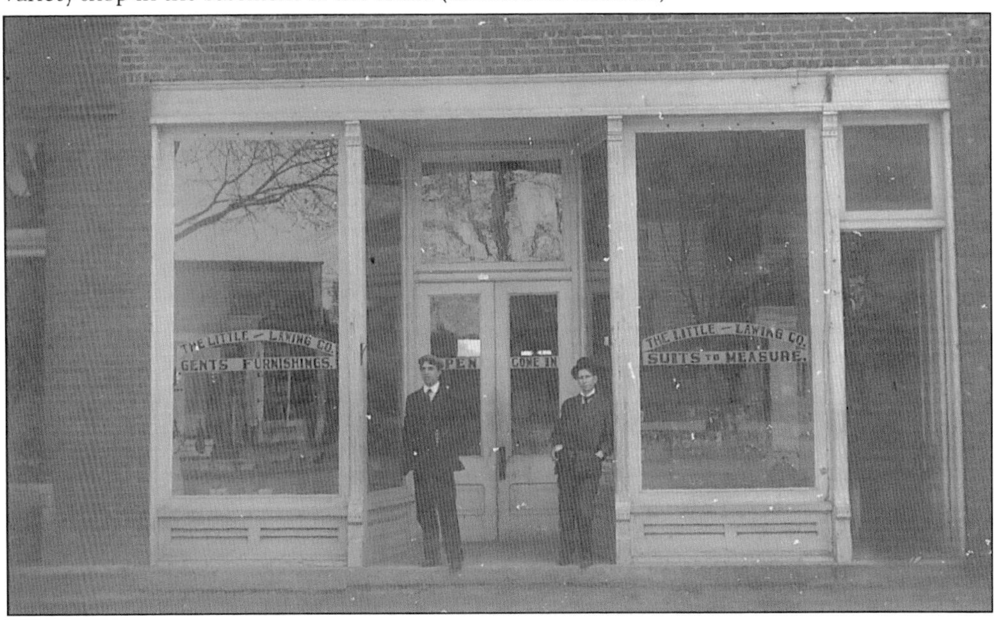

M.L. Little and W.L. Lawing stand on the front step of their clothing store at 106 East Main Street in the early 20th century. Little partnered with Lawing in this business venture before opening his grocery store a few years later in the same block on East Main. (Ermintrude Mullen.)

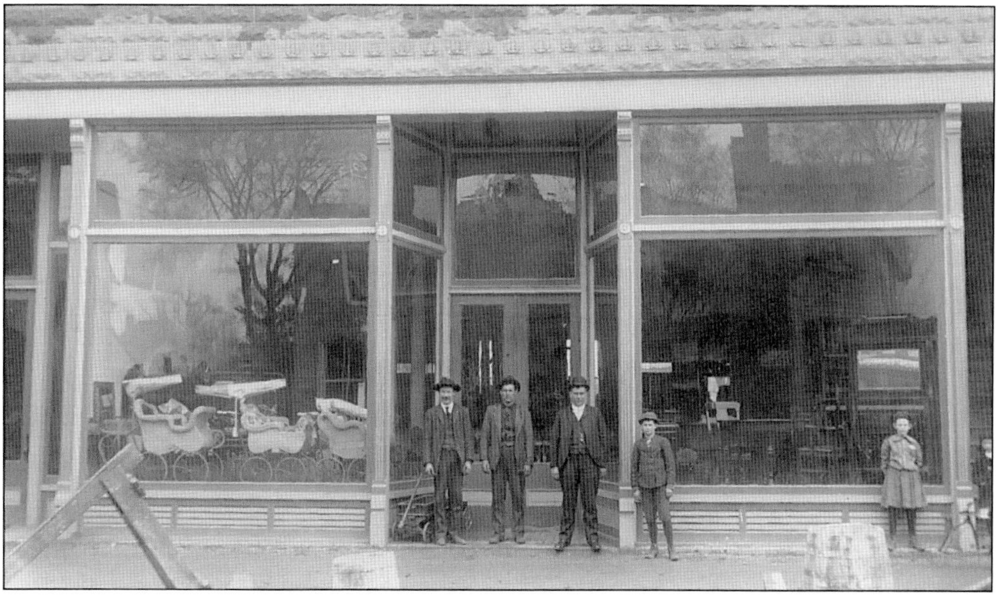

E.C. Baker, the gentleman on the right in the doorway, opened Baker Furniture and Undertaking around the turn of the 20th century at 122 East Main Street as the first commercial undertaking establishment in Lincolnton. Baker followed the typical arrangement by displaying furniture on the first floor and caskets on the second. Fire destroyed the building in 1929. (David C. Heavner.)

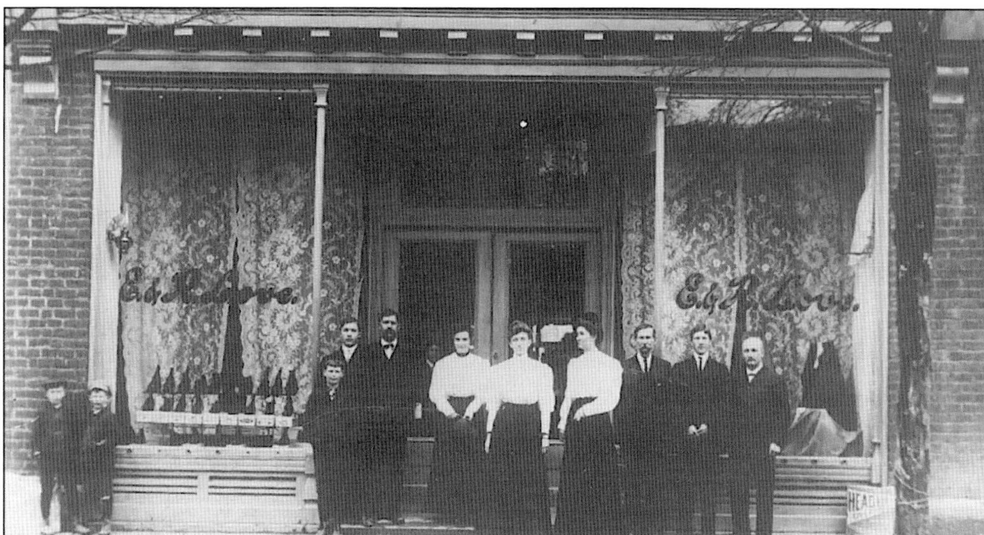

The bold red letters reading "E & R Love" are just as striking as the uniforms worn by the employees in this photograph taken in the early 1900s in the first block of East Main Street. Edgar Love, a Gastonia-native who came to Lincolnton in 1892, owned the store along with his brother Robert, who oversaw its management. William Sherrill, author of the *Annals of Lincoln County*, described Love as a "community builder who was willing to be taxed for needed improvements, for better school facilities, for paved streets, for the city water and light systems, and for modern school buildings. He held positions as mayor, chairman of the school board, and as a state legislator for two terms (1917 and 1919)." (Jim Love.)

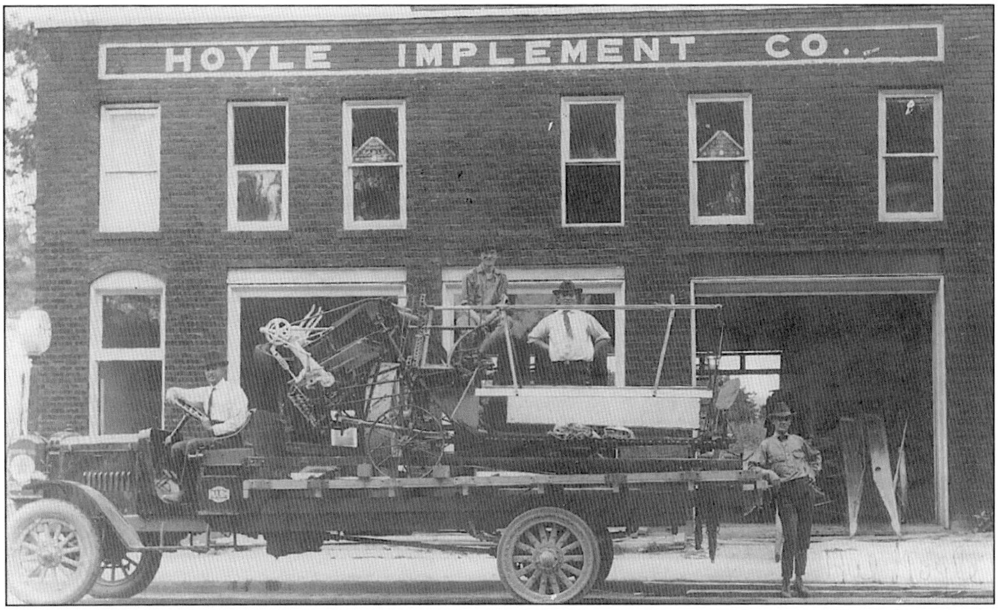

Loaded and ready to deliver some farming implements, members of the staff of the Hoyle Implement Co. park in front of their building in the second block of East Main Street for this photograph during the 1920s. Marcus Hoke, while living in a large Victorian House 4 miles from Lincolnton in an area called "Turkey Foot," farmed and sold horse-drawn farm machinery. Seeking a better outlet for his equipment, he purchased the former E.C. Baker house at 206 West Main Street during the 1910s. He moved his family into the house and his inventory of equipment on the back of his lot. The brick building pictured was constructed by Hoyle and sons Fitzhugh and Hal at 227 East Main Street in 1919. He began selling Fords in 1928. Hal Sr. was a local Ford dealer from 1928 to 1983. Pictured, from left to right, are Marcus Hoyle (driver), Fitzhugh Hoyle, Dewey Hoyle, and Hal Hoyle Sr. (John Hoyle.)

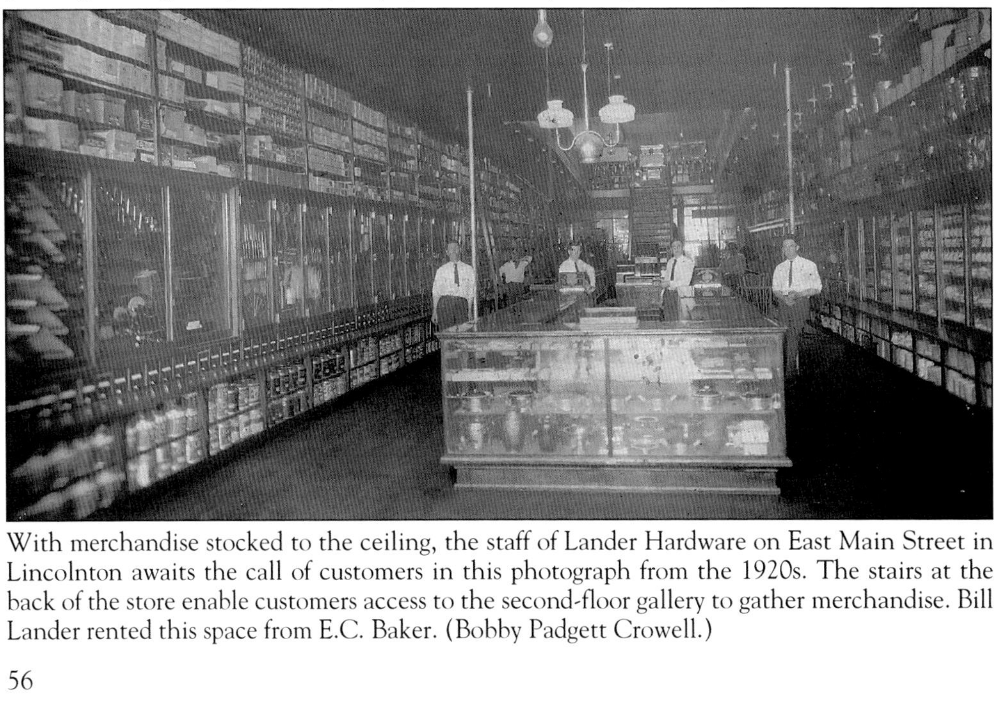

With merchandise stocked to the ceiling, the staff of Lander Hardware on East Main Street in Lincolnton awaits the call of customers in this photograph from the 1920s. The stairs at the back of the store enable customers access to the second-floor gallery to gather merchandise. Bill Lander rented this space from E.C. Baker. (Bobby Padgett Crowell.)

Three

STRIKE UP THE BAND
IT'S A PARADE

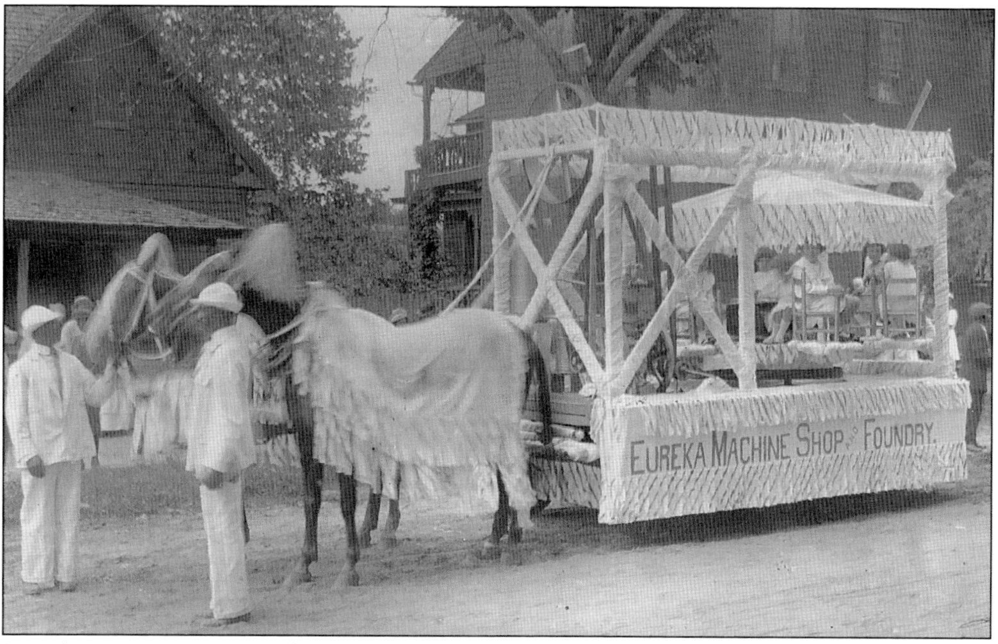

Seen here on Main Street during a Fourth of July parade, two gentleman hold the reins of the lead horses with their elaborate drapings while the float passengers await the ride. The kids are sitting atop a carousel that is turned by a pulley system built by the Eureka Machine Shop and Foundry. Located in Lincolnton, Eureka produced iron implements and tools. (Lincoln County Museum of History.)

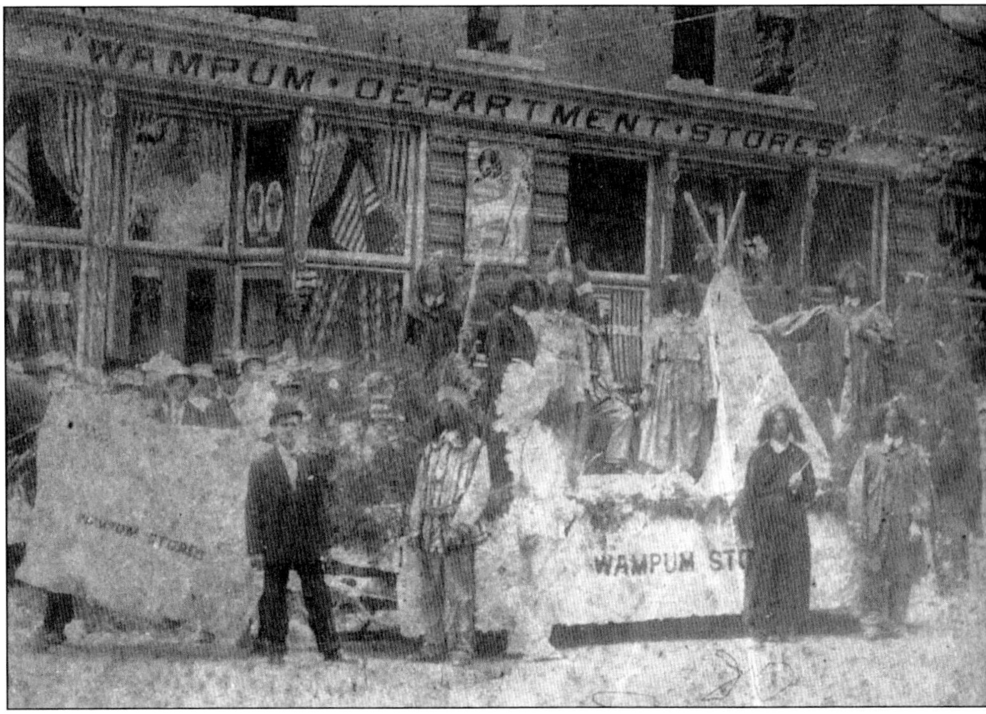

The patriotic theme of the Fourth of July Parade on July 4, 1909, is evidenced by the flags in the windows of the Wampum Department Store, situated at the corner East Main and Academy Streets in Lincolnton. The store's parade float was adorned with a tepee and individuals dressed in Native American attire. (Jack Dellinger.)

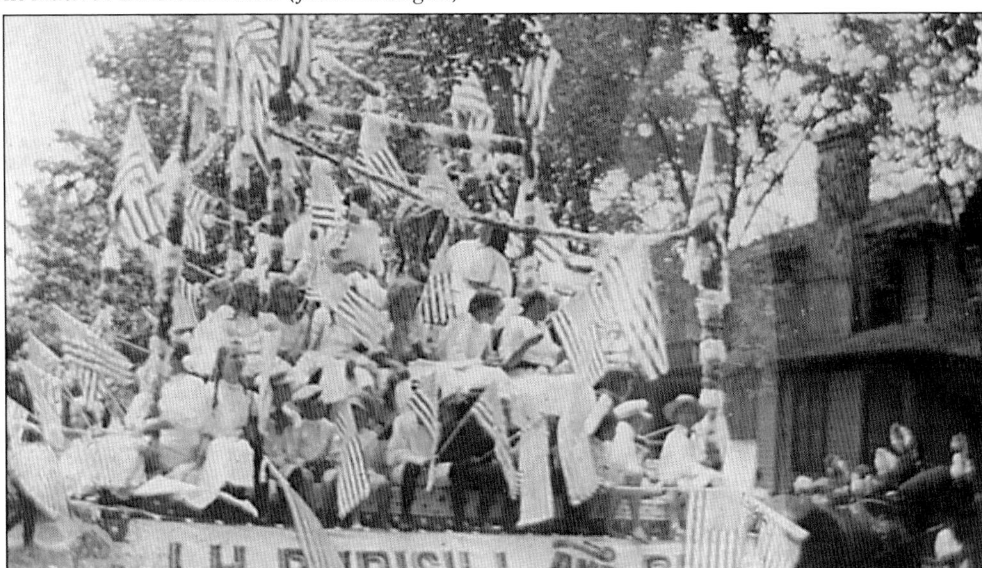

In typical parade fashion, the J.H. Rudisill and Company float brandishes a decorative cover to participate in an annual parade in Lincolnton. Located on the north-northwest corner of the courtsquare, once described as the busiest corner in Lincolnton, J.H. Rudisill and Company sold general merchandise during the 1920s. (Bobby Padgett Crowell.)

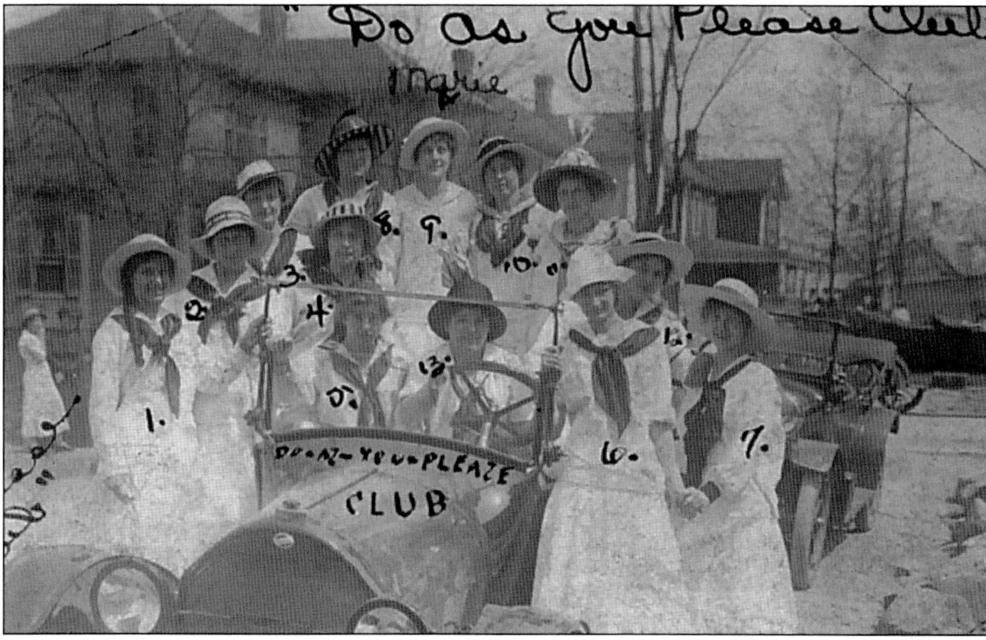

The "Do As You Please Club" stands in full force behind the wheel for the local "Bickett for Governor" Democratic rally of 1916. Those pictured are as follows: 1. Willie Costner (Mrs. E.W.G. Hoffman); 2. Sallie Lee Nixon (never married); 3. Flora Camp (Mrs. Jim Merritt); 4. Naomi Ensor (Mrs. Grady Crowell); 5. Georgia Heavner (Mrs. J. Thos. McLean); 6. Ruby McLean (Mrs. Luther House); 7. Grace Sherrill (Mrs. Erskine Willis); 8. Corinne Crowell (Mrs. Jean Schenck); 9. Marie Rudisill (Mrs. Hal Hoyle); 10. Lois Yoder (Mrs. Ruel Newton); 11. Marie Motz (Mrs. Heath); 12. Lena Dellinger (Mrs. Richard Mullen); and 13. Ruby Padgett (Mrs. Roger Hickman). Their claim was the following: "This club was in name only, as we never did get to do as we pleased!" (John Hoyle.)

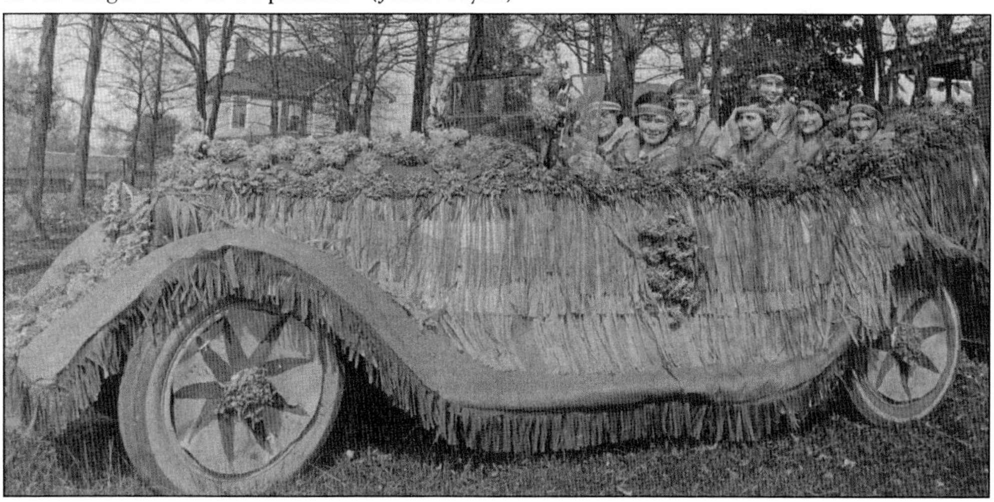

A group of women from Lincolnton pause for a moment en route to a Fourth of July parade on East Main Street. Looks of pride beam from their faces for the time they spent adding the fanciful decorations to their car. They are, in no particular order, Margaret Dover Love (driver), Lelia Reinhardt, Mrs. Hunter Mauney, Mrs. Ed Kale, Mrs. C.S. Little, and Mrs. J.M. Shuford. (Jim Love.)

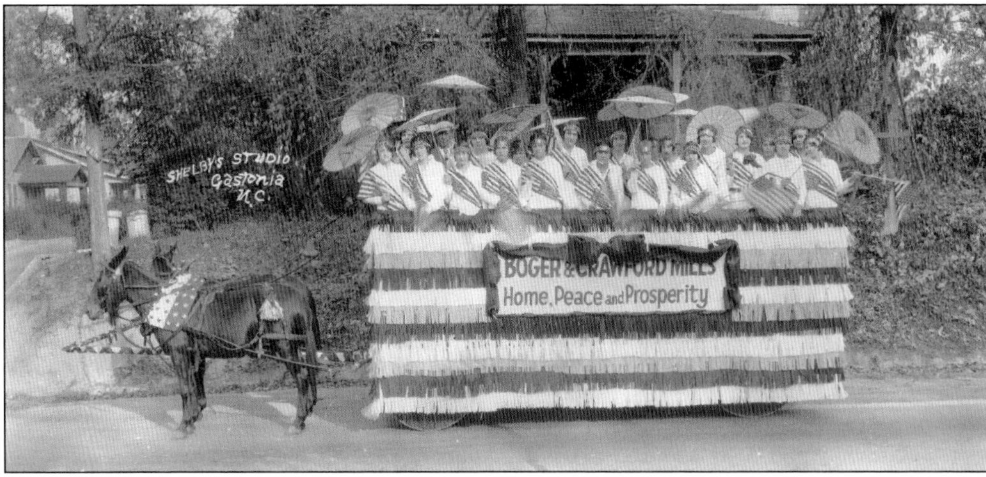

This float is thought to have appeared in a parade at the county's sesquicentennial celebration on October 10, 1935. It is assumed the participants were employees or members of employee families from Boger and Crawford Mills, smiling as the float approaches the Flint Street intersection heading up East Main Street into town. The company sponsored a semi-pro baseball team and an annual field day for employees, and emphasized education for their children. The house behind the float is the current home of Eckerd Drugs. (Lincoln County Museum of History.)

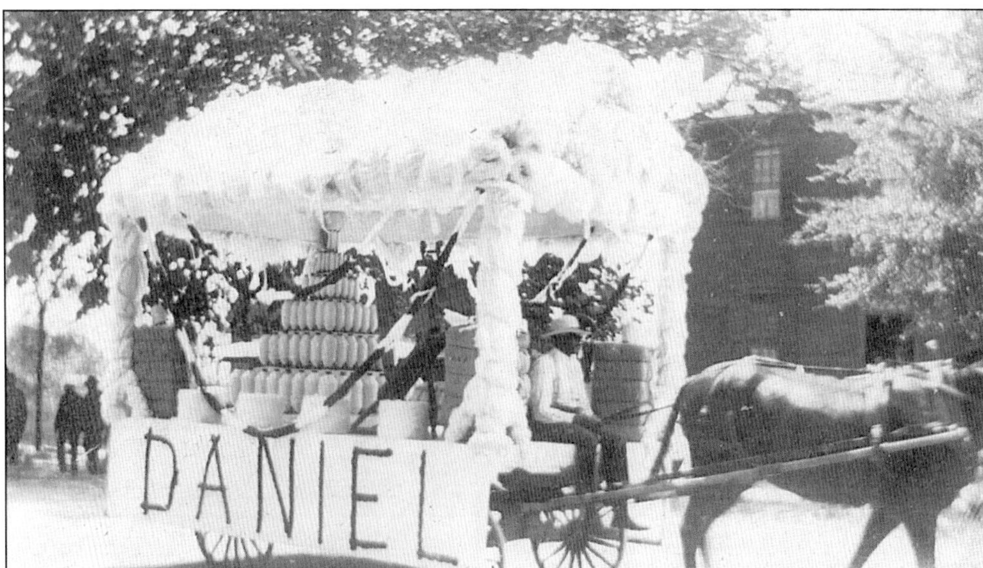

Loaded down with decorations and cotton spools, the Daniel Cotton Mill float rolls down East Main Street in Lincolnton during a celebration of July Fourth. Parades have been for many years an avenue for celebration in Lincoln County. Beginning with the sesquicentennial celebration in 1935, reported to have drawn the largest crowd up to that point, other parades have commemorated the return of soldiers from World War I and World War II, and the 100th anniversary of the Emancipation Proclamation. (Jim Love.)

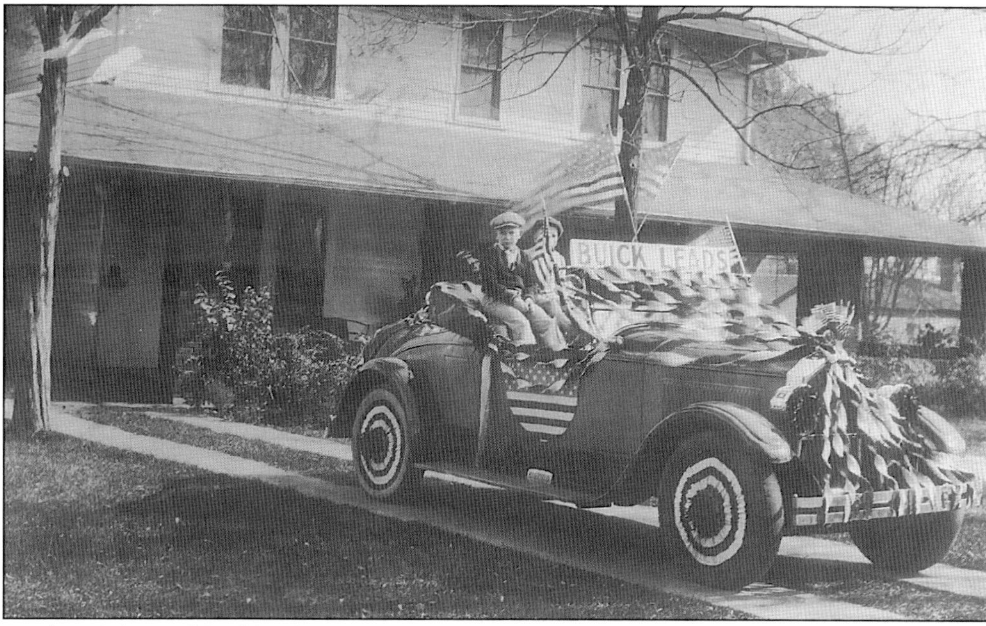

Brothers John and Roddy Cline sit atop a classy Buick from their family's dealership, awaiting entry in one of Lincolnton's Fourth of July parades. Their house stands at the intersection of West Sycamore and North High Streets in Lincolnton. (Mike Cline.)

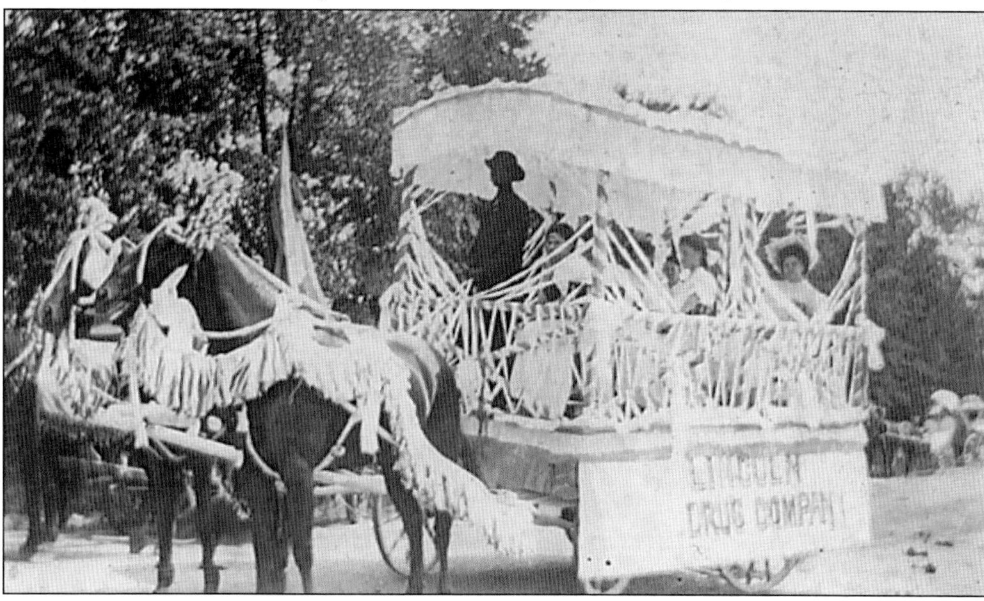

The Lincoln Drug Company float is standing ready to begin the festivities of another Fourth of July parade in downtown Lincolnton. This company began in the 1930s, when Mr. C.B. Phillips acquired the building, previously operated as the Wampum Department Store and Efirds Department Store, and opened it as a retail drugstore and pharmacy. A registered pharmacist, Phillips held ownership of the building until the 1940s, at which time James A. Abernethy Jr. purchased the property and operated it as Lincoln Cut Rate Drugs. It is currently operated as Lincoln Drugs, Inc. at the corner of East Main and South Academy Streets. (Bobby Padgett Crowell.)

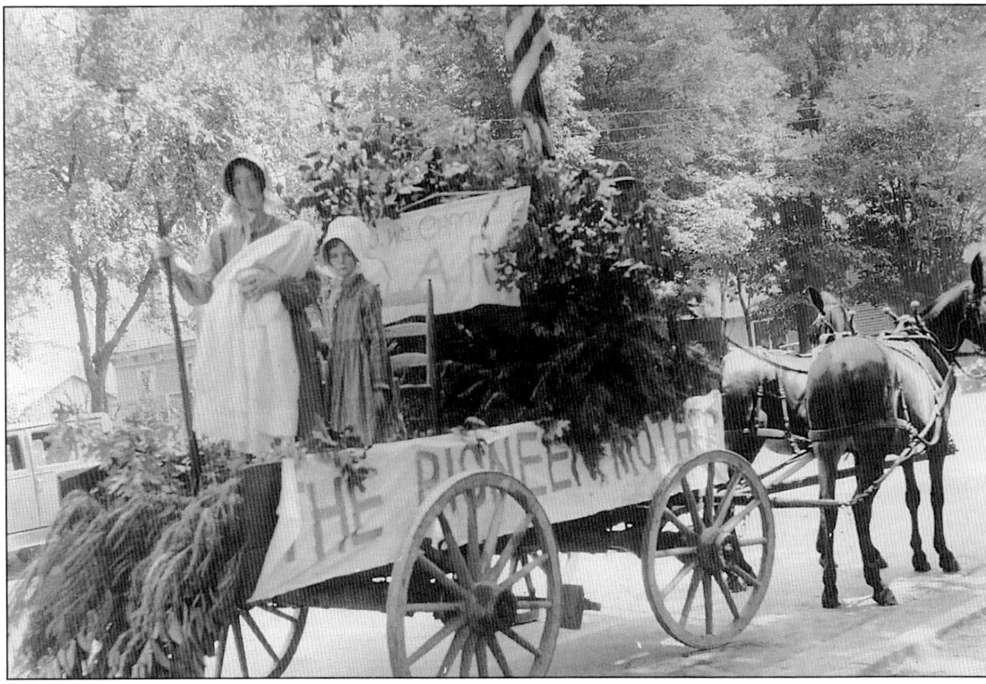

Barbara Bowen poses as the mother and Nancy Willis Massey as the child on this sesquicentennial float titled "The Pioneer Mother" in downtown Lincolnton. The J. Wm. Chronicle Chapter of the Daughters of the American Revolution entered their float in the parade commemorating the 150th anniversary of the Battle of Ramsour's Mill (June 20, 1780), celebrated on June 20, 1930. (Lincoln County Museum of History.)

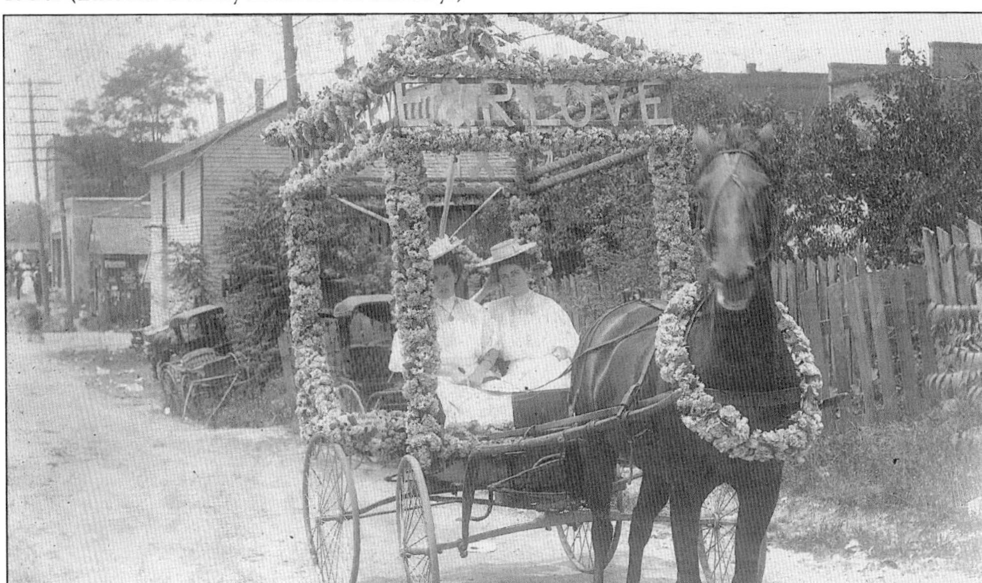

Dressed in the day's finest, two ladies ride along one of Lincolnton's back streets preparing for a Fourth of July parade. The E&R Love store is well represented with the decorations of greenery and flowers draped around the neck of the horse on a wreath and adorning the buggy. (Jim Love.)

Four

Lincoln County at War

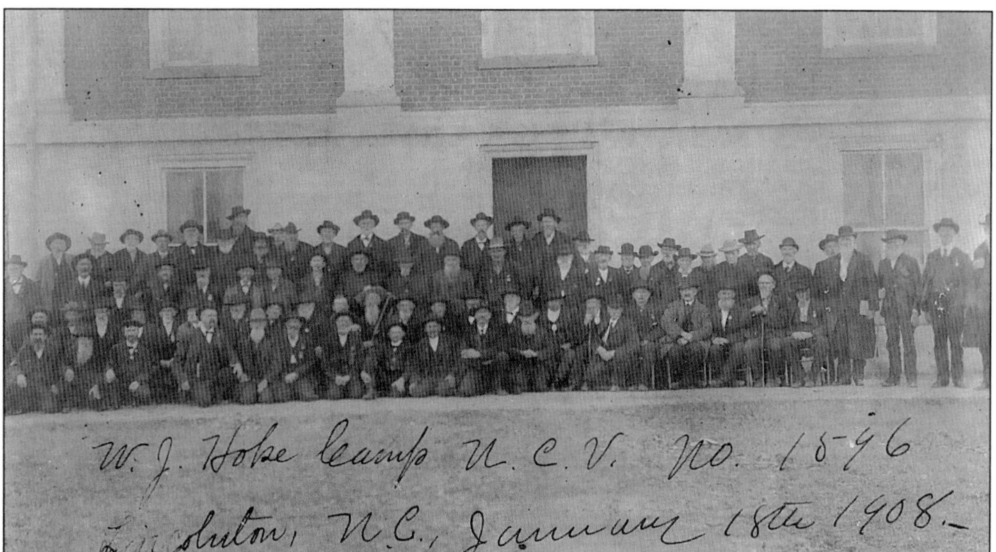

Lincolnton's Courthouse, completed six years before the beginning of the War between the States, is a fitting background for this photograph taken on January 18, 1908, of the W.J. Hoke Camp No. 1596, United Confederate Veterans of Lincolnton. Lincoln County furnished nine full companies to the Confederate Army. With a population under 6,000, 1,311 patriots took arms to fight for the Southern states. The Southern Stars, the first military company from Lincolnton and composed of 97 men, was organized on April 22, 1861, and took part in the first battle of the war at Bethel. (Lincoln County Museum of History.)

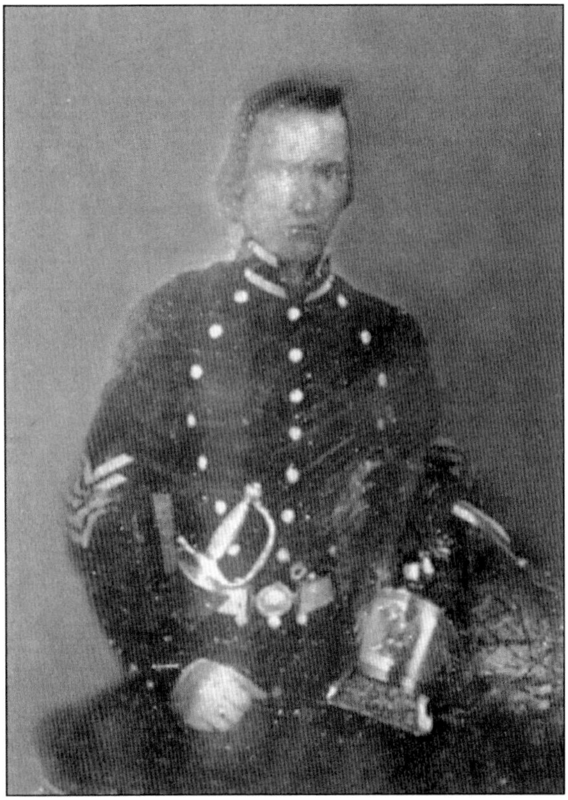

Major Hull (October 27, 1834–January 19, 1929), son of Major Hull (1790–1856) and Margaret "Peggy" Gross Hull, poses for this daguerreotype in the late 1850s. Hull is believed to have been part of the Lincoln Stars, a pre-war militia company, also referred to as the Lincoln Guards. At the outbreak of the War between the States, this company changed their name to the Southern Stars to alleviate any association with President Abraham Lincoln. Eventually, this company became Company K of the First Regiment, North Carolina Volunteers (the Bethel Regiment). (Lincoln County Museum of History.)

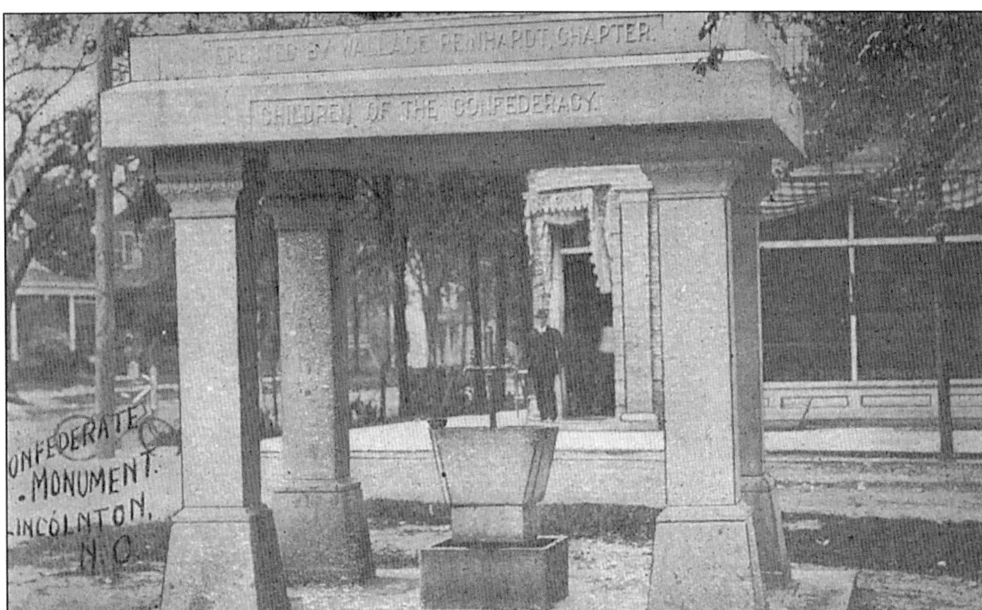

Lincolnton's Confederate Monument, unveiled May 11, 1911, was erected in honor of the soldiers who served and died in the War between the States. The Wallace Reinhardt Chapter, Children of the Confederacy, under the leadership of Miss Lena Reinhardt, raised the funds to erect a monument that would serve the citizens as a water fountain. (Linda Graham.)

Major General Stephen Dodson Ramseur (1837–1864) graduated from the U.S. Military at West Point in 1860, after a year of Davidson College, and entered the Confederate Army in 1861. He reached the rank of brigadier general after being wounded at Malvern Hill, and was cited for bravery at Chancellorsville, Gettysburg, and Spotsylvania Courthouse. He was the youngest Confederate soldier from West Point to be awarded the rank of major general. Mortally wounded at Cedar Creek, General Ramseur died on October 19, 1864, one day after the birth of his child. (NC Museum of History.)

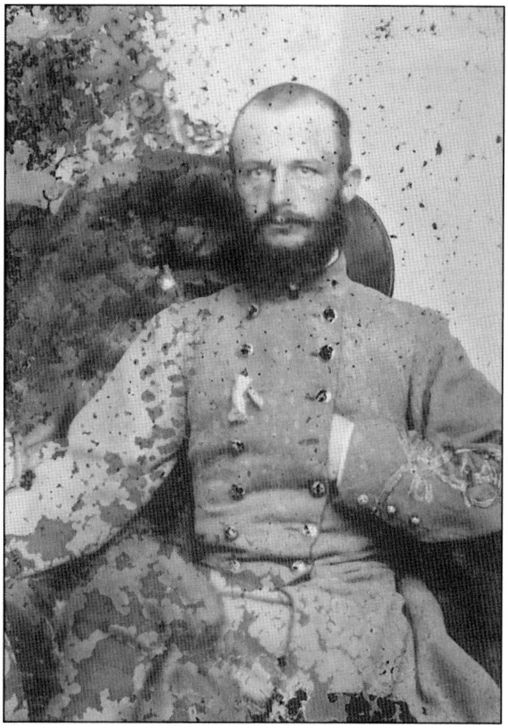

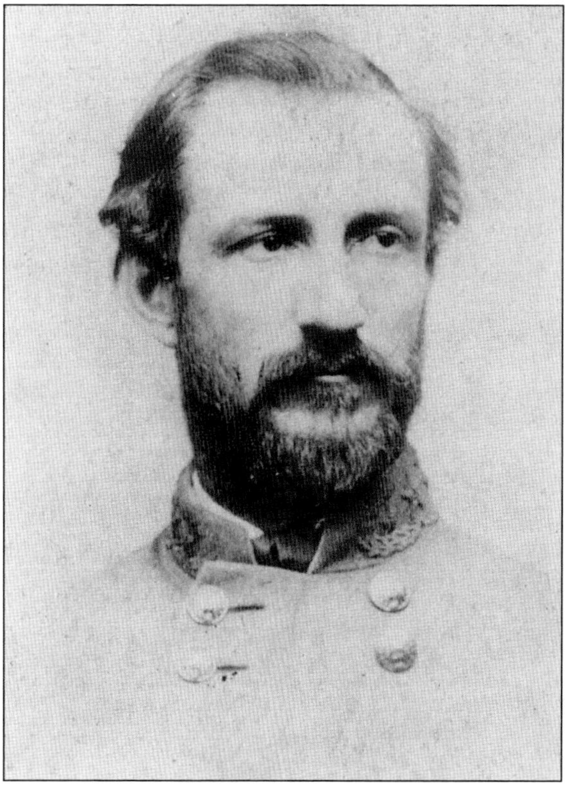

Major General Robert Fredrick Hoke (1837–1912), referred to as "the most distinguished soldier this state supplied to the Civil War," served North Carolina and the Confederacy with gallantry and outstanding leadership. Educated at the Pleasant Retreat Academy in Lincolnton and the Kentucky Military Institute, General Hoke entered service in April 1861 as a second lieutenant in Lincoln County's first company, the Southern Stars. He is recognized as one of two major generals in the Confederacy from Lincoln County, and one of eight from North Carolina. After the war, Hoke operated the Cranberry Iron Works, served as director of the North Carolina Railroad, and as president of the North Carolina Insurance Company. (Southern Historical Collection, Wilson Library, UNC Chapel Hill.)

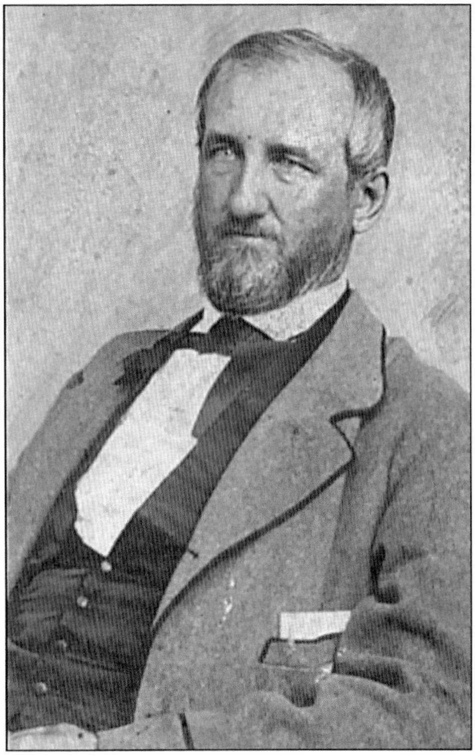

Colonel William James Hoke (October 5, 1825–October 11, 1870) casts a pensive gaze in this photograph taken after the War Between the States in the late 1860s. Hoke married Georgianna Turner Sumner (March 22, 1831–July 27, 1903), daughter of Benjamin and Sarah Hunt Sumner, on January 8, 1851, at St. Luke's Episcopal Church in Lincolnton. Entering service in the Confederate Army as captain of the Southern Stars of Lincolnton, Hoke fought at Bethel, Chancellorsville, and Gettysburg. W.J. Hoke died while living in Columbia, South Carolina, and is buried in the St. Luke's Episcopal Church Cemetery in Lincolnton. (Lincoln County Museum of History.)

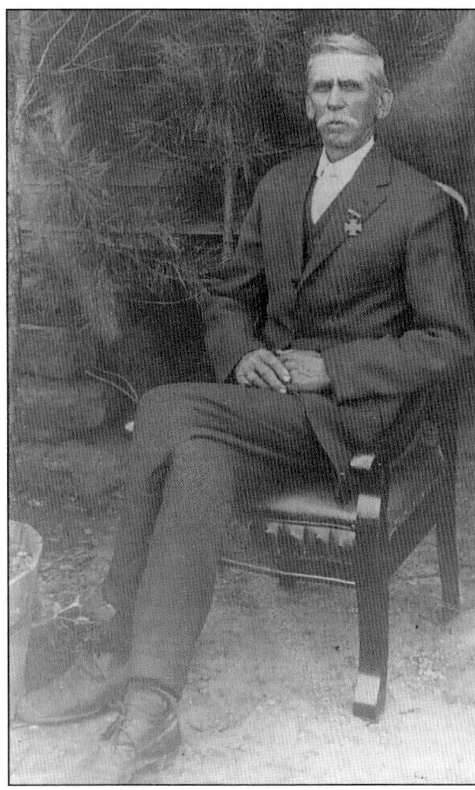

As the last surviving Confederate veteran from Lincoln County, Elias Calvin Huss (February 1, 1847–February 10, 1938), the son of David and Sarah Hallman Huss, wears his medal of service to the Confederacy in this undated photograph. Huss entered the Confederate Army on May 22, 1864, as a member of Company I, 72nd Regiment. After the war, he was appointed by Governor Ehringhaus as a member of the Lincoln County Pension Board. (Mary Ramsey.)

Joseph Long, a native of Thomasville, stands at attention dressed in his military uniform with rifle in hand while in service to the United States during the Spanish-American War at St. Simon's Island, Georgia. Long enlisted and was mustered into service with the Second Regiment of Volunteers from North Carolina in Company K on June 23, 1898. He was mustered out in Wilmington on November 18, 1898. Coming to Lincolnton, Long worked as a foreman at the Ideal Chair Company and upon retirement wrote a column titled "Old Rambler" in the local paper. (Robert Long.)

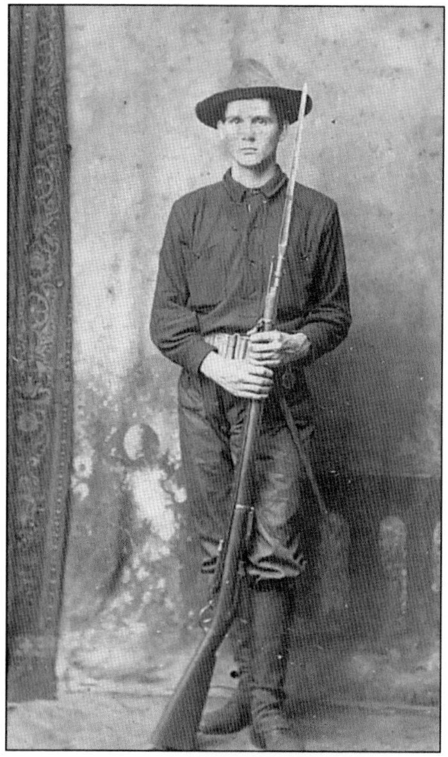

First Lieutenant Harry Page and Second Lieutenant Sam Bell sit in their chairs under a small tent while in Havana, Cuba, during the Spanish-American War. (Edward Little.)

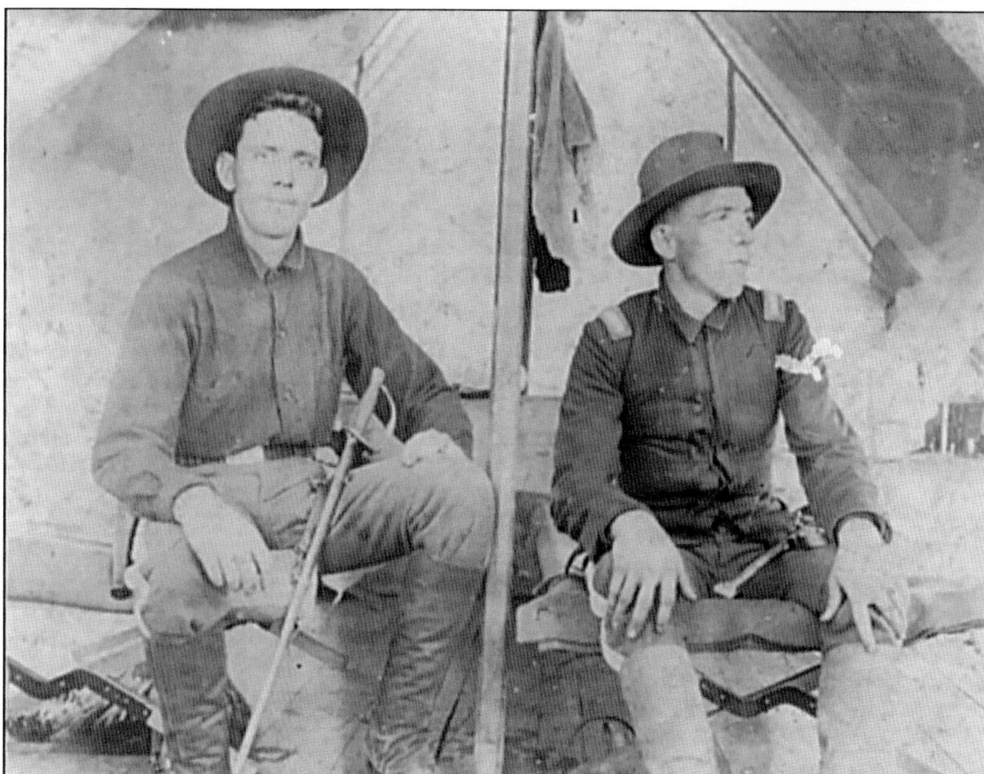

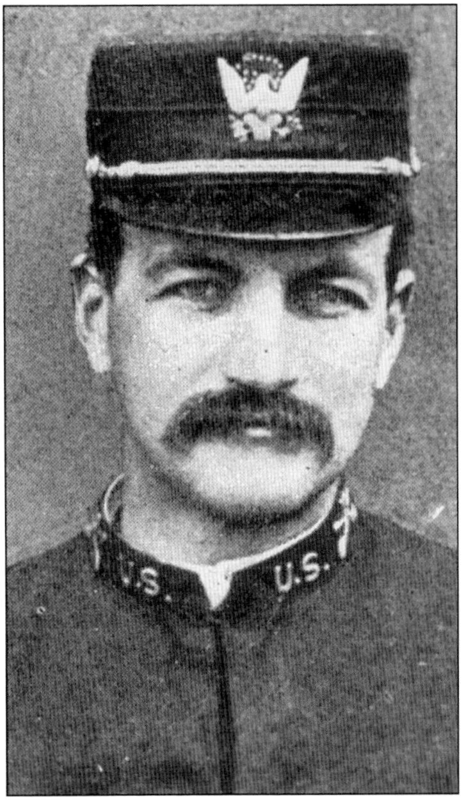

One of Lincolnton's most highly regarded heroes, William Ewen Shipp (August 23, 1861–July 1, 1898) was assigned to duty with the Tenth U.S. Cavalry, which was stationed in the Southwest Territories of the United States. In 1886, he accompanied the military expedition responsible for capturing Geronimo, Medicine Man of the Chiricahua band of the North American Apache Indians. On July 1, 1898, Lieutenant Shipp was killed in action while leading his troops in the charge up San Juan Hill near Santiago. In this charge, Lieutenant Shipp's troops were credited with saving the day for Lieutenant Theodore Roosevelt and his famous Rough Riders. (North Carolina Division of Archives and History.)

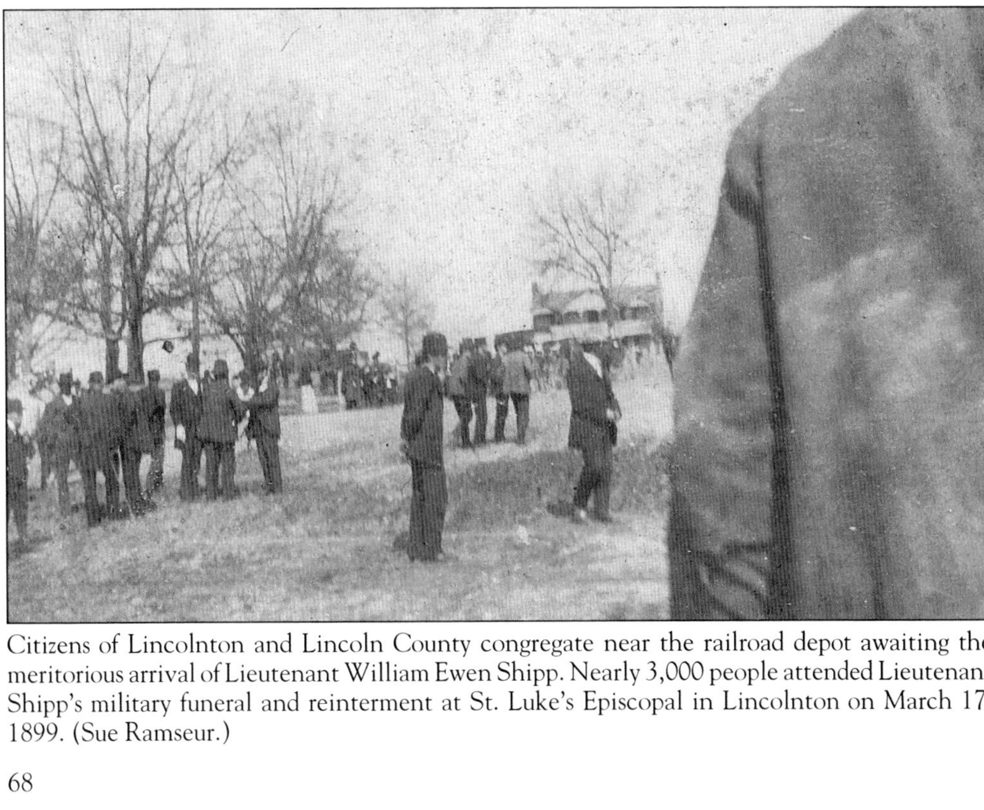

Citizens of Lincolnton and Lincoln County congregate near the railroad depot awaiting the meritorious arrival of Lieutenant William Ewen Shipp. Nearly 3,000 people attended Lieutenant Shipp's military funeral and reinterment at St. Luke's Episcopal in Lincolnton on March 17, 1899. (Sue Ramseur.)

The Confederate veterans of Lincoln County stand in a patriotic and military formation near the courthouse in Lincolnton as escorts for the funeral procession of Lieutenant William Ewen Shipp. (Sue Ramseur.)

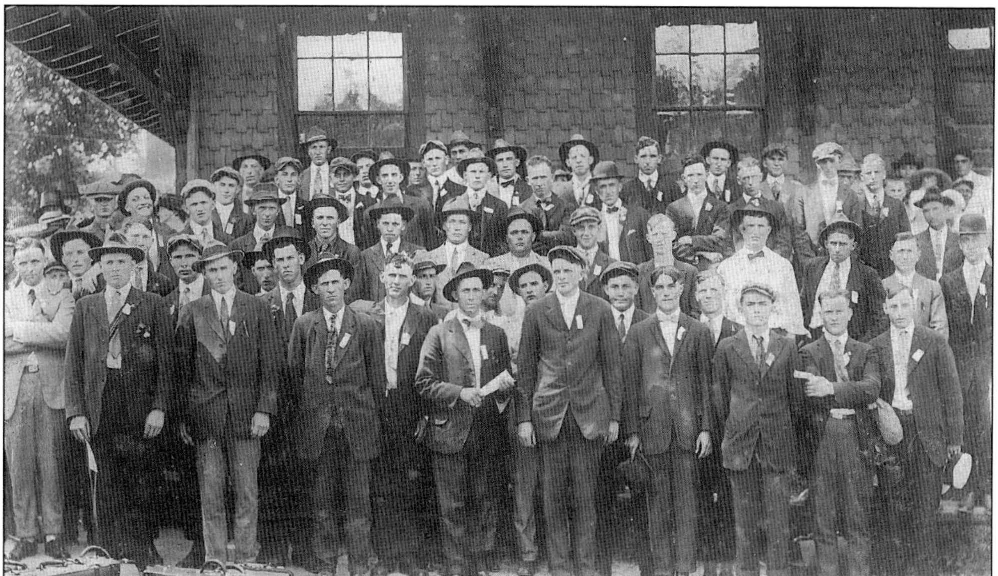

As war broke out in Europe in July 1914, President Woodrow Wilson took precaution and attempted to maintain our neutrality. The strain of foreign relations, particularly with Germany, and the sinking of the *Lusitania* by a German submarine in April 1916, plunged the United States into WW I on the side with Britain. The first contingent of men from Lincoln County boarded the train and headed to training camp in Columbia, South Carolina, on September 18, 1917. The five men called to duty were Melvin L. Sipe, George Clifton Warlick, William C. Talent, Jacob Emmanuel Miller, and Fred Ray Kiser. David Milo Wright was the first Lincoln County man to die in WW I; he died in France on May 29, 1918. With suitcases ready, this large group of patriotic men from Lincoln County waits at the Depot in Lincolnton for their opportunity to serve their country. (Lincoln County Museum of History.)

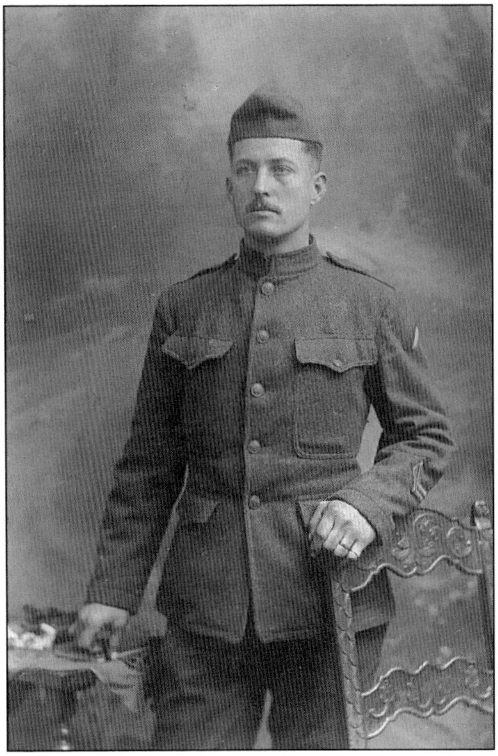

Private Patrick Winslow Goodson (April 23, 1891–January 4, 1976) stands for a photograph to send home to his mother, E.V. Goodson, and family in eastern Lincoln County. Goodson served in Company E, 67th Infantry, A.E.F. (Lincoln County Museum of History.)

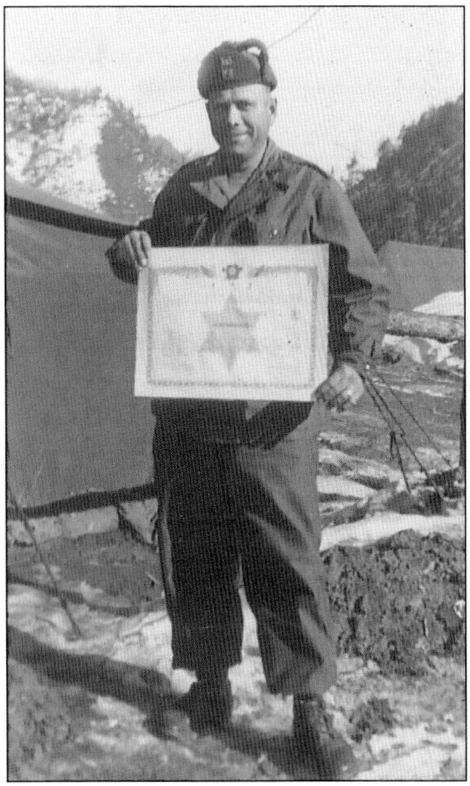

Captain Harold Craig enlisted in Company A, Lincolnton National Guard in 1939. Called in to active duty in September 1940, he served overseas during World War II in the 378th Combat Engineers Battalion. He moved quickly up the ranks and was promoted to captain in 1946. He advanced to the rank of major in 1962. His 30 years of service with the Lincolnton National Guard is the longest period of service of any member of the unit. A list of his medals and citations include the following: Good Conduct Medal, American Theater (Asiatic and Pacific, five campaigns), (Philippine Liberation, two campaigns), (Korean Conflict, five campaigns), Army Reserve Medal, and the Bronze Star for action in the Korean Conflict. Seen here, Captain Craig holds a certificate presented to his company by the Korean government. (Faye Craig.)

James Frank Love was born in Gastonia on July 31, 1894, and attended the University of North Carolina. During WW I, he served as an ambulance driver in a unit of the Medical Ambulance Corps of the United States Army. He received an honorable discharge in 1919 after 14 months of active overseas service with the American Expeditionary Forces. Soon after his return from service, Love became secretary and treasurer of Saxony Spinning Company, and became president when his father, Edgar Love, died in 1920. (Jim Love.)

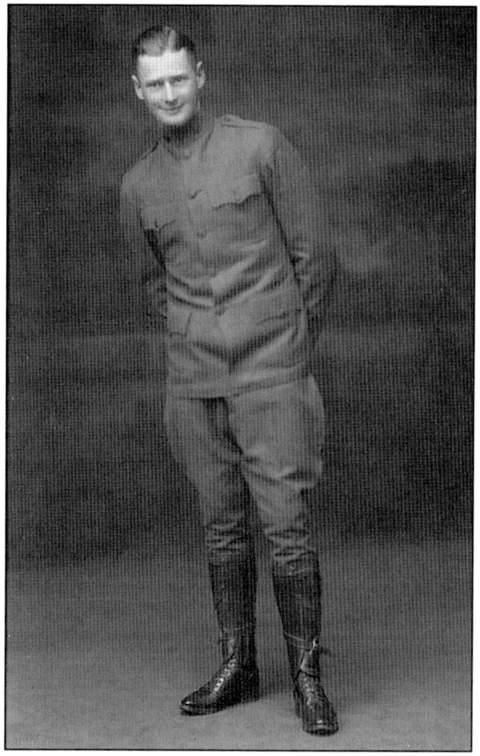

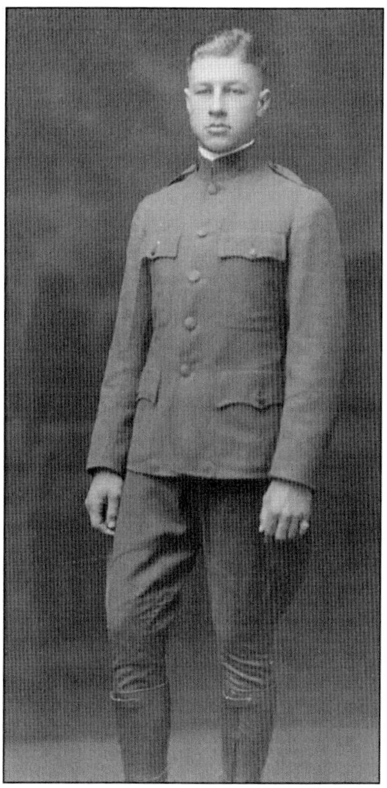

Dr. Gordon Bryan Crowell (1895–1926) stands before the camera with a pensive look for this photograph taken during his service in WW I. Crowell, son of Dr. L.A. Crowell Sr., was born and reared in Lincolnton, graduating from the Lincoln Graded School in 1912 and later from the University of North Carolina. He studied medicine at the University of Pennsylvania and afterwards, returned to Lincolnton to practice as a physician and surgeon. He was married to Frances Geitner of Hickory. Dr. Crowell died on May 9, 1926, from post-operative shock during gallbladder surgery. His daughter was four years old at the time of his death. Dr. L.A. Crowell changed the name of Lincoln Hospital to Gordon Crowell Memorial Hospital in honor of his son. (Gordon and Frances Crowell.)

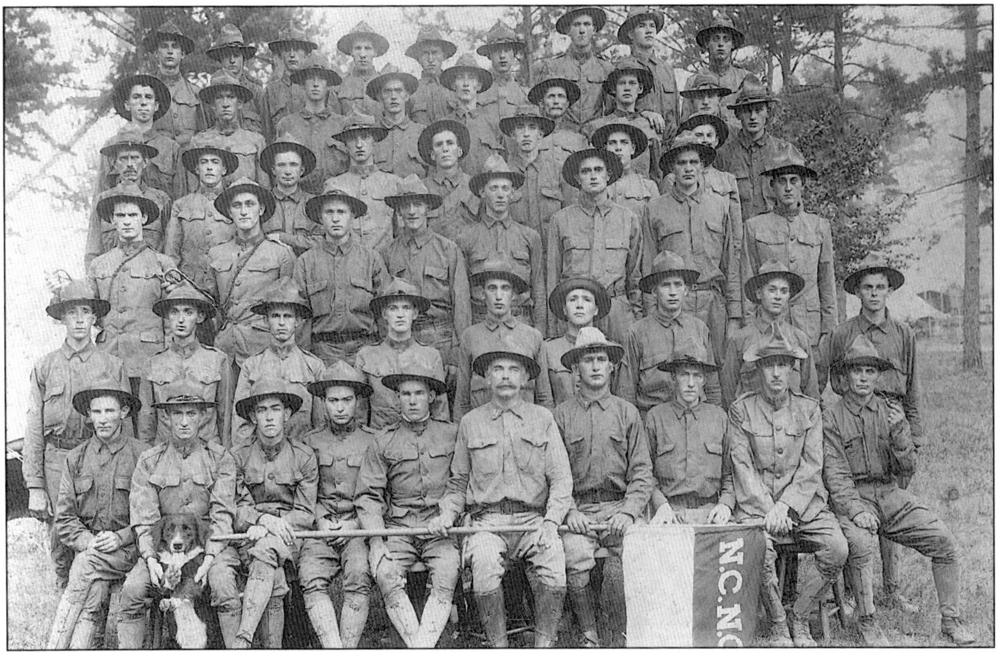

In February 1912, Captain W.A. Fair organized Troop A of the North Carolina National Guard in Lincoln County. The troop performed their weekly drills and encampments until the spring of 1916, at which they answered the call to service in the conflict with Mexico. Leaving Lincolnton on June 20, 1916, the troop was on active duty around El Paso, Texas, until their arrival back home on March 21, 1917. Five months later, the troop reported to Camp Sevier, South Carolina, for another major assignment. The troop served in France with distinction as an M.P. unit in the 30th Infantry. They were mustered out at Camp Jackson on April 14, 1919. (Lincoln County Museum of History.)

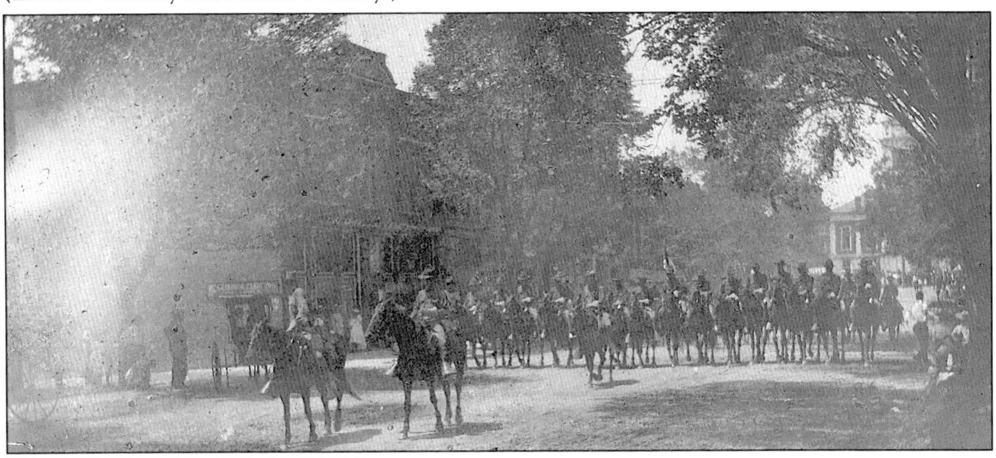

Troop A rides down East Main Street, possibly on maneuvers, as local citizens look on from the edge of the road. On January 21, 1920, the unit was reorganized as Troop I, 109th Cavalry. The local National Guard made their home at various places throughout their time of service, some of which are East Water Street at the Old County Fairgrounds, Boger City, and the present National Guard Armory. As Company I, the guard made its last charge in Mecklenburg County in 1938 under the command of Wiley Pickens. On March 31, 1938, the cavalry became engineers. (Linda Graham.)

Staff Sergeant John A. Reynolds volunteered for service in 1940 and served one year with the Engineers Corps at Fort Jackson. He came home shortly after but re-entered the service in March 1942. He trained at Fort Jackson; Fort Bragg; Fort Knox, Kentucky; Fort Riley, Kansas; Desert Training Center, California; and left Camp Polk, Louisiana, for overseas duty in August 1944. Reynolds distinguished himself when he and two other soldiers pushed hundreds of pounds of TNT into the Rhine River on March 7, 1945, after they hauled it out of the stone piers at each end of the Remagen bridge. These actions prevented the immediate destruction of the bridge and enabled First Army to establish a bridgehead on the east bank of the Rhine River—the event credited with hastening the end of WW II. He was killed by a sniper on April 15, 1945. John Reynolds is pictured third from the left. (Glenn Reynolds)

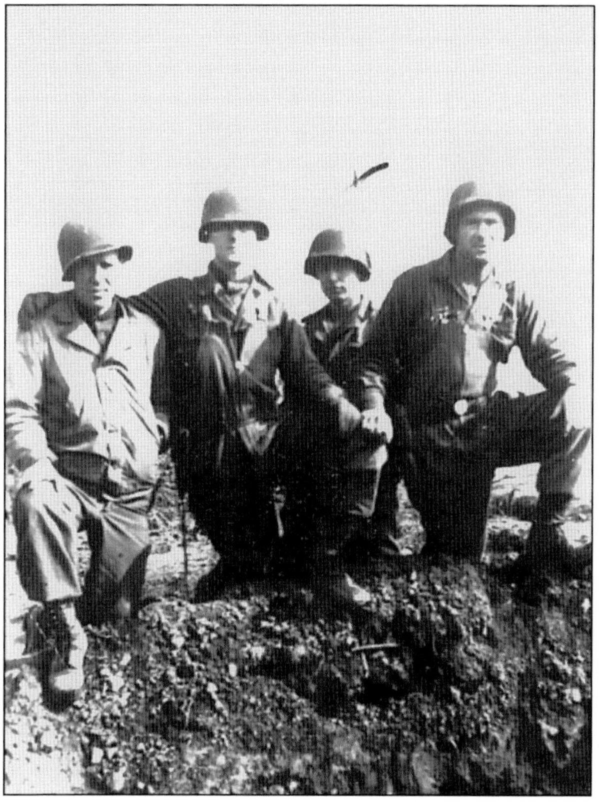

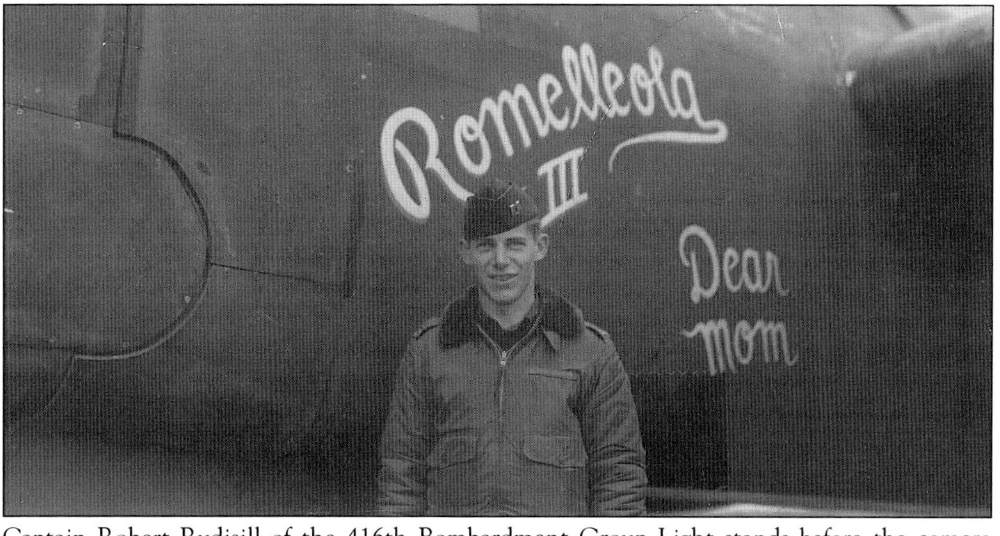

Captain Robert Rudisill of the 416th Bombardment Group Light stands before the camera while in England in 1944. His A-20 bears the named "Romelleola," appropriately named for his wife, Romel, and his mother, Leola. Captain Rudisill flew 65 missions in A-20s, flying close to the ground troops. (Robert Rudisill.)

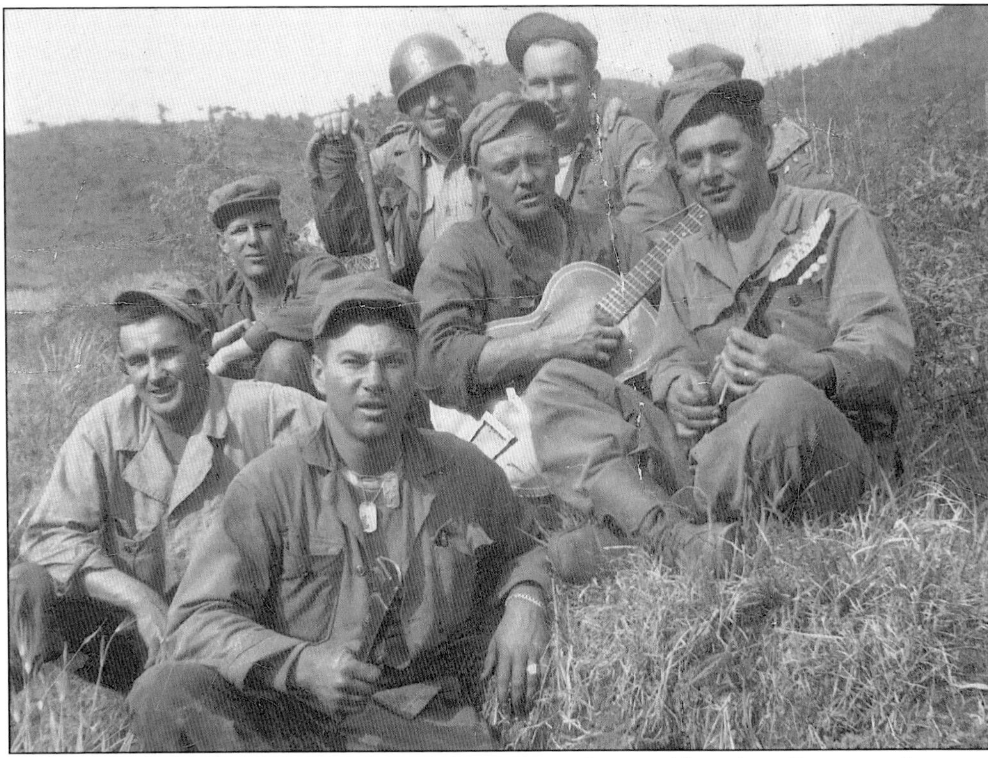

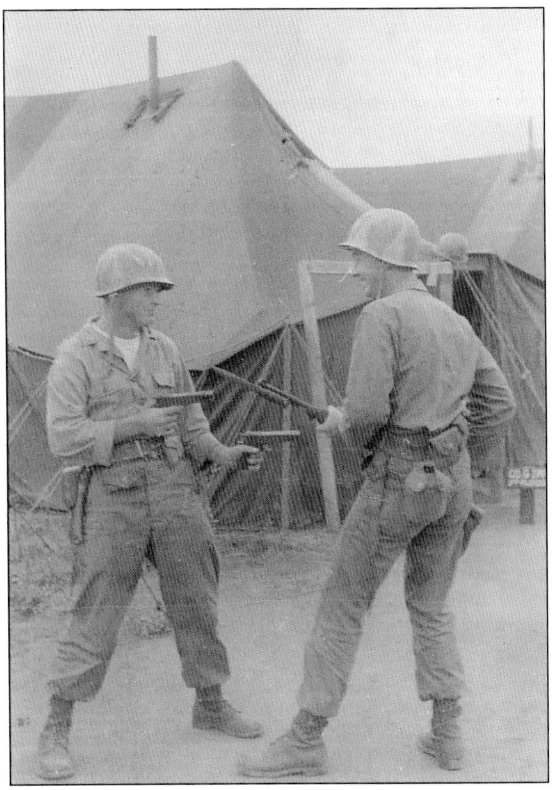

Some soldiers from Company A., 378th Combat Engineers, Lincolnton National Guard, rest on a bank with instruments "killing time" while waiting on ammunition trucks during the time of their service in Korea. They are, from left to right, as follows: (first row) "Jasper," and Rayford Beam; (second row) Houser Beam–holding a mandolin, Ford Pendleton–holding guitar, and Carroll Carpenter; (third row) Dare Reese Beam and Arnold Tarr–with helmet and cane. (Houser Beam.)

Corporal Bob Keener stands with pistol on fellow soldier Lutz while encamped in Korea. Keener was drafted into service on January 24, 1951. He trained three months at Camp Polk and was sent overseas on June 8, 1951. His ship landed on Hokpaido Island, where he trained for Korea until December 23, 1951. Corporal Keener landed in Korea on December 28, 1951, and by January 15, 1952, was on the front lines. (Bob Keener.)

Mrs. Mary Leila Willis (November 11, 1856–July 6, 1949) rocks in her chair as she knits for the Red Cross. During WW II, while living with her son-in-law and daughter, Thomas F. and Grace Abernethy, Mrs. Willis played a role in supplying the soldiers with wool socks. She was a member of the Daniel's Reformed Church and came to live at the Abernethy family farm in 1920s. (Robert and Martha Abernethy.)

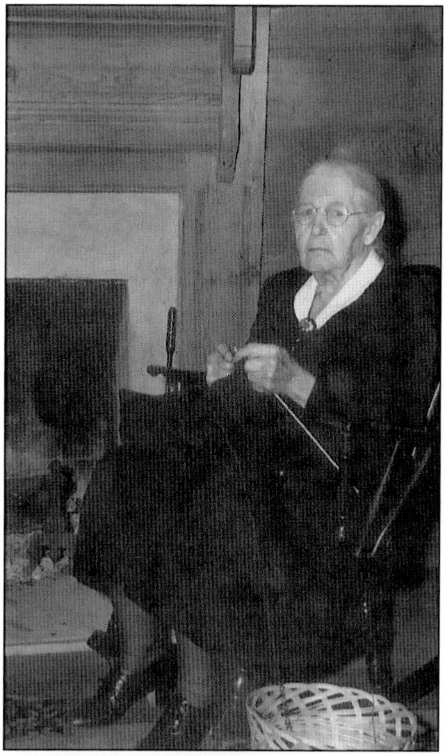

On September 7, 1951, Corporal Jerry K. Crump killed two enemy soldiers with his bayonet during an assault and distinguished himself by diving on and absorbing the blast from an enemy grenade to save the lives of his comrades. Corporal Crump is one of the youngest men to receive this award. Members of his family pictured include his mother and father, Mr. and Mrs. Harvey L. Crump, and twin brothers, Private (first class) Harry Crump–at center, and Boyd Richard Crump. Corporal Jerry K. Crump, a member of Company L, 7th Infantry Regiment, U.S. Army, visited the White House on June 27, 1952, to receive a Congressional Medal of Honor for his service in the Korean Conflict. (Teresa Schwab.)

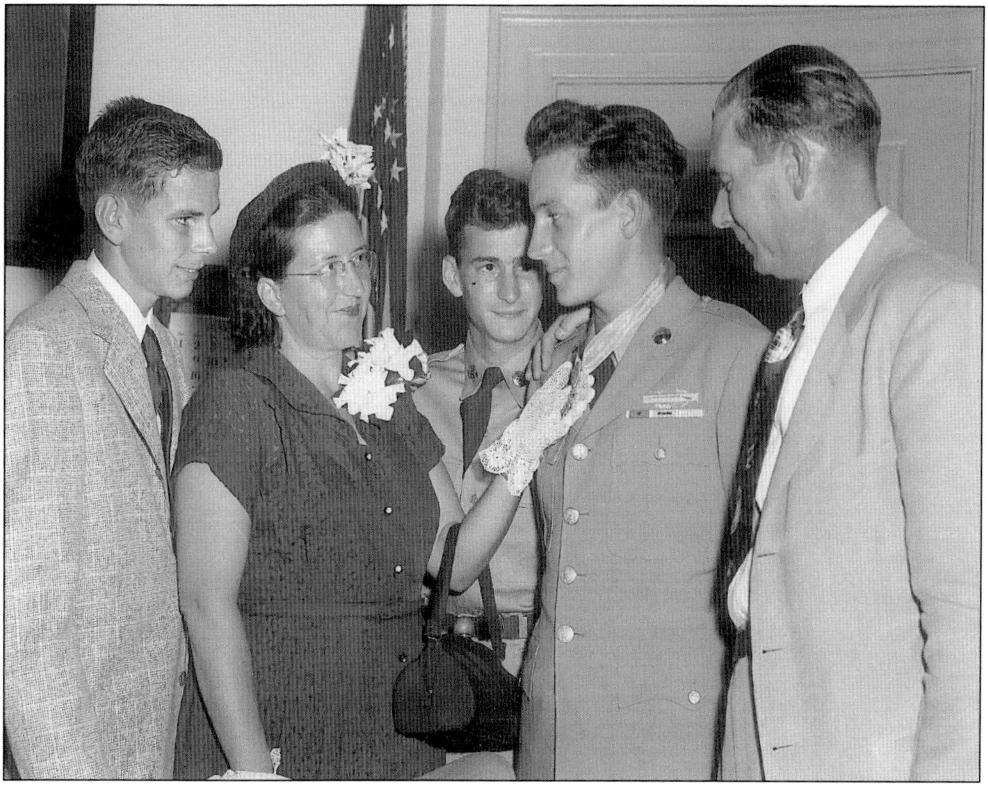

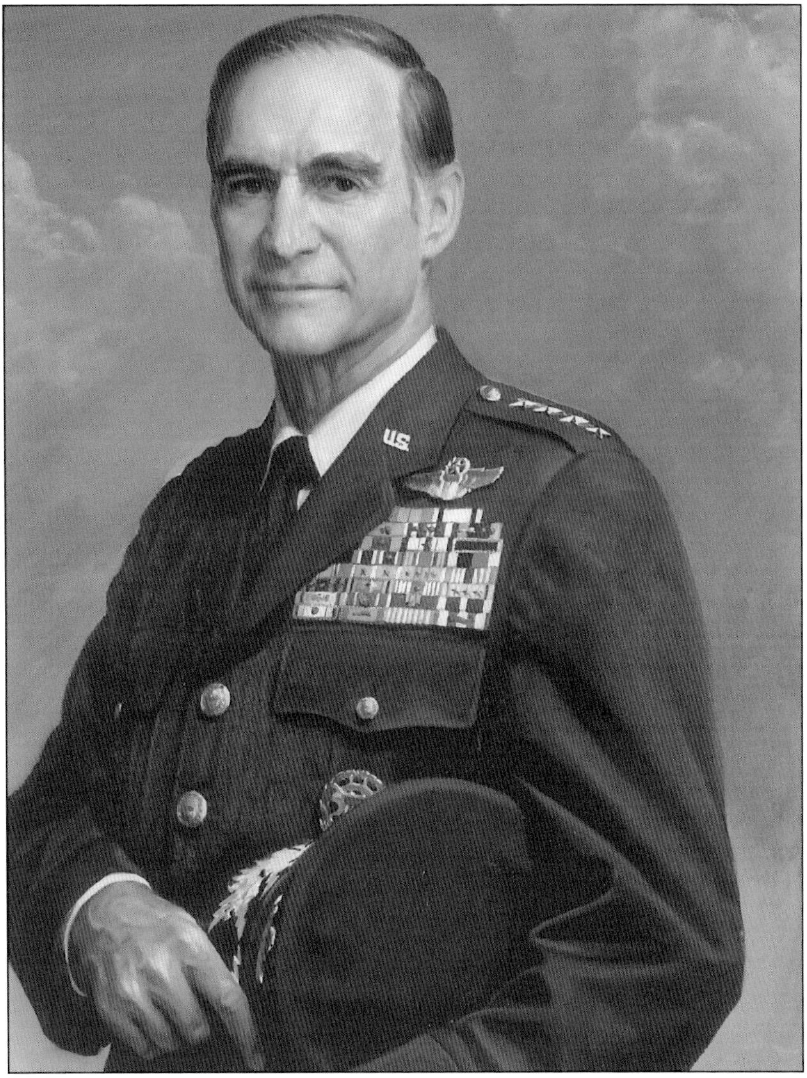

General Charles A. Gabriel was born in Lincolnton on January 21, 1928, to Paul and Lettie Goodson Gabriel. He received his education at Lincolnton High School and Catawba College before graduating from the U.S. Military Academy in 1950. After pilot training he was assigned to duty in South Korea. In 1963, he earned an M.S. degree in engineering management from George Washington University. Gabriel graduated from the Command and Staff Course at the Naval War College in 1962 and the Industrial College of the Armed Forces in 1967. He served as deputy chief of staff for operations at Headquarter Tactical Air Command, Langley Air Force Base, Virginia, from February 1975 to August 1977. He then became deputy commander-in-chief, U.S. Forces Korea and deputy commander-in-chief, U.N. Command, Seoul, Korea. In April 1979, he returned to Air Force headquarters as deputy chief of staff for operations, plans, and readings. Gabriel was promoted to general on August 1, 1980. He served as commander-in-chief, U.S. Air Forces in Europe and commander of Allied Air Forces Central Europe at Ramstein Air Base, Germany, from August 1980 to June 1982. Ronald Reagan appointed him to chief of staff of the U.S. Air Force in July 1982. General Gabriel retired in 1986 after 36 years of service in the Air Force. Lincoln County awarded him the Lincoln County Distinguished Citizen Award. (Betty Ross.)

Five

Religion

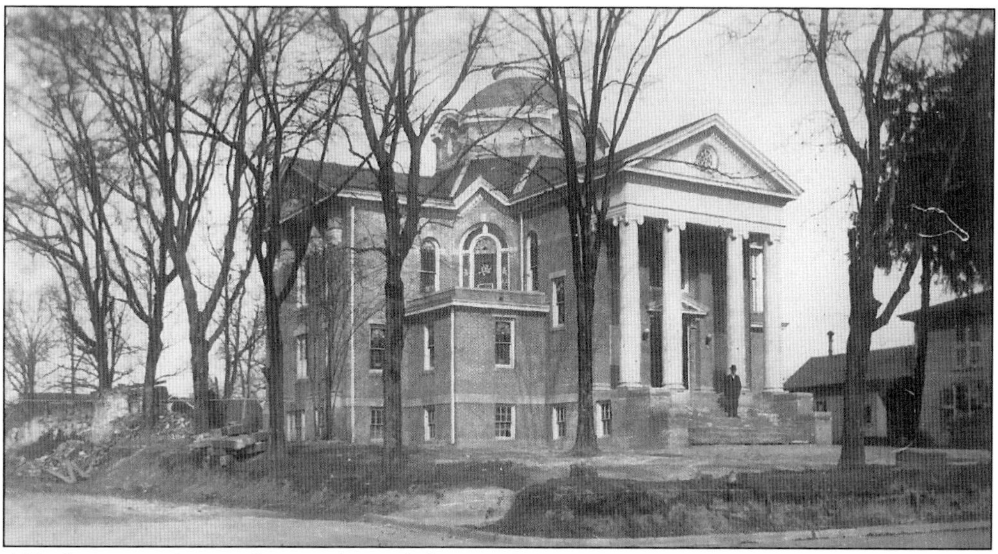

Alfred Nixon admires the neoclassical design of the First Baptist Church in this photograph taken after completion in 1922. Designed by J.M. McMichael, noted Charlotte architect, this structure served as the congregation's third building since its organization on May 28, 1858. The church added a large addition on the back of the building in 1951 before moving to a new church in 1979. This building is now the home of the Lincoln Cultural Center, housing the Lincoln County Historical Association, the Lincoln Arts Council, the Lincoln Theater Guild, the Lincoln Choral Guild, and the Lincoln Chapter of the North Carolina Symphony. (Linda Graham.)

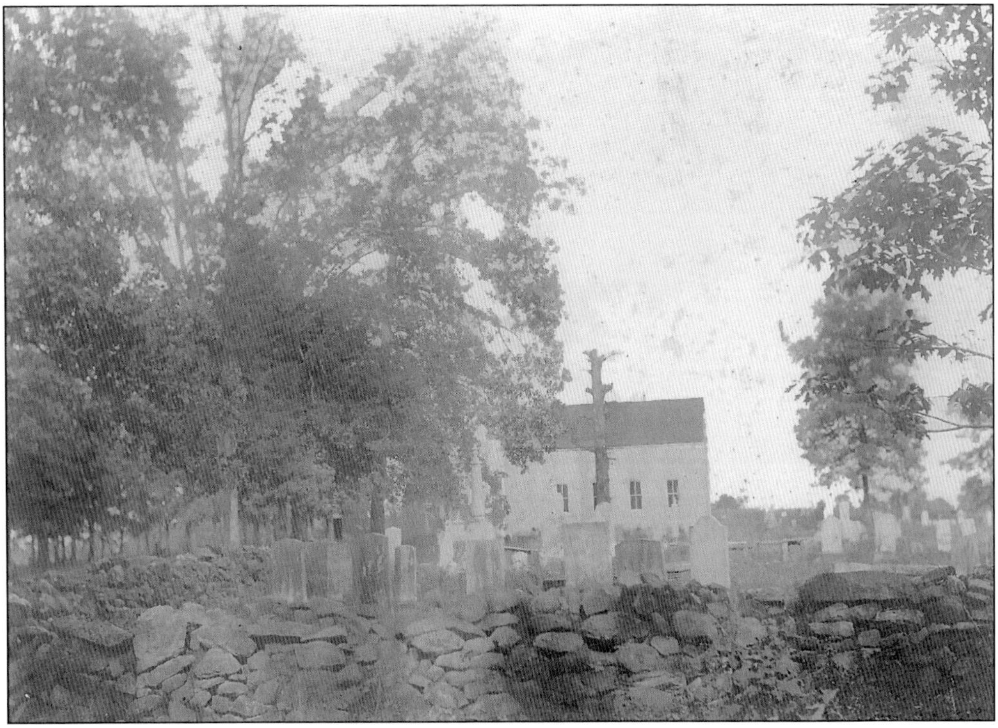

A look through the cemetery of Unity Presbyterian Church shows the church in the background. The building shown here was the third structure used by the congregation, from 1833 to 1931. Unity was established in 1796 as the pioneer religious organization in the Beatties Ford community. Reverend Humphrey Hunter, pastor from 1796 to 1803, was the first Presbyterian minister to serve a church west of the Catawba River. (Linda Graham.)

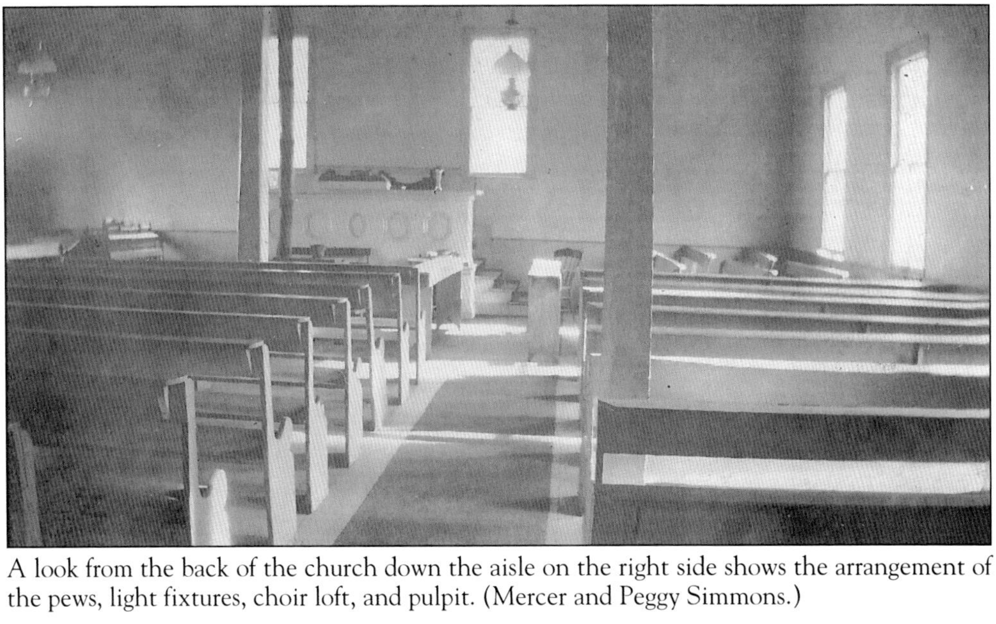

A look from the back of the church down the aisle on the right side shows the arrangement of the pews, light fixtures, choir loft, and pulpit. (Mercer and Peggy Simmons.)

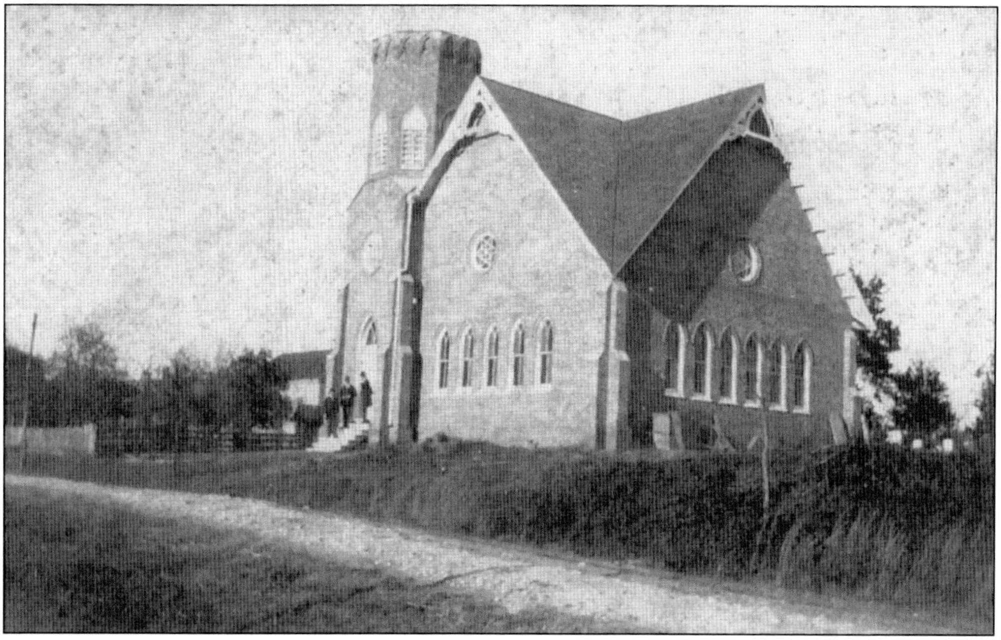

Lutherans and German Reformed congregations began their worship services in a log structure built in 1788 on a 2-acre plot in Lincolnton. A second story was added to this building in 1819 and the original portion of the building was weatherboarded and painted white, thus the Old White Church name. The church burned in 1893, and the Lutherans built the brick church pictured above on the site of the old church. This served as their place of worship until the present Emmanuel Lutheran Church was constructed across the street in 1920. (Mike Cline.)

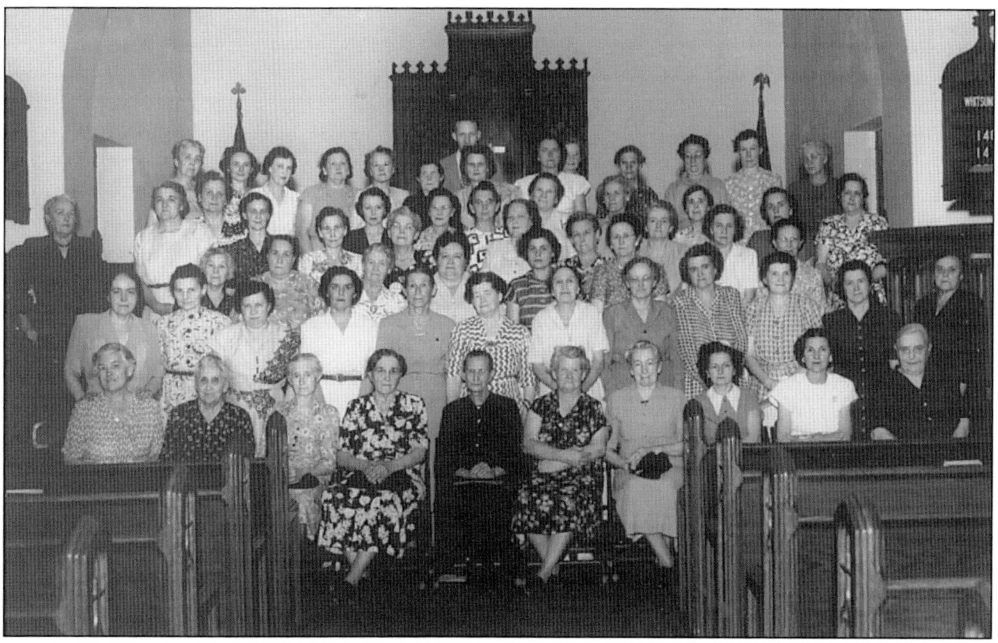

On the afternoon of June 6, 1949, the members of the Women's Missionary Society of the Emmanuel Lutheran Church of Lincolnton pose for an organizational photograph. (Ermintrude Mullen.)

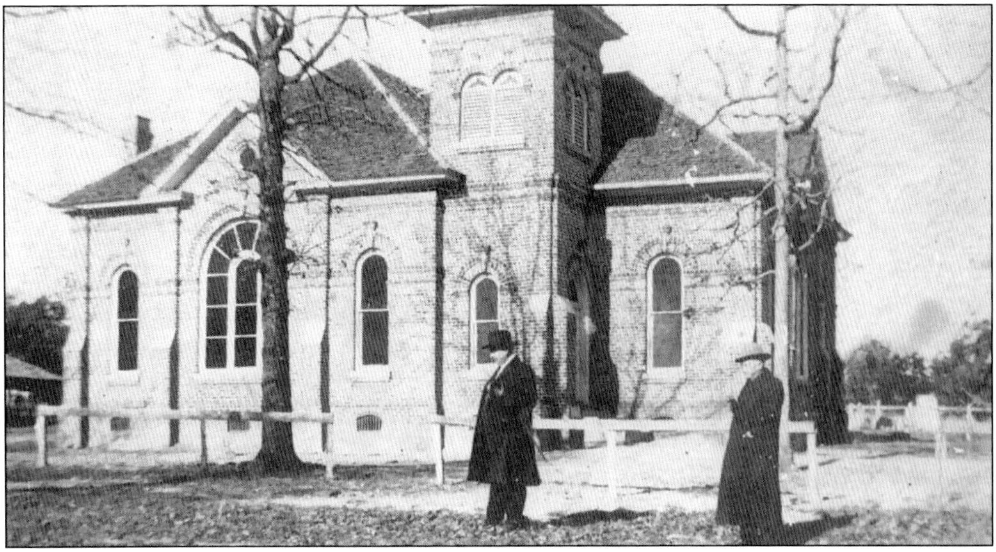

Under the leadership of Reverend John G. Fritchey, the German Reformed segment of people from the Old White Church in Lincolnton organized St. Matthews Church on May 3, 1837. Alfred Nixon and an unidentified individual stand on the land donated to the church by John Ramsour, who with John Coulter, was elected trustee. Ramsour and Joseph Finger, along with John Blackburn and Jacob Summerow, were appointed to a committee to build a church building–30 feet by 40 feet for $265. The church held annual camp meetings under a brush arbor until a substantial wood arbor was built in 1845. (Linda Graham.)

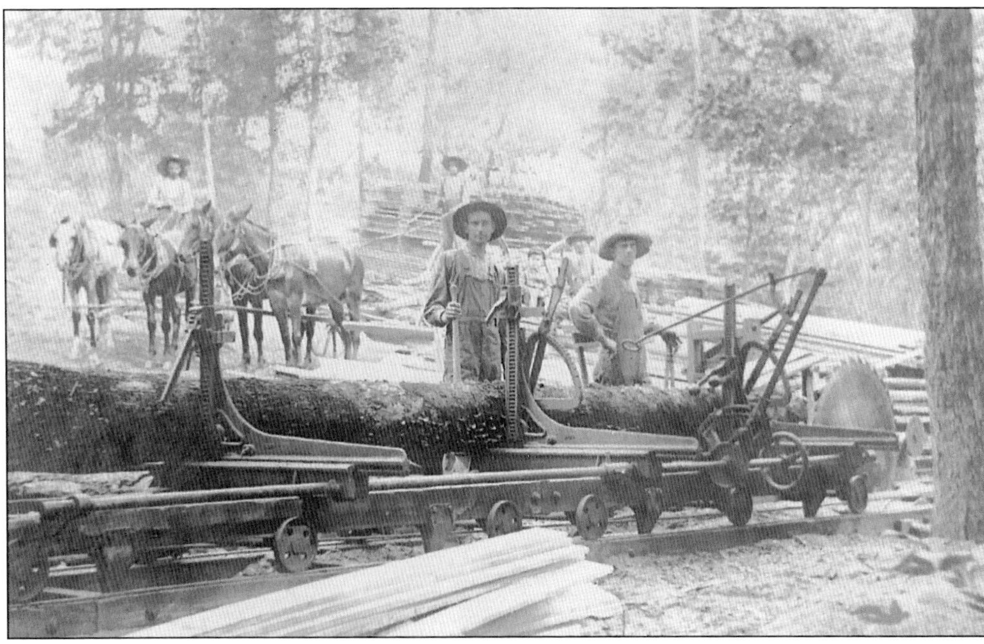

Two gentlemen pause for a moment to have their image captured while sawing logs for the St. Matthew's church building in 1906. The congregation used handmade bricks from the farm of Levi Schrum, a few hundred yards southeast of the church site, in the construction of the church, completed in 1908. The church gathered for the groundbreaking and laying of the cornerstone on Ascension's day in 1908. (Buddy Funderburk.)

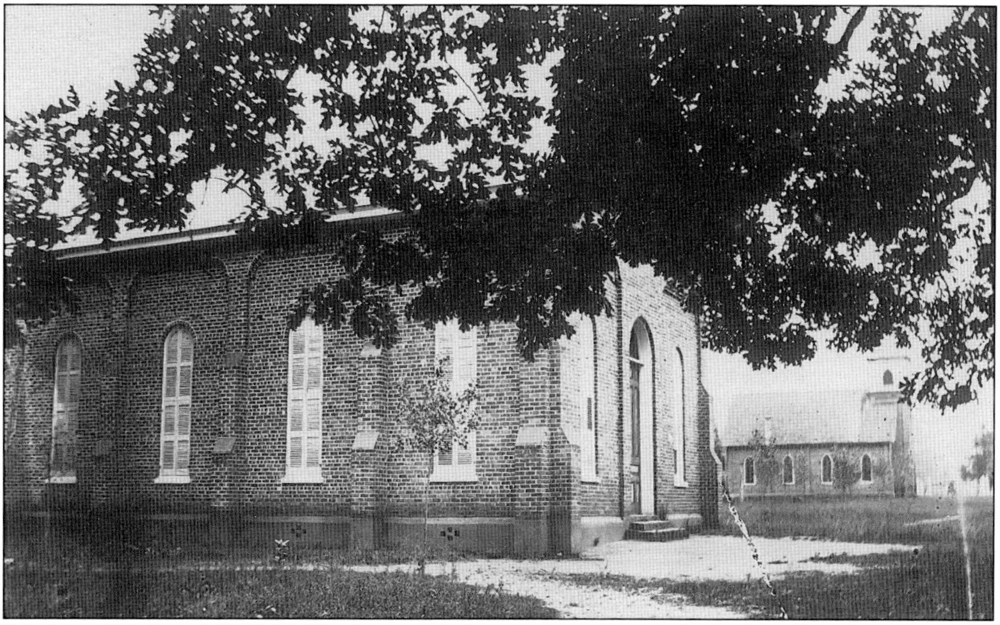

On July 15, 1768, Matthew Floyd, in consideration of ten pounds sterling, conveyed 50 acres of land to Nicholas Warlick, Frederick Wise, Urban Ashebraner, Peter Stotler, Peter Summey, and Peter Hafner, trustees of the United Congregation of the Lutheran and German Reformed Churches. Both congregations shared the first two churches built on this site until the Lutherans decided to build a new and separate church. The first church in the left of the picture was the separate church built by the Lutherans in 1889, and the brick Reformed church was built in 1894. (Robert and Martha Abernethy.)

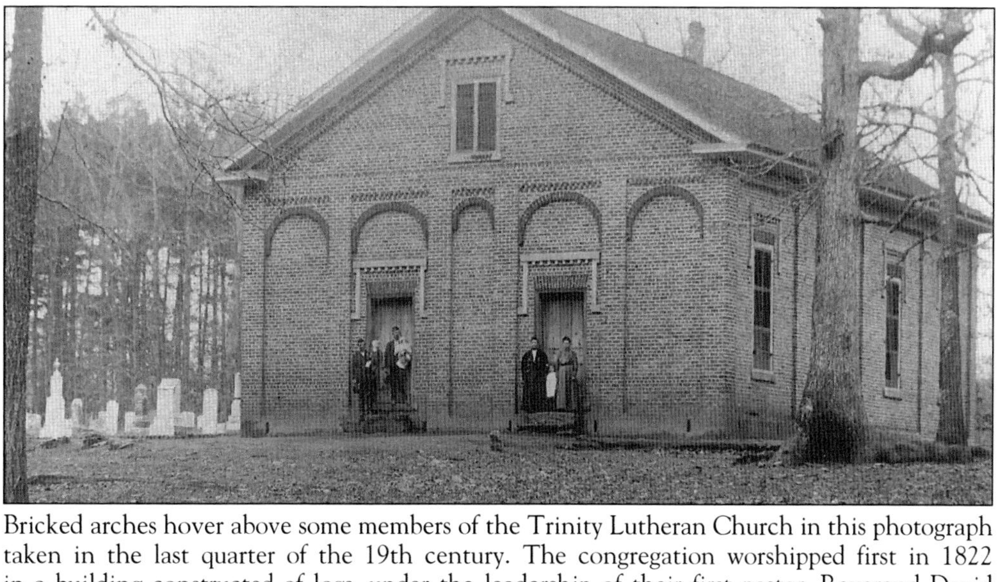

Bricked arches hover above some members of the Trinity Lutheran Church in this photograph taken in the last quarter of the 19th century. The congregation worshipped first in 1822 in a building constructed of logs, under the leadership of their first pastor, Reverend David Henkel. The building pictured above was constructed during the pastorate of Reverend M.L. Little (1876–1882), with handmade bricks made by the congregation. The church saw further alteration with enlargements in 1911, 1927, and 1943. An educational building was added in the 1950s to bring the church to its present state. (Lincoln County Museum of History.)

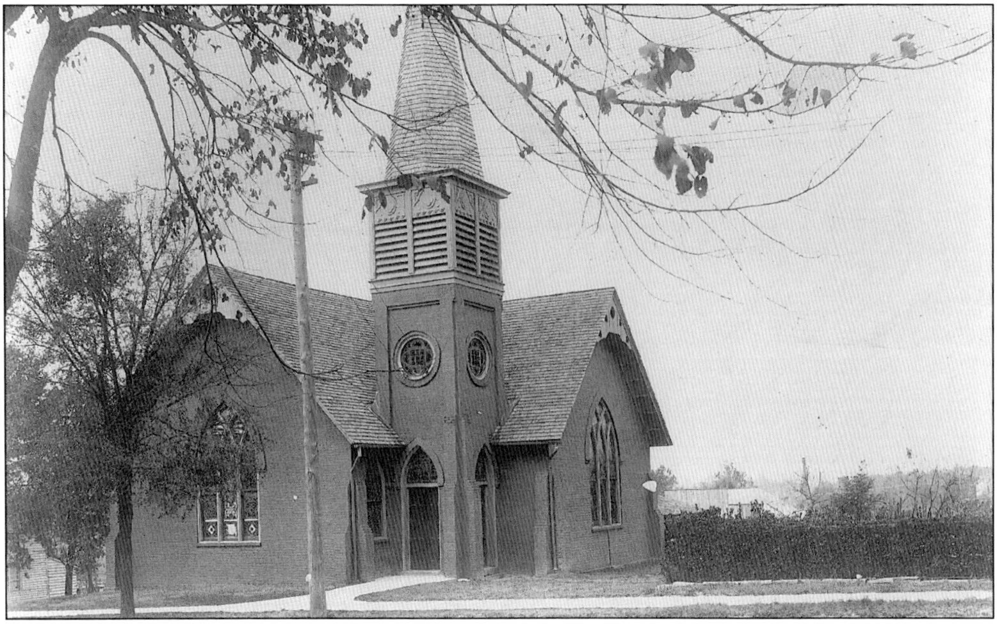

The first Presbyterian congregation in Lincolnton was organized in 1823 with Reverend Joseph Bell as its pastor and Colonel John Hoke, David Ramsour, Peter Summey, Michael Reinhardt, and Charles E. Reinhardt as its elders. This congregation worshipped under Reverend Humphrey Hunter at the Old White Church until they built a church in 1834 on West Water Street. The photograph shows the third structure built for the congregation in 1891. The first worship service in this church was conducted on July 10, 1892. In 1917, this building was razed to make way for the present edifice. (First Presbyterian Church, Lincolnton.)

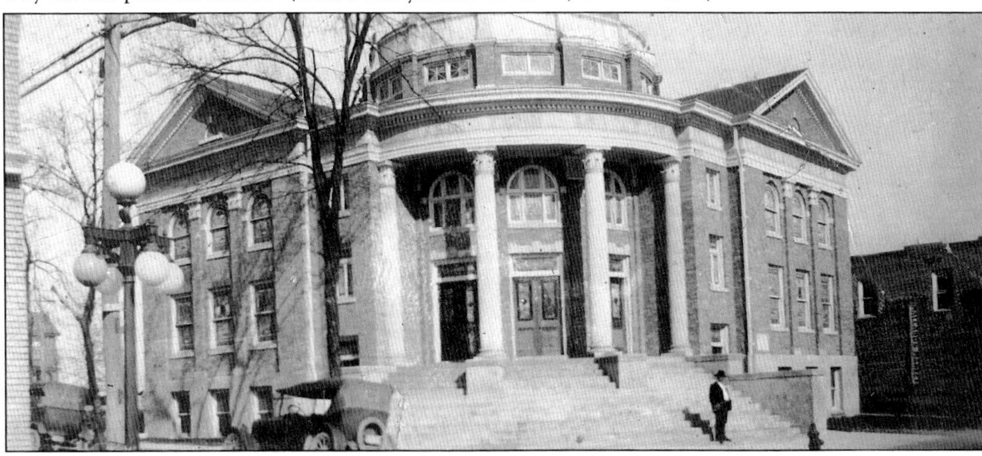

The neoclassical features of the First United Methodist Church of Lincolnton emanate from the four two-story Corinthian columns. The first church was a wooden structure built about 1828 on what is now South Aspen Street. Shortly before his death, Reverend James Hill preached the first sermon in the new building. In 1857, the wooden church was replaced by a brick structure. At this time, the congregation was part of the Lincolnton circuit, with one pastor serving several area churches. In 1902, the Lincolnton church was set aside as a separate station. Built in 1919 at a cost of $55,000, the church featured in the photograph is the third structure to serve a Methodist congregation since the time of formation in Lincoln County in 1824. (Linda Graham.)

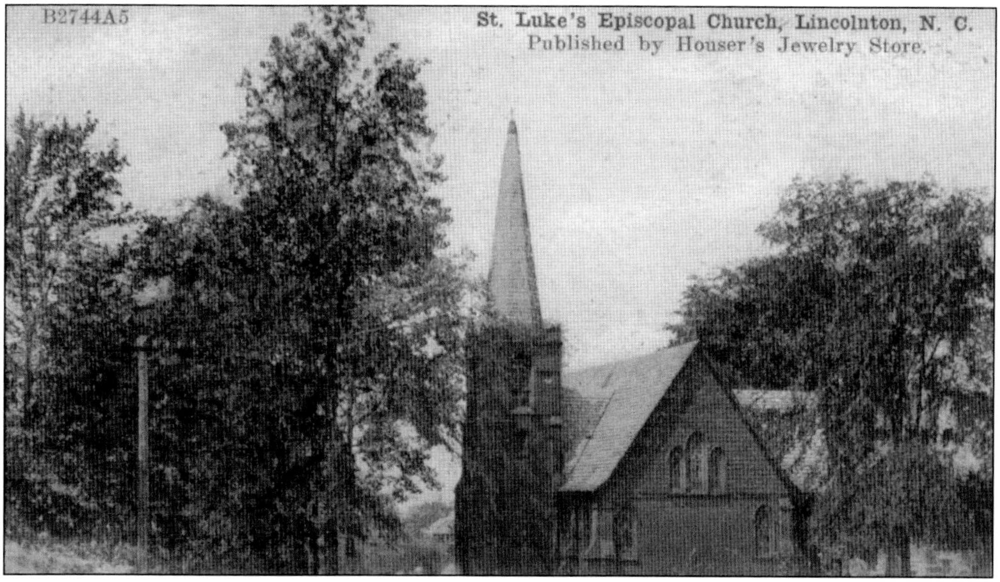

St. Luke's Episcopal Church was established in Lincolnton in 1842 on its present site, and was the first church of its denomination in the city. A hand-carved altar and choir stall of Gothic Revival design adorn the interior of the sanctuary. Haywood W. Guion, attorney and vestryman, drew up the plans for the church and oversaw the construction. In 1849, the tower was rebuilt, and in 1886, the entire body of the church was rebuilt, with only part of the tower retained. Other alterations occurred in 1917 and 1923. (Lincoln County Museum of History.)

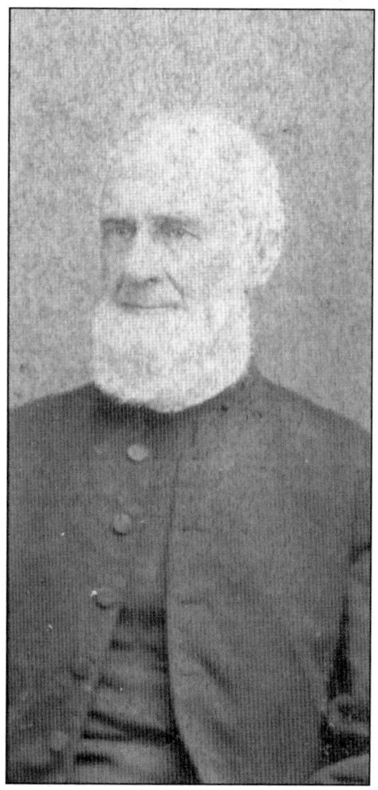

Reverend Dr. W.R. Wetmore (November 23, 1834–March 24, 1904) came to Lincolnton in the latter half of 1862 as rector of St. Luke's Episcopal Church and was ordained a priest by Bishop Thomas Atkinson on September 21, 1862. In addition to ministerial work, Reverend Wetmore served alongside Professor H.H. Smith at the Male Academy in Lincolnton. St. Luke's was virtually rebuilt and a new cornerstone laid during his rectorship in 1886. He is buried in the St. Luke's Episcopal Church cemetery. (Bobby Padgett Crowell.)

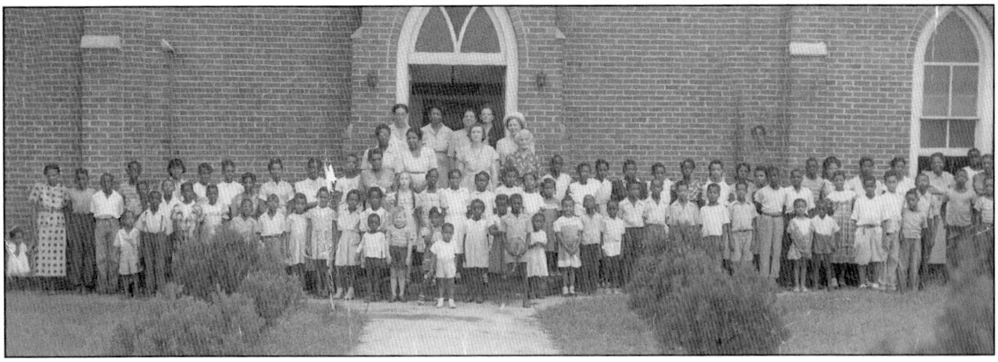

Children from the Sunday school classes at Pine Street Presbyterian Church squeeze to fit into this photograph taken at the Moore's Chapel A.M.E. Zion Church on East Main Street of Lincolnton. Pine Street Presbyterian was established by Reverend David Stephen Baker of Sharpenburg, Pennsylvania, as the Second Presbyterian Church. Reverend Baker brought Reverend I.D. David to serve the church in 1883. This church is the second oldest church building of black churches in the county. (Leroy Magness.)

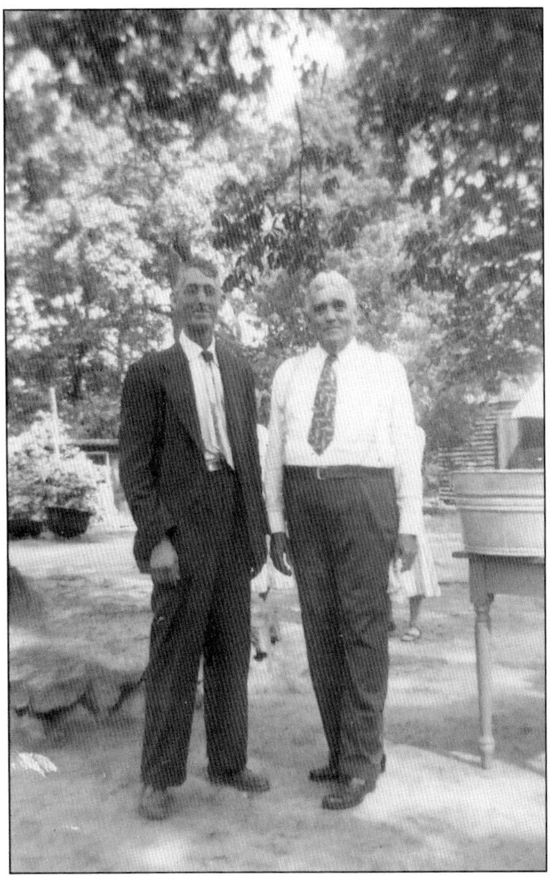

Smiles emanate from the faces of Reverend C.H. Little and J.C. Killian in this photograph taken in 1945. Reverend Little once pastored the Unity, Macphelah, and Castanea Churches, and often preached at Martha's Chapel and in eastern Lincoln County. Reverend Little attended Davidson College at the insistence of his older brother, E.H. Little. E.H. could not attend college because he had to work on the family farm, and C.H. had crippling in one of his legs that restricted his labor. E.H. rode C.H. to Davidson each morning from their family farm, since they had only one mule, and returned later in the day to pick him up. (Frances Hampton.)

Six

Education and Athletics

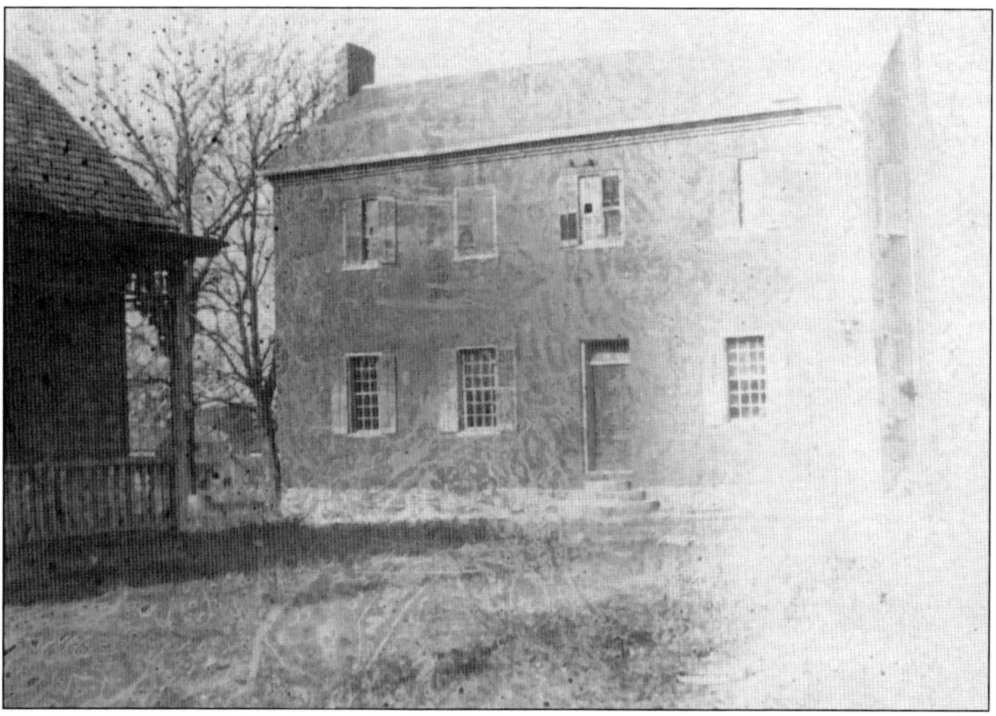

Chartered in 1813 and constructed between 1817 and 1820, the Pleasant Retreat Academy stands as the earliest brick structure in the city of Lincolnton. Before closing its doors as an educational institution between 1878 and 1884, this early-19th-century academy counted some of the county's most famous figures among its students. (Linda Graham.)

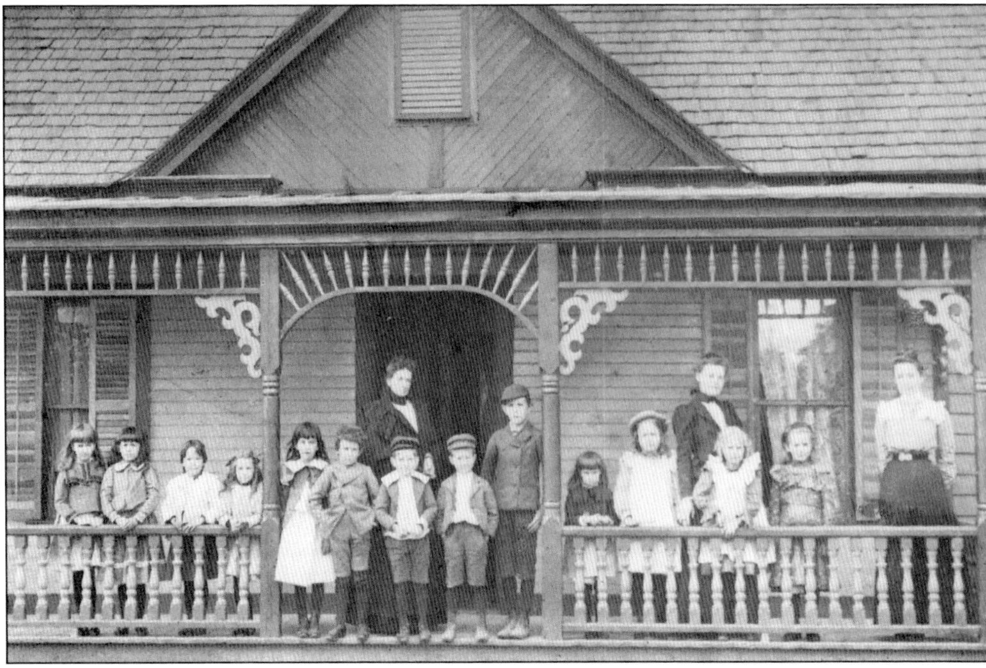

Founded in 1900 by Catherine Cameron (Miss Kate) Shipp and her sister, Anna C. Shipp McBee, the Mary Wood School, named in memory of their former teacher, Mary Wood Alexander, accommodated both boarding and day students. The school closed in 1904 when Miss Kate Shipp decided to return to school for an advanced degree. (Lincoln County Museum of History.)

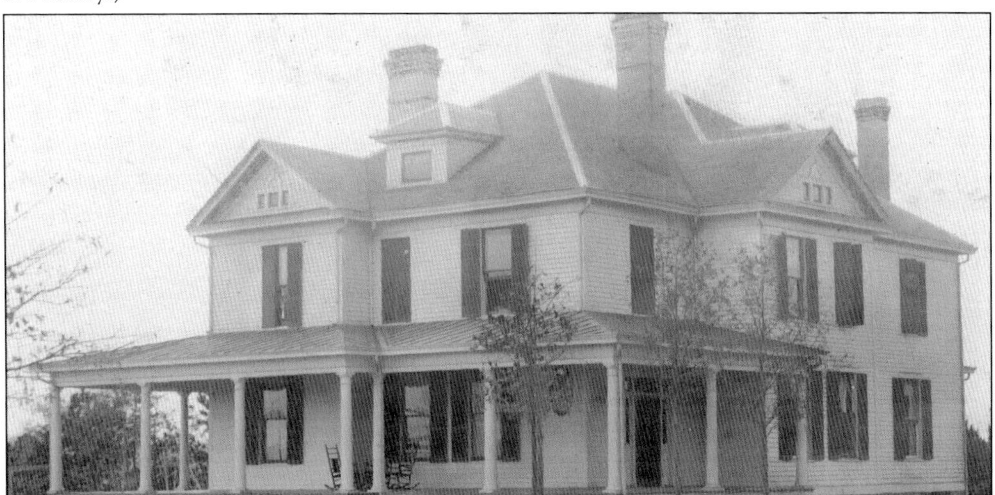

Fassifern "Miss Kate Shipps" School was established in Lincolnton in 1907 by Miss Kate Cameron Shipp and her sister, Mrs. Anna C. McBee. Miss Shipp named the school after the "Fassifern Castle," the ancestral home of the Camerons in England. The two sisters ran the school until Mrs. McBee's death in 1923. In 1925, the demand for larger equipment prompted Miss Shipp to sell the school in Hendersonville to Reverend Joseph Sevier. The building was moved to Hendersonville, where a much larger student body found suitable accommodations. (Ermintrude Mullen.)

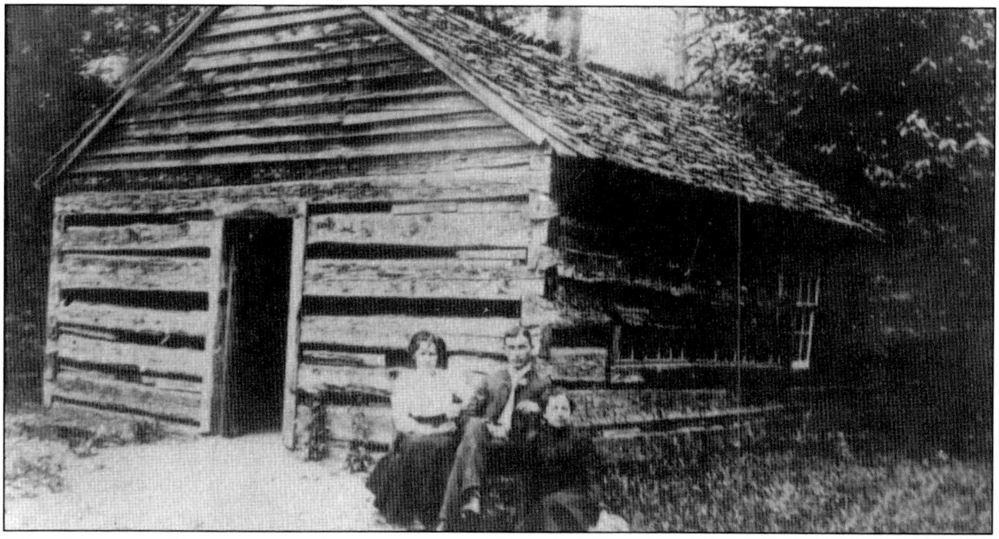

Mrs. Augustus Heavner, teacher, and an unidentified gentleman rest near the entrance of the Leonard's Fork School near Lincolnton in the 1890s. As a one-room log building, the school taught the young children of the area the primary requirements of reading, writing, and arithmetic. The school got its name from a stream that ran near the school and the Leonard's Fork Baptist Church, which sat across the road. In 1918, Gus Heavner, who lived beside the church, moved the building behind his house for usage as a tenant dwelling. The building burned a few years later. (David C. Heavner.)

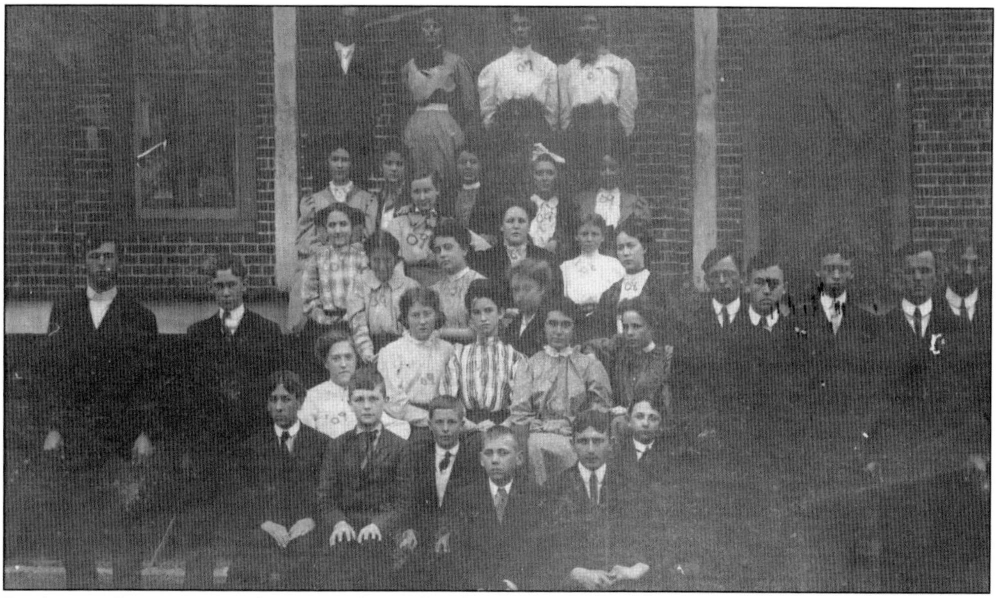

Piedmont Seminary students, grades eight through ten, gather on the steps of the old Female Academy for this photograph taken March 12, 1907. Some of the students pictured are John Ramsour, Zed Crawford, Catherine Crawford, Margaret Cobb, Nora Lander, Ethel Long, Annie Nixon, Harry Shuford, Hamp Childs, Jessie Caldwell, Macon Epps, Henry McLean, Mary Dellinger, Nell Rudisill, Mae Rhodes, Florence Mauney, Mattie Camp, Rose Hinson, Fan Shuford, Martin Hovis, Mary McKee, Stella Tilson, Fannie Carpenter, Eva James, Ross Sigmon, Sam Dellinger, Peg Nixon, and Ethel Courtney. (David C. Heavner.)

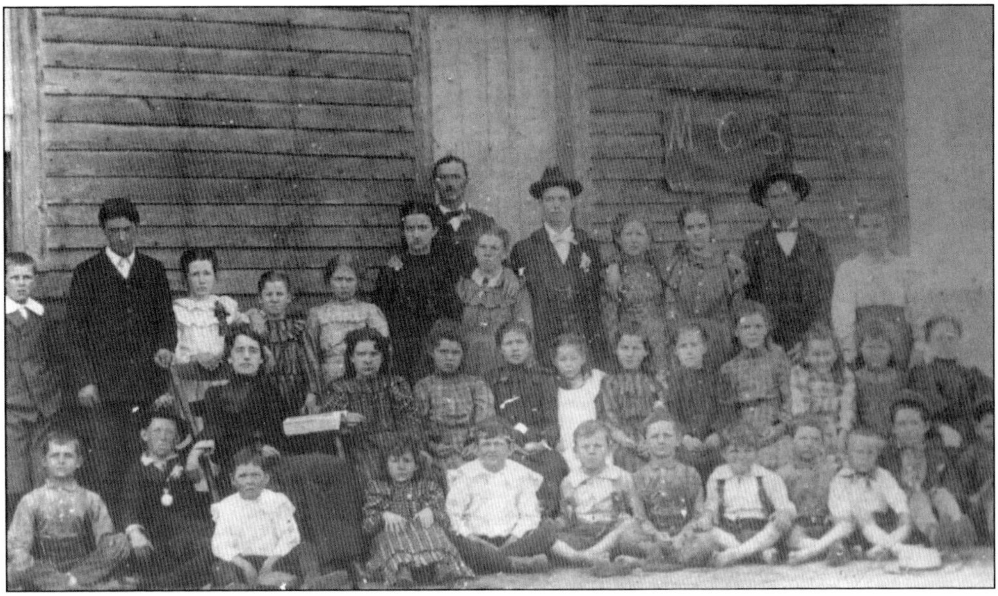

During the 1899–1900 term, a group of students ranging from 6 years to 20 years of age poses outside their one-room school in eastern Lincoln County. Labeled "M.C.S." on a primitive sign attached to the exterior, the McLean School, located on the corner of the Old Cowan's Ford Road and the Moore's Ferry Road, served children from various families in the area: Siffords, Nantzs, Moores, Hagers, Duckworths, McConnells, Jones, McIntoshs, and Edwards. The school's teacher, Miss Minnie Alexander, is seated in the chair among her students. Some years later, Miss Alexander went to India as a missionary. (Frances Hampton.)

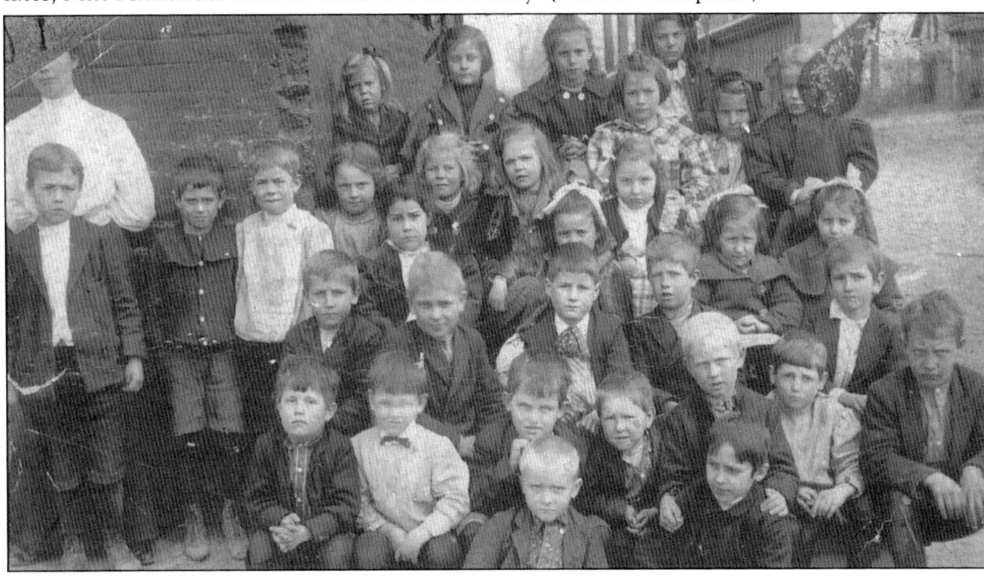

A primary school group poses on the steps of the old Pleasant Retreat Academy (Male Academy) for a group photograph in 1906. Marie Rudisill stands as the only identified member from the group on the top row as the second student from the left. This group moved to the Lincolnton Graded School when it was built in town in 1909. Many of these students played a role in the laying of the cornerstone and the assemblage of the time capsule sealed in the graded school's foundation. (John Hoyle)

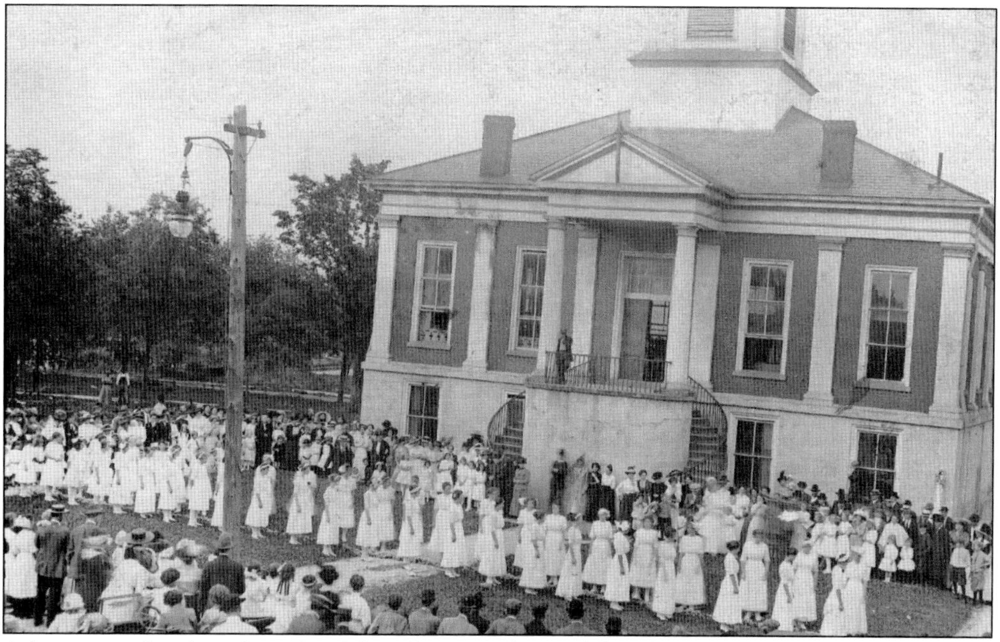

A large crowd gathered on East Main Street in front of the old courthouse for the Lincolnton Graded School Commencement in May 1913. (Jack and Ellen Shuford.)

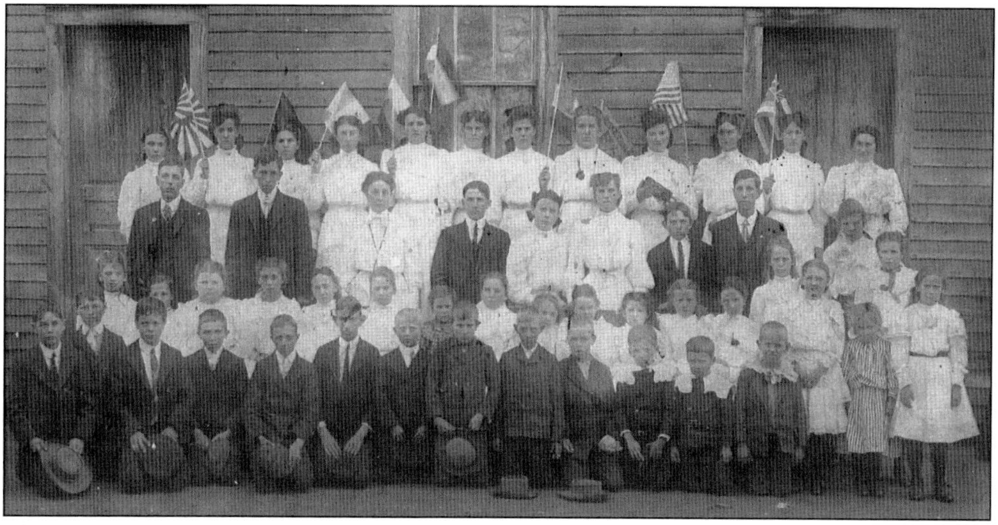

The Ridge Academy School group shows their patriotism during a class photograph. Members of this year's class are as follows: (first row) Jessie Massagee, Press Lingerfelt, Johnny Rudisill, Solon Leonard, Dall Sain, Blair Yount, Fred Sain, Loy Rudisill, Alvin Goodman, Carol Yount, and some Yount children; (second row) Lula Yount, Mae Carpenter, Lula Seagle, Minnie Leonard, Clemmie Leonard, Clara Lynn, unidentified, Bryth Wyant, unidentified, Blanche Massagee, Mable Yount, Ula Lingerfelt, unidentified, Lois Heavner, Nannie Clyde Leonard, Carrie Rudisill, unidentified, and Eva Lefevers; (third row) Horace Hoyle, Ernest Hoyle, May Houser, Lee Seagle, Ethel Rudisill, Nora Sain, Alvin Goodson, Wesley Houser, and Nettie Rudisill; (back row) Myrta Leonard, Junie Houser, Londie Goodman, Petti Wyant, Maggie Beam, Alice Yount, Minnie Beam, Jennie Wyant, Hattie Yount, and Mrs. Smathers (teacher). (Marie Whitener.)

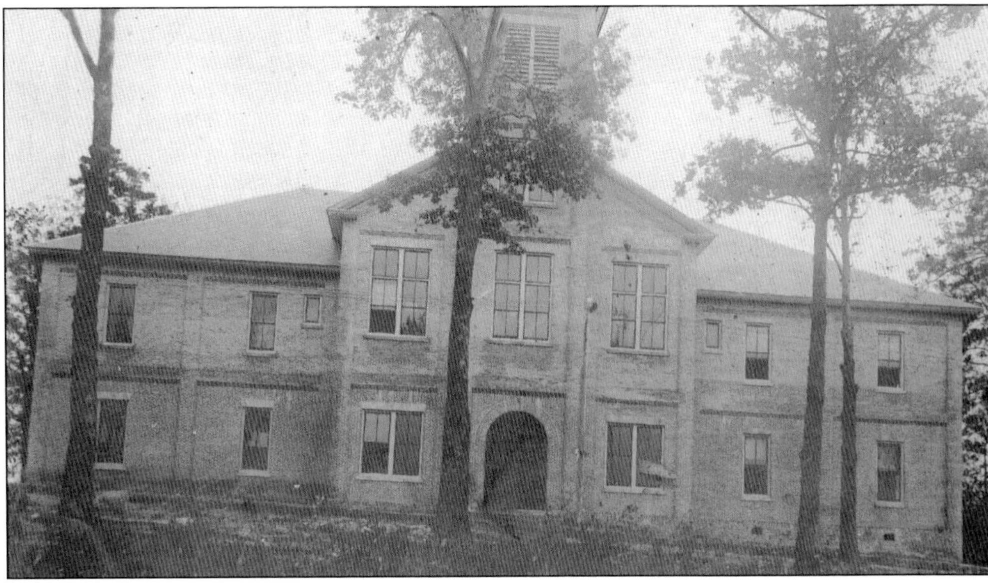

The Lincolnton Graded School, designed by Reverend Robert A. Yoder (member of Lincoln County School Board, pastor of Emmanuel Lutheran Church, and first president of Lenoir-Rhyne College), was constructed in 1907–1908 at the corner of Congress and Academy Streets in Lincolnton. The building housed the entire Lincolnton school system until 1916. It later served as an elementary school, as part of Lincolnton High School, and in later years was commonly referred to as the Grammar School. (Ermintrude Mullen.)

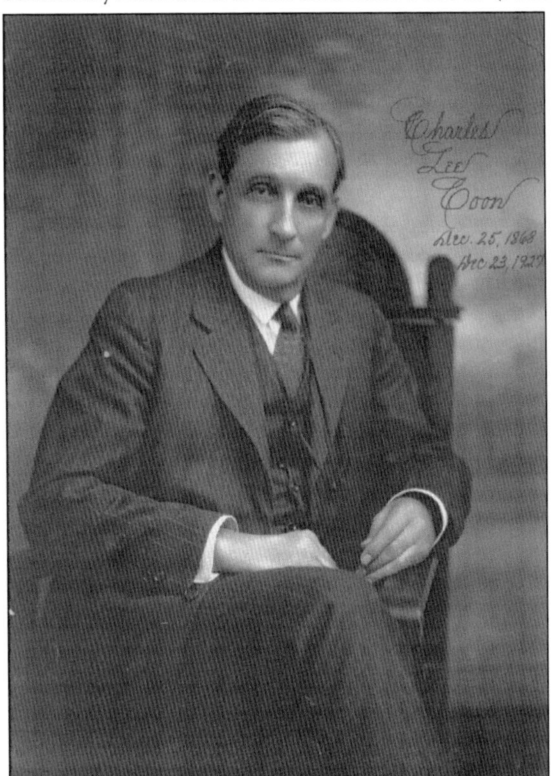

Charles Coon (1869–1927) became a teacher after his graduation from Conover College in 1887. Some of his positions in the field of education include principal, Denver Academy 1889–1891; teacher, Conover College 1891–1896; principal, Lincolnton Schools 1896–1897; teacher, Charlotte Schools 1897–1899; superintendent, Salisbury Schools, 1899–1903; secretary, Bureau of the Southern Educational Board, Knoxville, Tennessee, 1903–1904; chief clerk, Office of the Superintendent of Public Instruction 1907; and superintendent, Wilson County School 1913–December 27, 1927. In 1908, he published *The Beginning of Public Education in North Carolina*, and in 1915, *North Carolina Schools and Academies, 1790–1840*. (Miriam Robinson.)

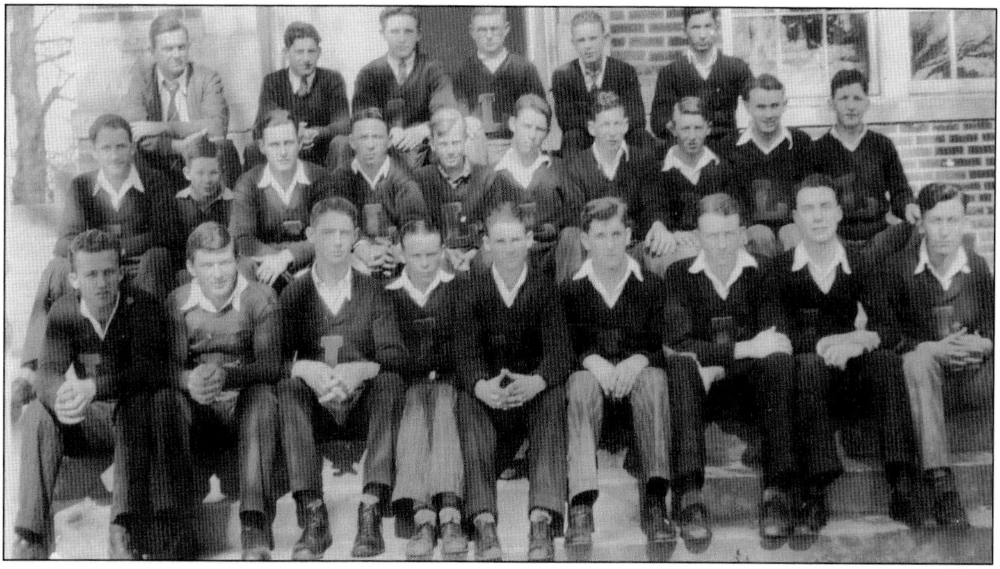

The "L" Club of Lincolnton High School poses for a 1930 photograph dressed in their club sweaters. Members include Thomas Armstrong, Carl Fortenberry, Howard Rudisill, Sam Hoover, Alexander Proctor, Kemp Huss, James Cornwell, Yates Ward, Kermit Cloninger, Ruffin Self, John Broome, Curtis Broome, Loy D. Elmore, Fred Rudisill, Hunter Mauney, Ralph Yoder, Ralph Crenshaw, Willie Ramsey, Jessie Robinson, Everett Mullen, Woodrow Blanton, Bill Jetton, John Rudisill, Melvin Lingerfelt, Bill Haynes, David Wilkinson, Harold Sherrill, Robert Allison, Frank Heavner, and George Page. The officers for the club are Hunter Mauney, president; George Page, treasurer; and C.D. Smith. (Lincoln County Museum of History.)

With the class motto "*Nihil Magnum Nisi Bonum*" (nothing great unless good), Lincolnton Graded School's graduating Class of 1909 stands on a bench in Lincolnton for a group photograph. Members of the graduating class include Mattie Camp, class president; Herbert Miller, valedictorian; May Rhodes; Mary McKee; Beatrice Bagley; Rose Hinson; Will Strider; Jack Rees; Henry McLean; and Zed Crawford. In honor of the class, Miss Eva James hosted a party at her home on South Laurel Street that featured musical selections, a poetic guessing contest, and banana cream and fairy sandwiches. (Bobby Padgett Crowell.)

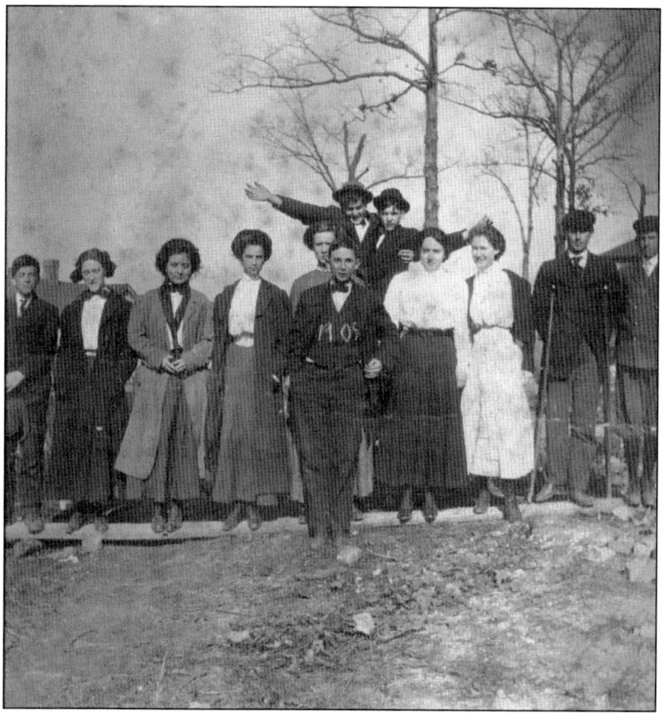

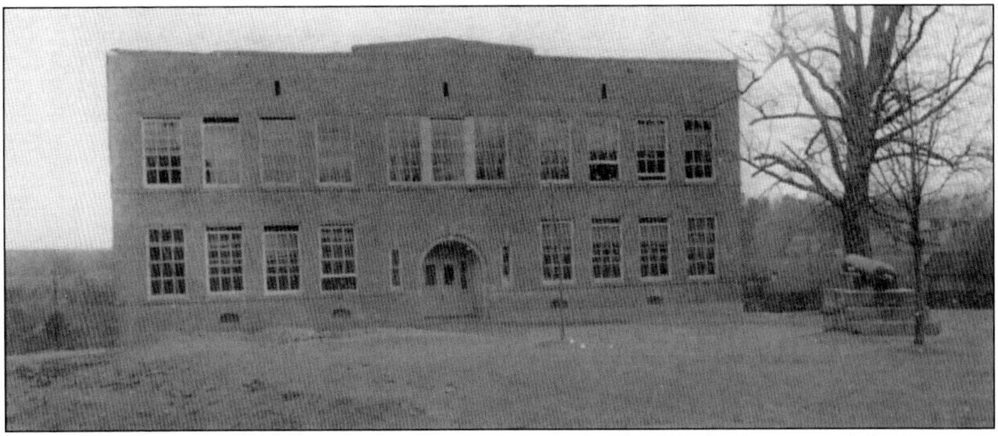

Since the early years of education in Lincoln County, schools of the highest regard, both private and public, have been established and conducted by instructors with highest level of education and excellence. During the early years of the 20th century, particularly the 1910s and 1920s, Lincolnton's public schools made great strides in advancing attendance and equipping their students with the academics to become successful and prosperous. Under the superintendency of Professor Wiley M. Pickens, enrollment in the town's four schools soared to around 1,500. The Academy Street Primary School (General Robert F. Hoke School), pictured above, was built in 1914 and ranked third in the group with 233, behind Lincolnton High School (General Stephen D. Ramseur) with 511; and Grammar School (Kate C. Shipp School) with 438. Behind Academy Street were Aspen Street School (General Robert D. Johnston School) with 93; and the "colored" schools with 214. (Lincoln County Museum of History.)

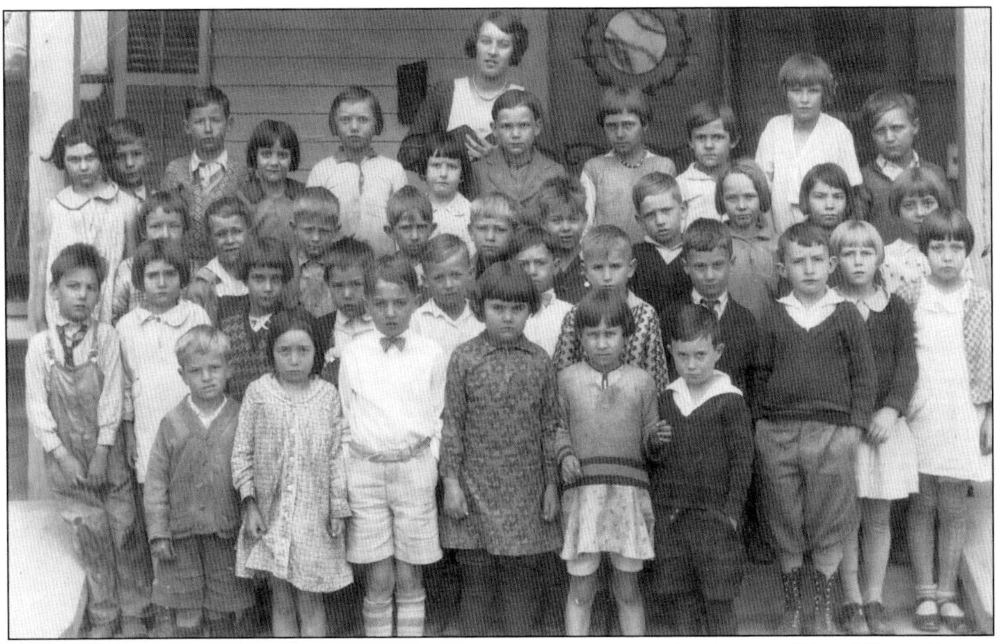

The Academy Street School group of 1929 stands on the steps at the home of Dr. J.W. and Jenny "Bessie" Sain, now Drum's Funeral Home, on North Academy Street for this class photograph. Though not all identified, some of the students include Leslie Yoder, ? Motz, Jimmy Hines, Bill Sigmon, Gene Modlin, Jerry Kistler, Hazel Craig, Margaret Dellinger, William Avery, and teacher Beatrice Boggs. (Margaret Dellinger.)

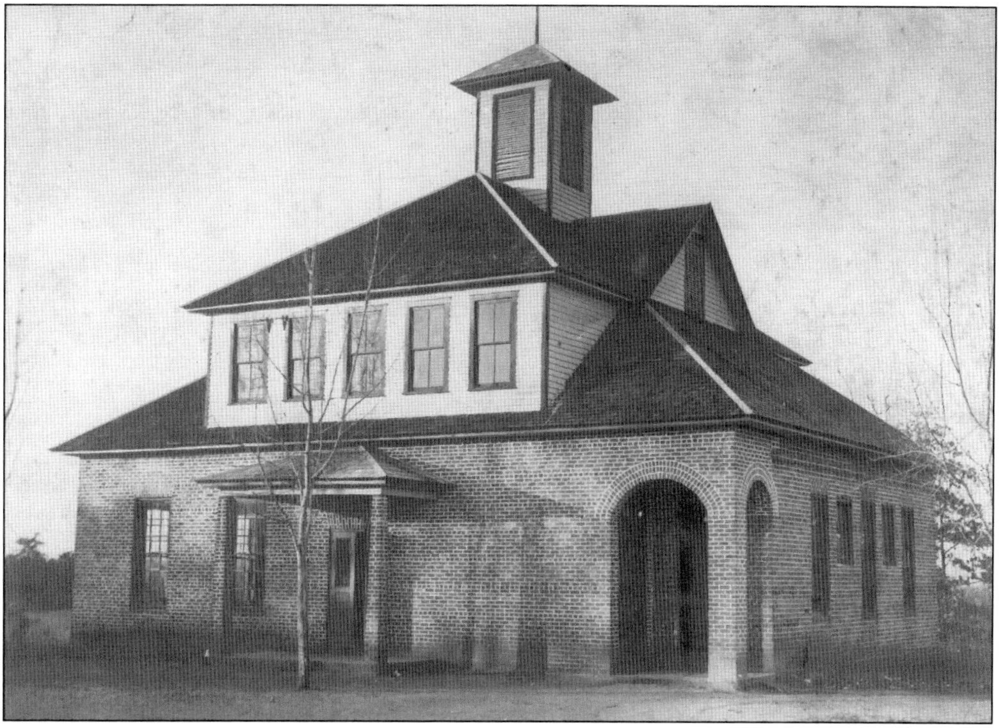

Daniels School was located in the vicinity of Daniels Lutheran and German Reformed Church on the Reepsville Road. A school in this location goes back to 1768, when both congregations obtained 50 acres of land for a church and school called Daniels. After this building burned in 1932, the Daniels and Hoover schools were consolidated into Union School. In 1932, the county's school population was 6,353 rural students and 1,647 in the Lincolnton city system. Out of the 34 schoolhouses throughout the system, 10 were one-room structures. (Lincoln County Museum of History.)

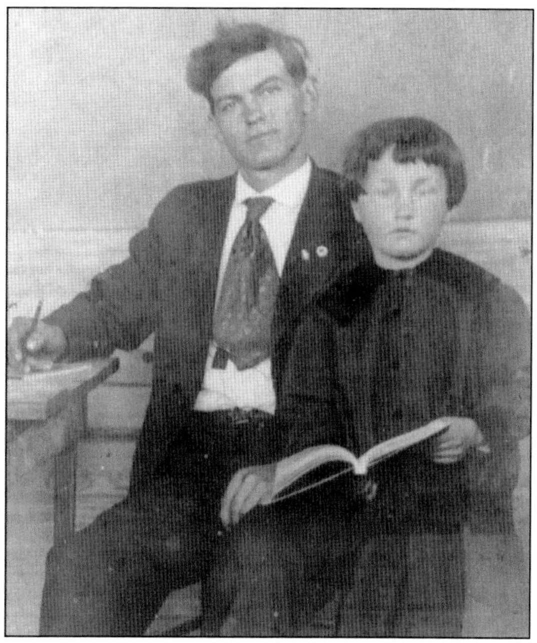

Alongside pupil Amy Sue Tillman, Willie Hull sits in a small desk in the Bushy Pine School during the 1920s. Hull received his early education at Cherryville High School while boarding with an aunt, and later at Lenoir-Rhyne College and by correspondence. Teaching for a remarkable 45 years, mainly in western Lincoln County, he spent the majority of his years instructing students in one- and two-room schools and at North Brook #3 School. Hull served on the Lincoln County Board of Education after his retirement from teaching. (Avis Peeler.)

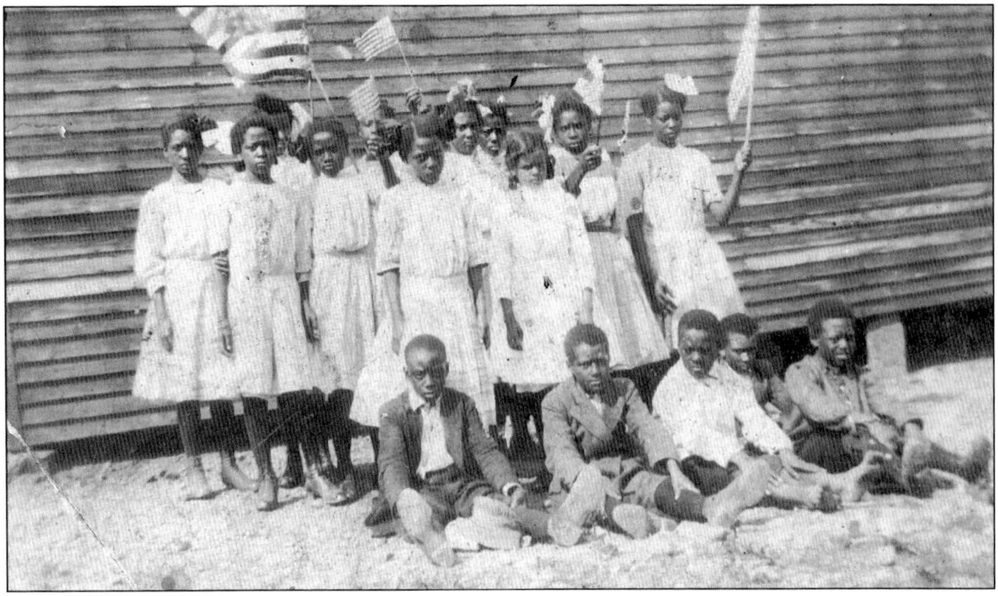

A third grade class at the Mt. Vernon Academy holds their flags high for this photograph taken during the 1914–1915 term. Built in 1902, this structure stood until a larger one was built with money from the Julius Rosenwald Fund. Rosenwald, a Chicago philanthropist and businessman, created the fund in 1917 to improve the opportunities and living conditions of American blacks. (Edith Lomax.)

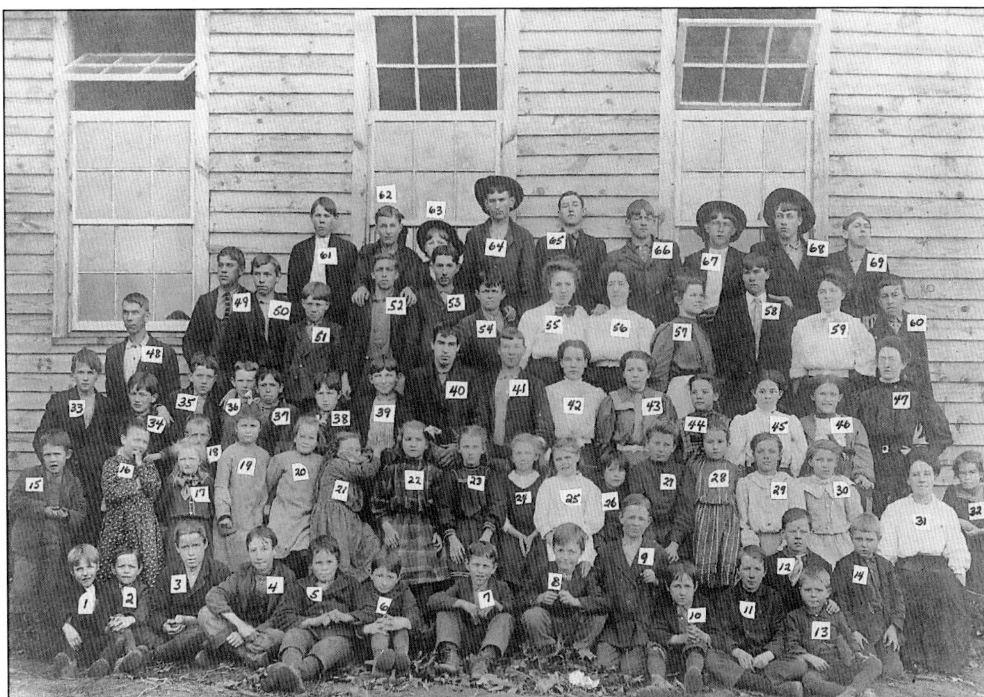

A large group of students from White Zion School pack together for a photograph taken during the 1909–1910 school term. Oscar Hartsoe built White Zion School and opened its doors in 1907. (Helen Peeler.)

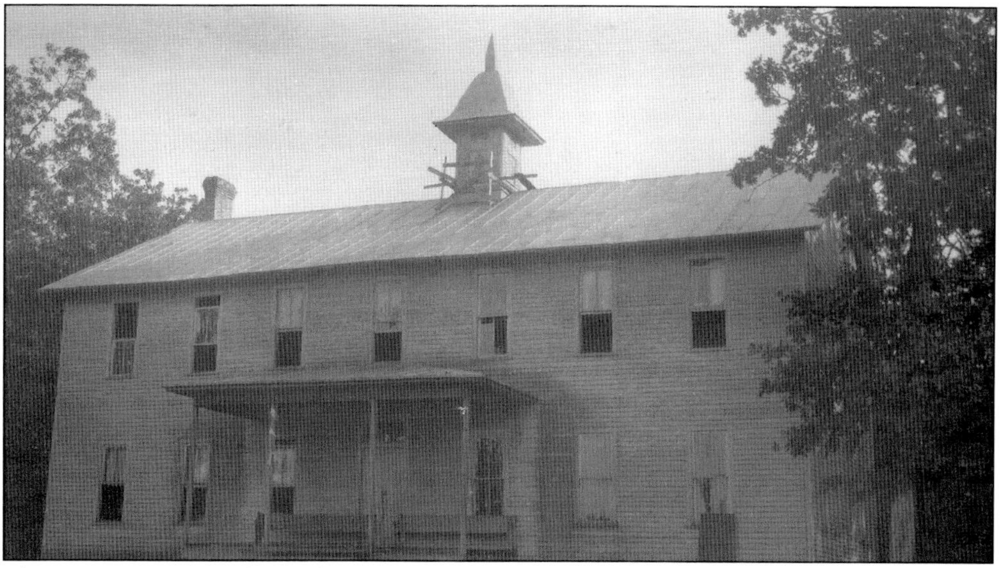

The eastern portion of Lincoln County saw schools established as early as the formation of O'Reilly's School located near Beatties Ford in 1826. In 1871 L.A.H. Wilkinson founded the Rock Springs Seminary in Denver. Wilkinson cut the logs to build the school, and before it opened, he hired a teacher to help with the instructions. Professor D. Matt Thompson took over the school in 1873 and conducted it as a boarding school before moving to Lincolnton in 1884 to work with the Lincolnton City Schools. A number of professors succeeded Thompson at Rock Springs, including James F. Brower, Charles L. Coon, Leon Cash, Sidney J. Whitener, and W.M. Brooks. In later years, a new school building was constructed with the name changed to Denver Academy (seen here). (Lincoln County Museum of History.)

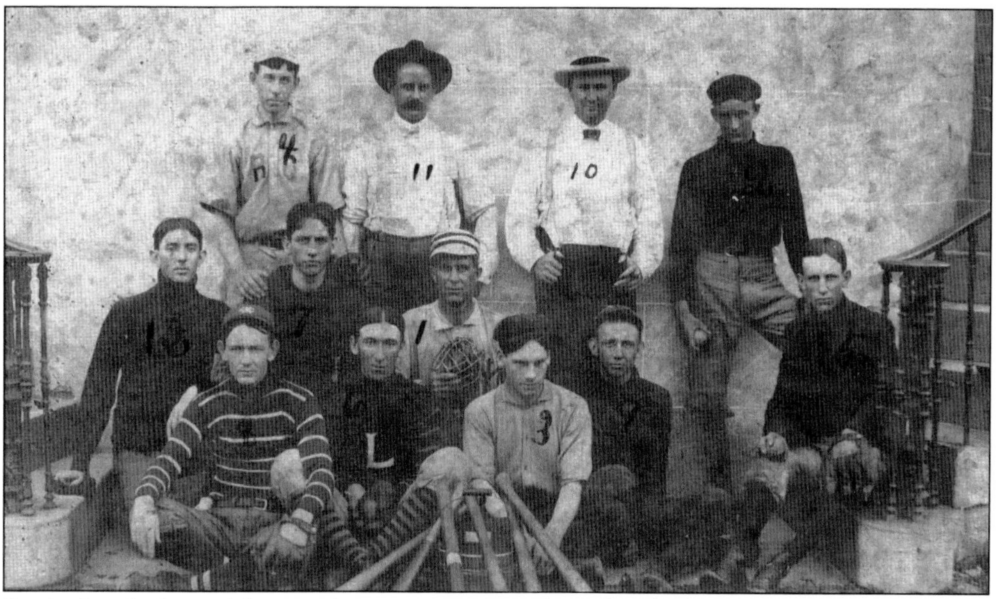

Perched at the base of the courthouse steps, a Lincolnton baseball team poses for a photograph around the turn of the century. They are, from left to right, as follows: (first row) Kemp Nixon, ? Cline, ? Shell, and Ben Hildebran; (second row) ? Cline, ? Burgin, and ? Davenport; (third row) Joe Nixon, ? Lineberger (umpire), ? Love (umpire), and two unidentified. (Mike Cline.)

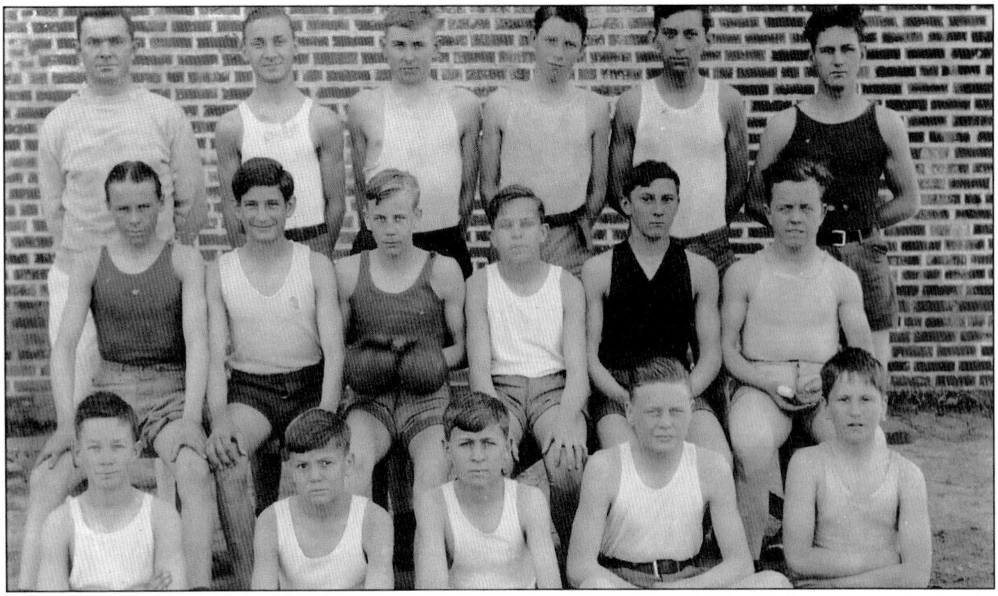

The Lincolnton High School boxing team shows their brawn in this 1928 photograph beside the school. Coach C.D. "Block" Smith" stands in top left of the photograph among the varsity squad: Merton Rudisill, David Wilkinson (captain), William Wilkinson, Loy D. Elmore, Kemp Huss, Woodrow Blanton, Ralph Crenshaw, John Rudisill, John Broome, Randolph Goodson, George Digh, Melvin Lingerfelt, Johnnie Lee, Bill Leonard, Daniel Philmon, Bell Jetton, and Howard Rudisill. Russell Mullen served as the team's manager. (Lincoln County Museum of History.)

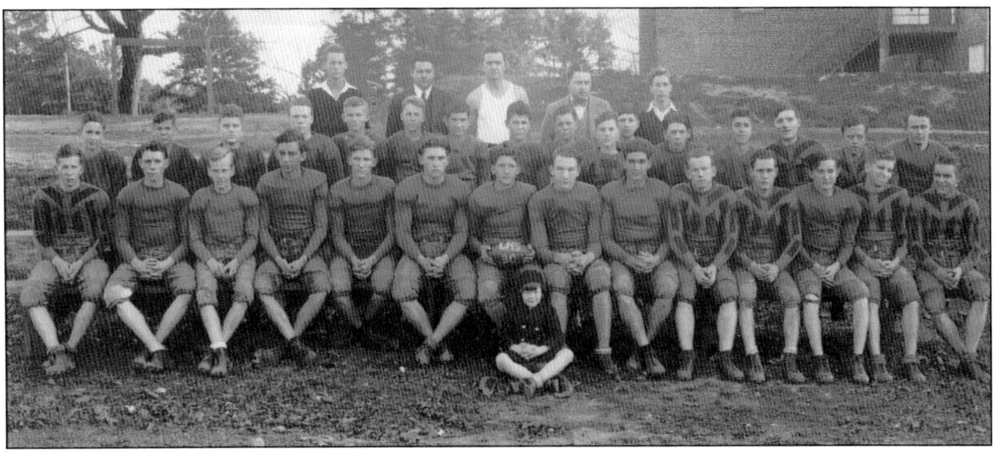

Suited up for the 1930 season, the Lincolnton High School football team awaits the flash from the camera with a stare. The roster, along with position, includes: Buck Mauney, quarterback; Kemp Huss, left halfback; John Rudisill, right halfback; Sam Hoover, fullback; David Wilkinson, left end; Pat Cashion, left tackle; Bud Paige (captain), left guard; Jessie Robinson, center; Fred Rudisill, right guard; Charles Smith, right tackle; and Loy D. Elmore, right end. The substitutes for the various positions are as follows: Ralph Yoder, quarterback; Guy Keener, left halfback; J.C. Pruitt, right halfback; Johnnie Lee, fullback; John Broome, left end; Harry Mullen, left tackle; Robert Little, left guard; Russell Mullen, center; Merton Rudisill, right guard; Clyde Cornwell, right tackle; and Howard Rudisill, right end. Charles D. "Block" Smith served as coach, and Charles Ramsaur, as manager. (Lincoln County Museum of History.)

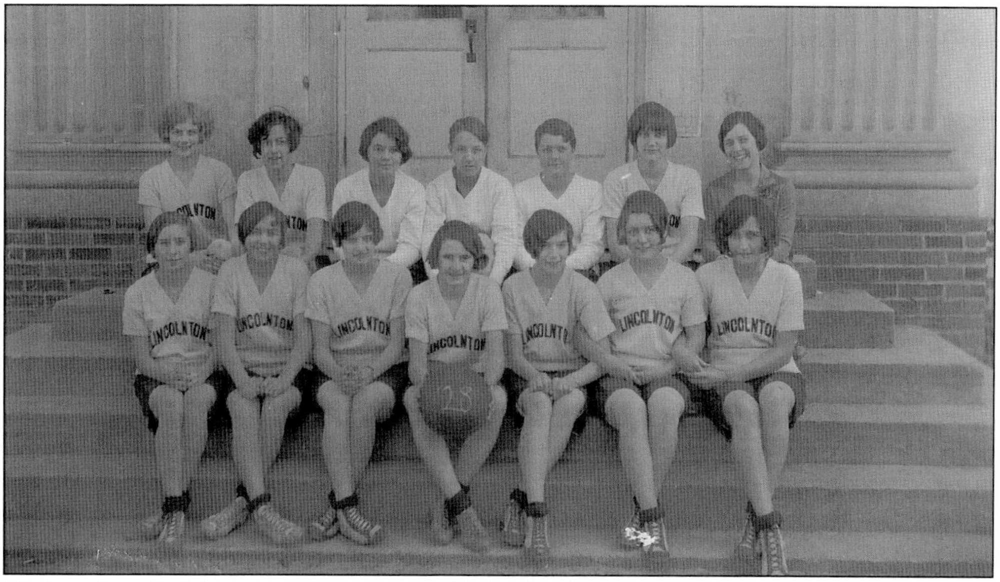

With socks rolled down and shoestrings pulled tight, the Lincoln High School girls' basketball team of 1928 poses for a team shot. The forwards are Marjorie Kate Abernethy, Lib Shuford, Toye Mae Harris, Milma Ramsey, and Lucille Lineberger. The long list of guards includes Juanita Saine, Eillen Padgett, Leanora Gamble, Frances Mauney, Emily Hunter (captain), Sue Ellen Shuford, Mary Frances Padgett, Elizabeth Hoyle, and Minnie Sue Erwin. Ruth Leonard stood also as the only center on the team. Miss Lib Hoke served as coach of the team. (Lincoln County Museum of History.)

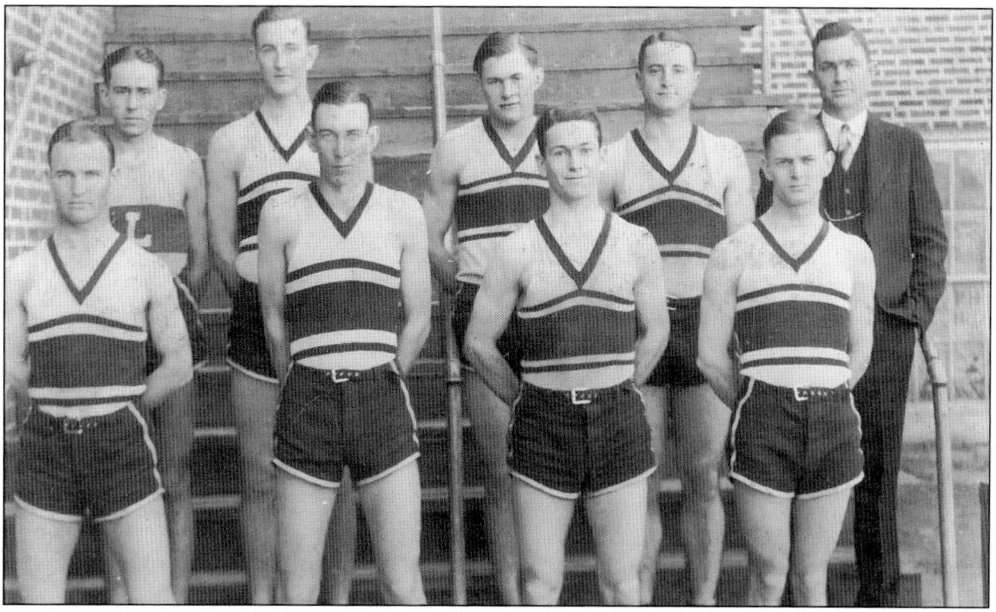

The Lincolnton City basketball team of 1927–1928 played in a league with Belmont, Dallas, and Clover. Pictured, from left to right, are the following: (front row) ? Cook, Elbert Combs, Edgar Love Jr., and Sidney McCutcheon; (back row) Goober Huggins, Tom Cornwell, "Country" Beam, Ernest Baxter, and C.D. "Block" Smith (coach). (Lincoln County Museum of History.)

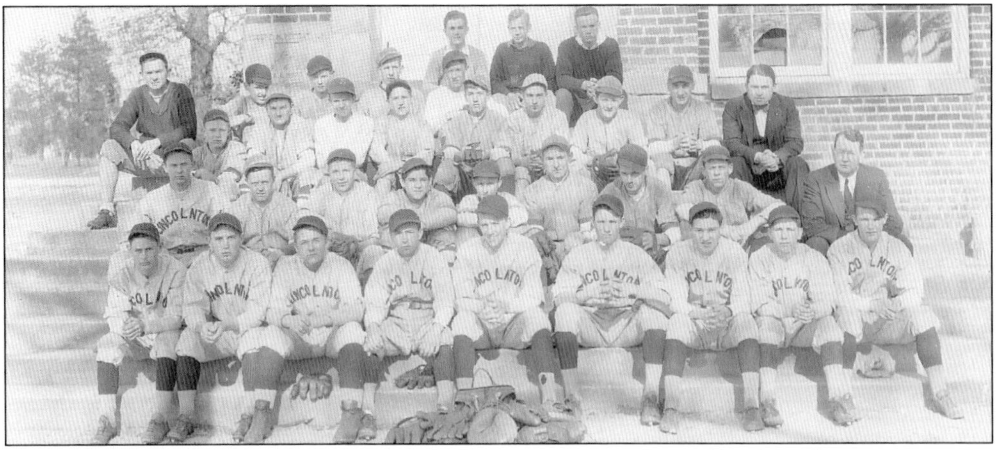

The Lincolnton High School boys' baseball team is pictured in 1931. Members are, in order by position, as follows: C. Smith, coach; D. Wilkenson, manager; J.C. Pruitt and J. Rudisill, assistant managers; L. Elmore, catcher; C. Broome, pitcher; J. Broome, first base; B. Mauney, second base; E. Goodson, third base; E. Rudisill, shortstop; Y. Ward, left field; R. Rudisill, center field; F. Rudisill, right field; J. Rudisill, pitcher; R. Little, sub-catcher; M. Lingerfelt, sub-pitcher; E. Caldwell, sub-first base; R. Yoder, sub-second base; W. Ramsey, sub-third base; B. Goodson, sub-shortstop; G. Digh, sub-left field; R. Mincy, sub-center field; J.C. Burke, sub-right field; and C. Dellinger, sub-pitcher. Also listed are the "Scrubs": B. Mauney, J. Reinhardt, S. Kale, J. Lee, G. Keener, F. Houser, and P. Kistler. (Lincoln County Museum of History.)

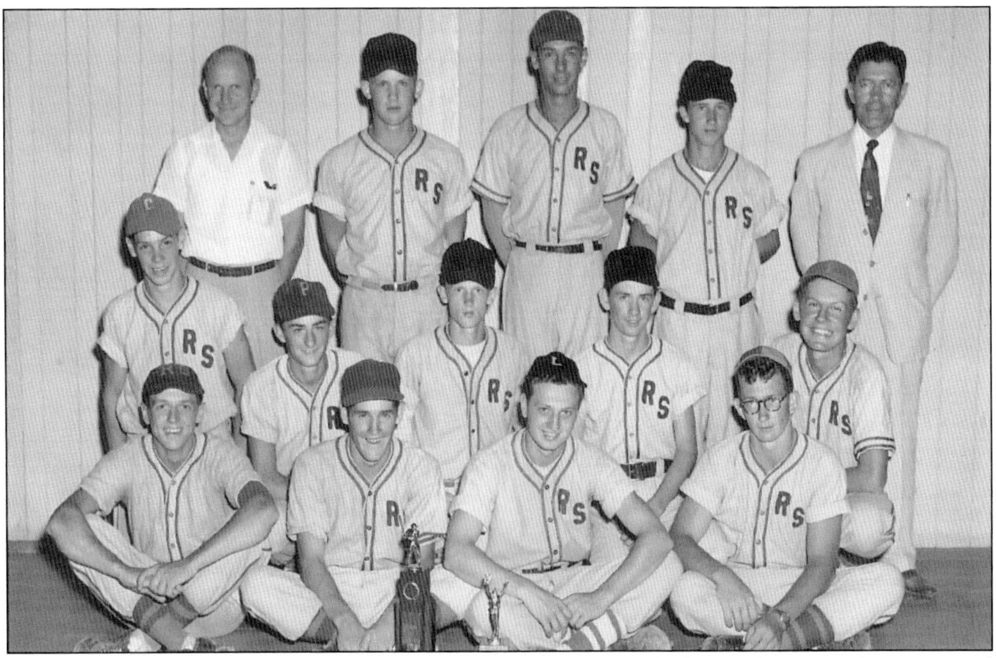

The Rock Springs High School baseball team of 1953 won both the Little Ten title, comprised of Gaston and Lincoln County teams, and the State Class A championship during their first year in the conference. Members are, from left to right, as follows: (first row) Ray Cloninger, Grady Barker, Junior Barkley, and Tommy Little; (second row) C.E. McCorkle, Herbert Loftin, Richard Sherrill, Walter Mundy, Kermit Sigmon; (third row) Lester Ballard, Jimmy Mundy, Donald Miller, Murray Sherrill, and W.T. Long, coach. (Lincoln County Museum of History.)

Seven

A Family Affair

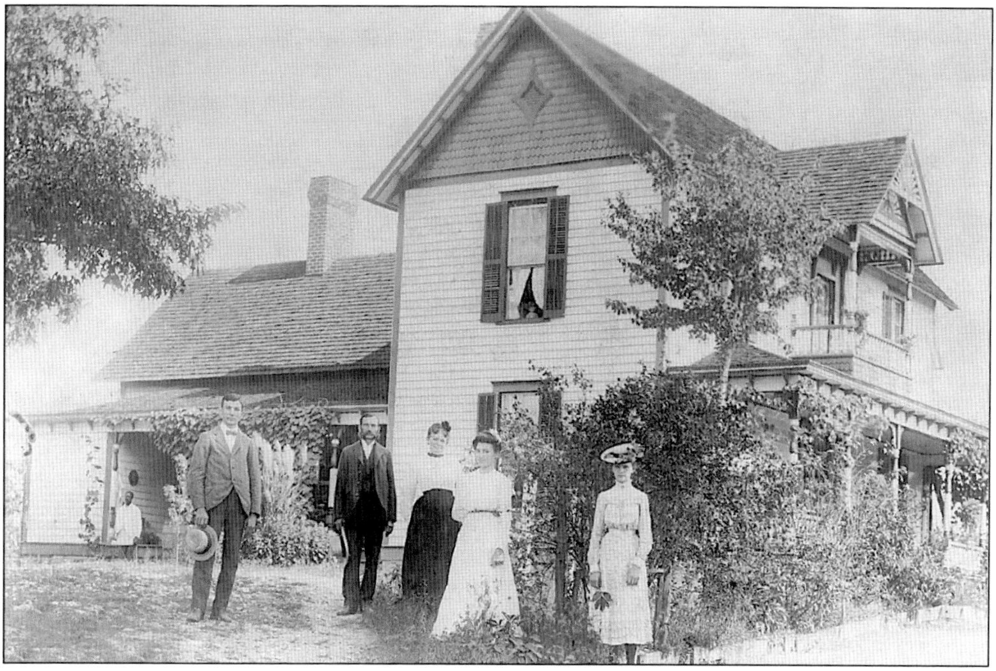

From a second-floor window of this stately Victorian house, a doll peers down on the Laban J. Rhyne family. Built in 1894 by D.E. Rhyne and brother-in-law, J.A. Abernethy, the gingerbread details of the house's front facade, combined with the grandiose attire of the Rhyne family, lend a sophistication to this photograph taken in 1900. Pictured, from left to right, are Nelson Logan (sitting on the porch), Paul, Laban J., Ellen, Lena, and Florence. (Ermintrude Mullen.)

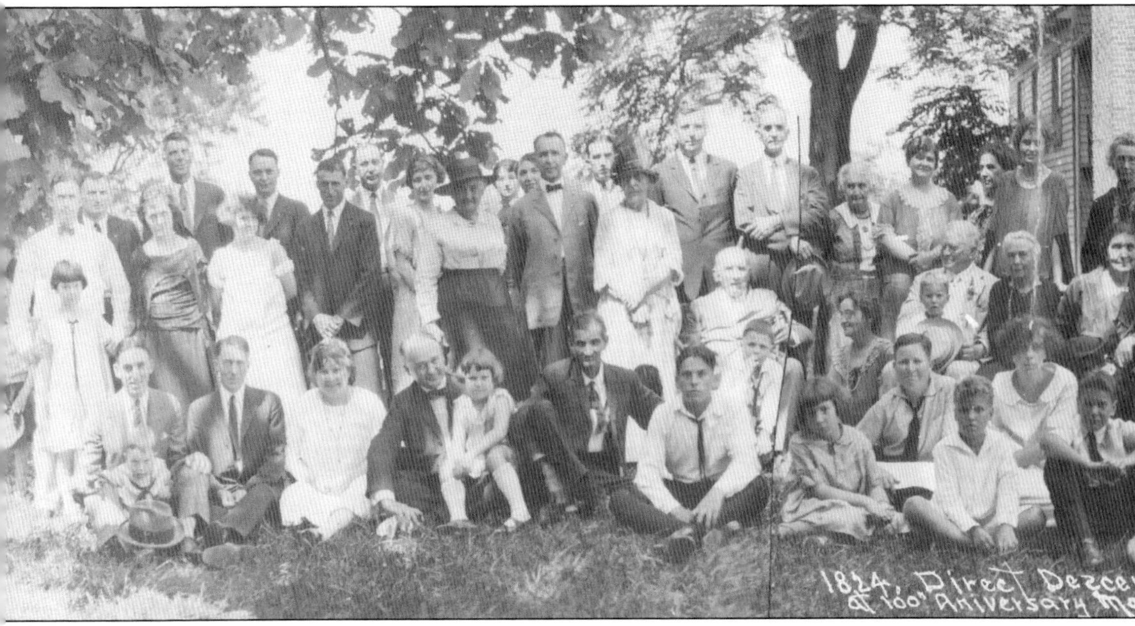

David Smith had this traditionally designed, three-room Quaker plan house known as "Magnolia Grove" built as his residence in Ironton Township in 1824. Descendants of Smith

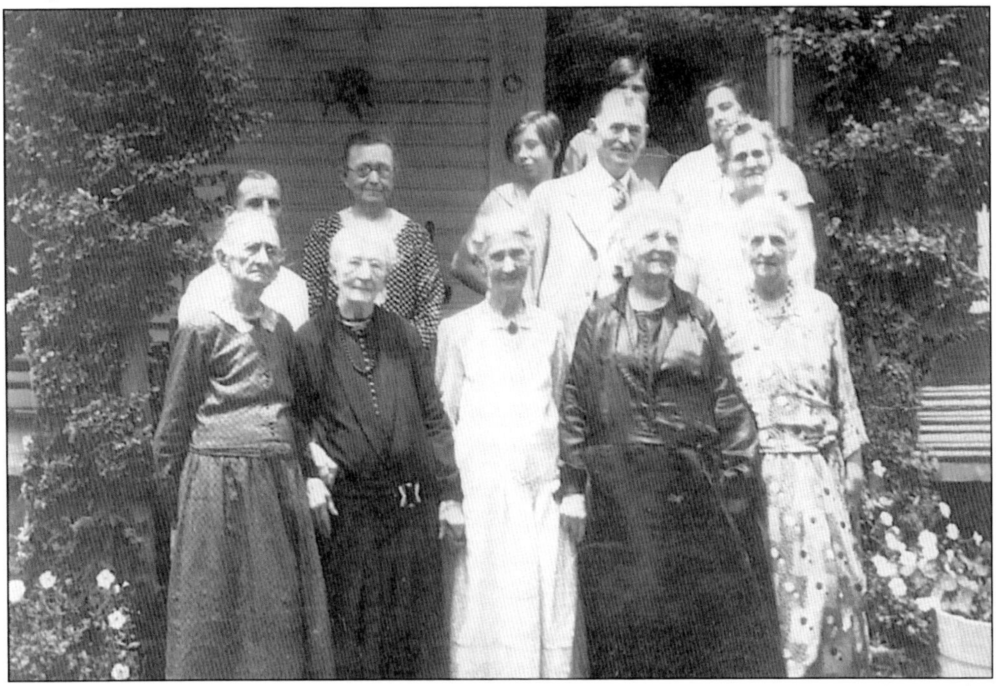

The daughters of Reverend Henry Asbury capture a brief moment in history during this photograph taken in the early 1900s. They are, from left to right, as follows: (front row) Mrs. Julia Ann Rebecca Asbury Robinson, Mrs. Melvina Asbury Thompson, Mrs. Jennie Asbury Goodson, Mrs. Sallie Asbury Duke, and Mrs. Ellen Asbury Bridges; (second row) Iola Jane Robinson Nixon; (couple on second row) Luckie Goodson Bolick, of Asheville, and her husband. (Mercer and Peggy Simmons.)

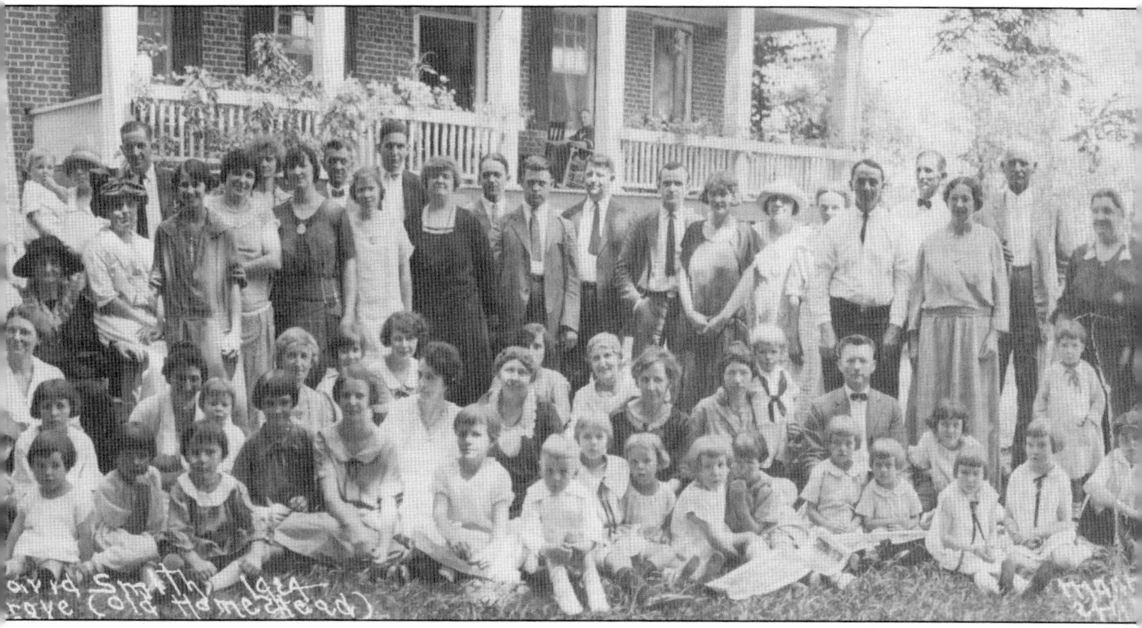
gathered for a reunion photograph in 1924 to celebrate the 100th anniversary of the building of his residence. (Lincoln County Museum of History.)

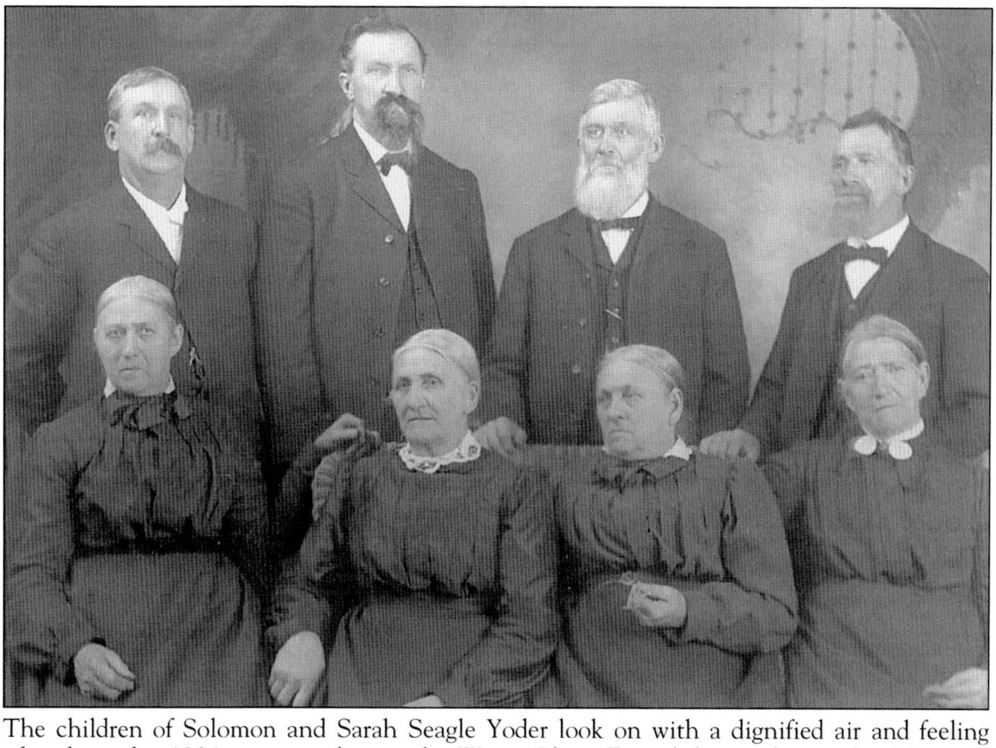
The children of Solomon and Sarah Seagle Yoder look on with a dignified air and feeling of pride in this 1904 portrait taken at the Wyant Place. From left to right are the following: (front row) Sarah Yoder Wyant, Elizabeth Yoder Petrie, Emmaline Yoder, and Mary Yoder Dellinger; (back row) Reverend Robert A. Yoder, Laban Yoder, David Yoder, and Daniel Yoder. (Sarah Yoder.)

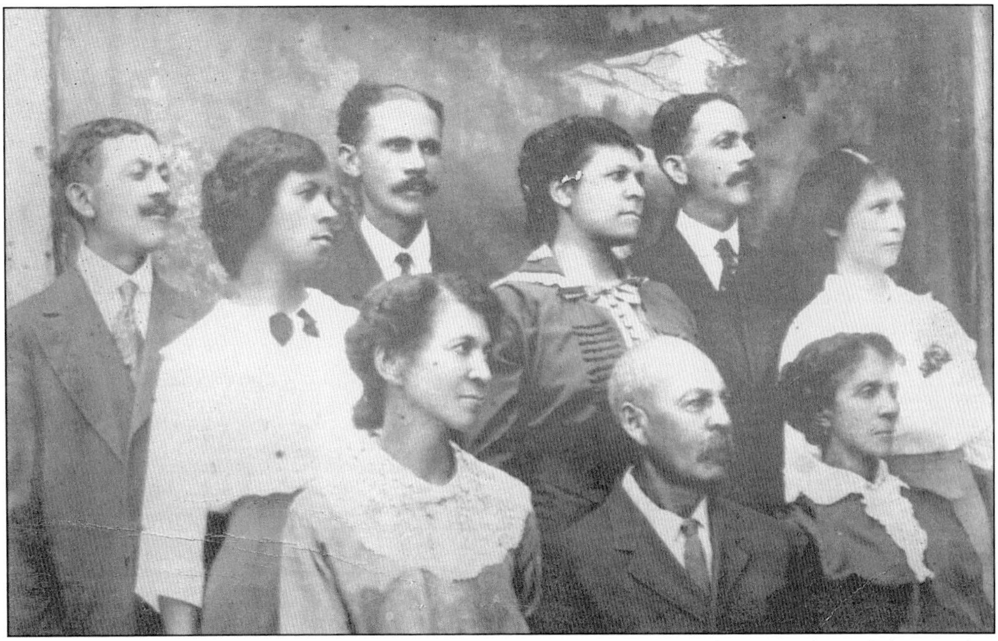

The Lander family lines up to capture a group portrait in 1916. They are, from left to right, as follows: (first row) Ella Lander Motz, Tench Lander, and Elizabeth Lander; (second row) Georgie Lander Burton, Mollie Lander Brooks, and Willie Rhodes; (third row) Tom Lander, Mark Lander, and Verlin Lander. (Leroy Magness.)

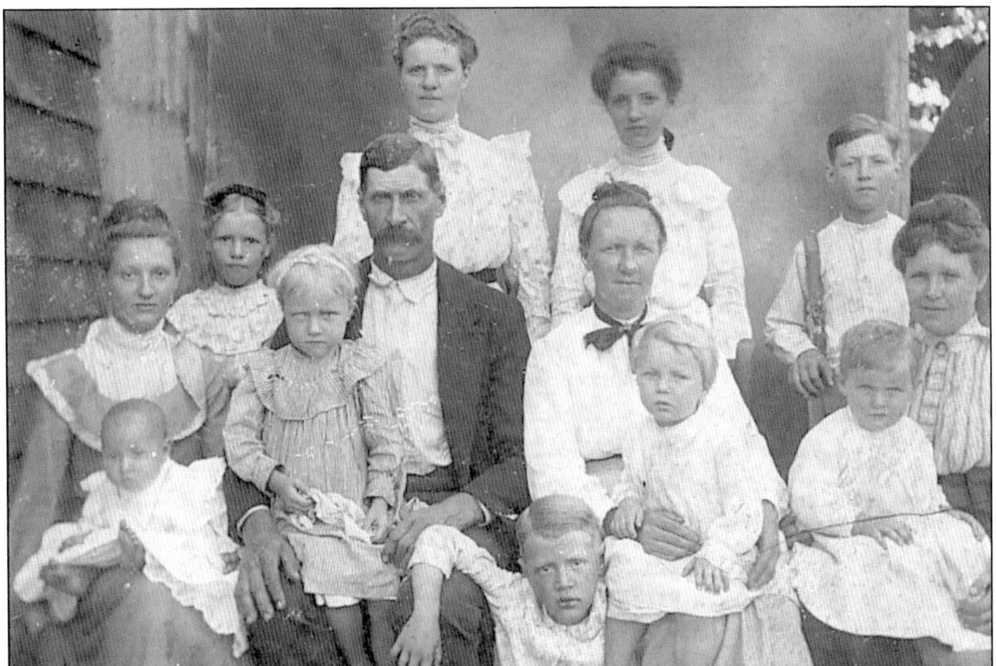

Members of the Reep-Lingerfelt family pose for this undated and untitled group photograph. Though not all identified, some of the members include Preston Lingerfelt, Lee, Grady, Ella, Nora, Minnie, Dallas, Goldie, and Lula. (Joyce Stroup.)

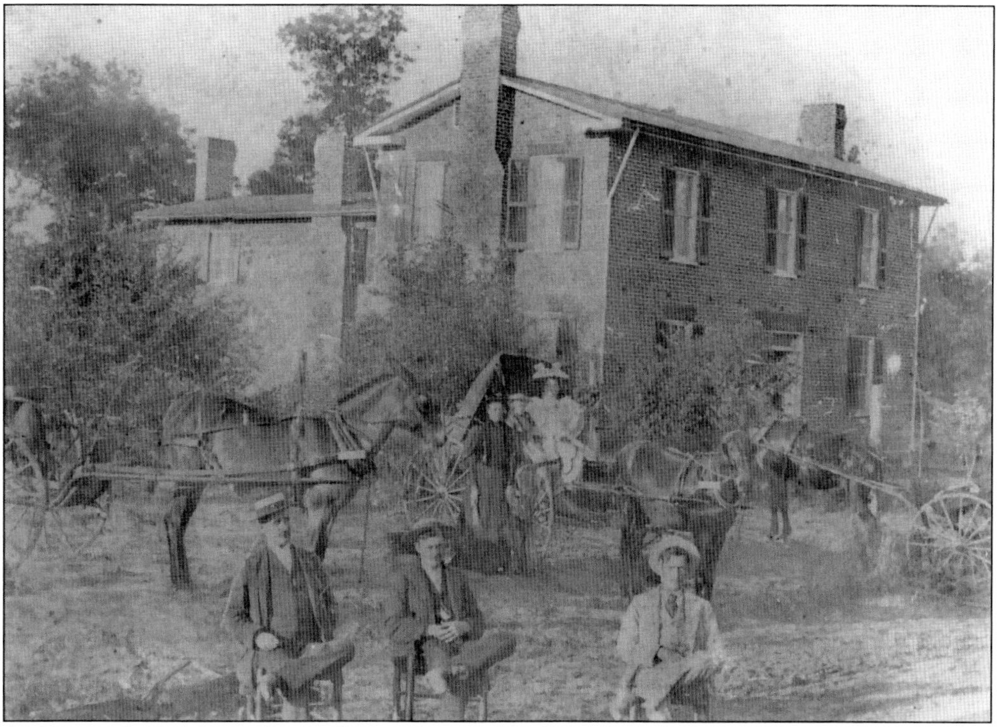

Built near Crouse around 1886 by Wesley Wells, the Lightfoot Williams Hoyle House adds a scenic backdrop to this unlabeled and undated photograph. The two-story rear ell was built first, with the two-story front block following the next year. Hoyle's business enterprises included a gristmill, cotton gin, and blacksmith shop. At one time there were about 25 frame outbuildings on the property. (Lincoln County Museum of History.)

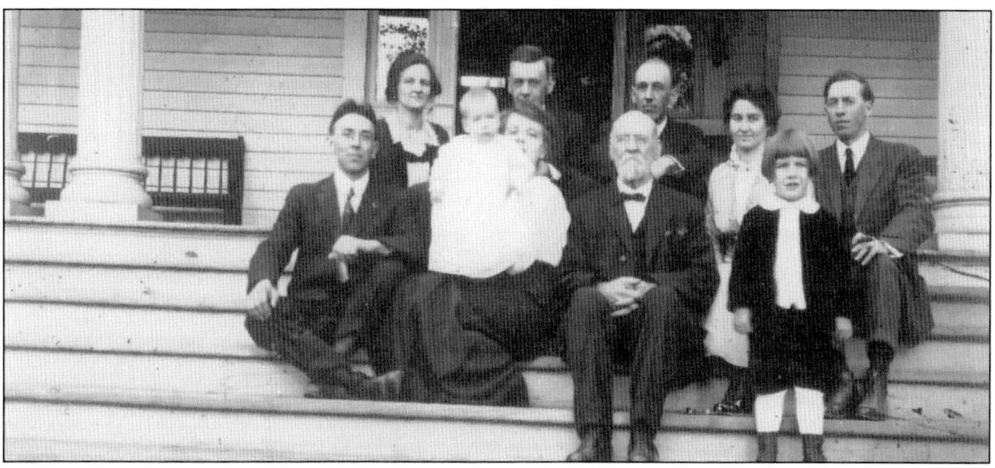

The recessed front doorway of the Michael Hoke House, birthplace of General Robert F. Hoke, lends its prominence as the earliest known example of Greek Revival–style architecture in Lincoln County to this photograph of H.E. Ramseur and family. H.E. Ramseur owned and operated Ramseur Hardware in Lincoln County and served as register of deeds from 1884 to 1888. Members of the family (from left to right) include (first row) John Ramseur, Charles (baby), Fetna Ramseur, Henry Ramseur, and Jack Ramseur; (second row) Mary Mac Ramseur, Fred Ramseur, Mont Ramseur, Jessie Ramseur, and Richard Ramseur. (Sue Ramseur.)

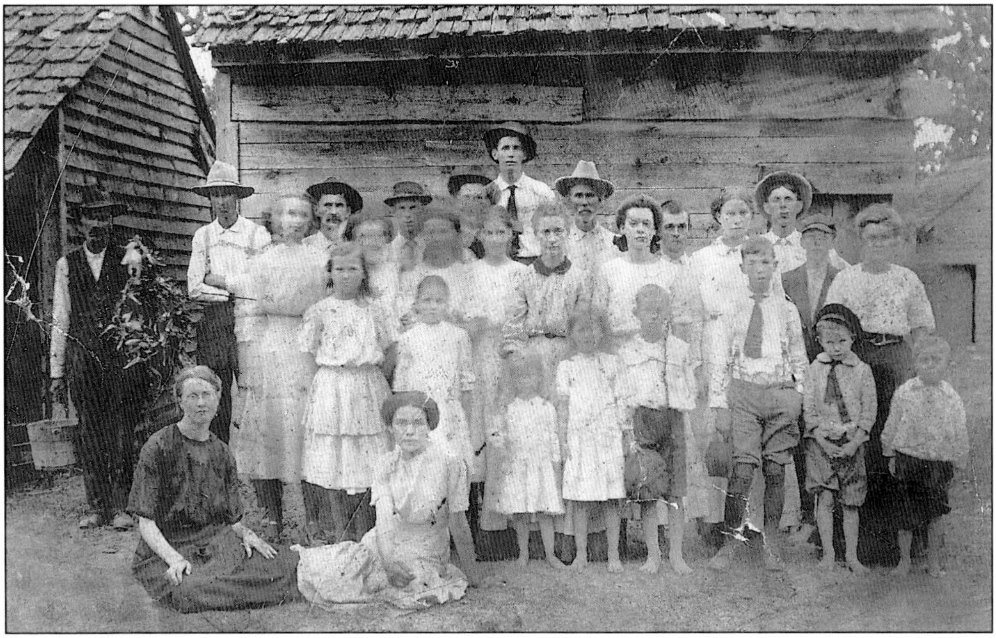

The simple majesty of the "tents" at the Rock Springs Campground provide lodging for the members who attend the annual camp meetings in eastern Lincoln County. A group of attendees stand in front of a typical "tent" in 1910. Some of the families represented in this photograph include Howards, Brothertons, Barkers, and Sherrills. Lewis Howard holds a bundle of fodder on his way to feed the group's horses and mules. (Terry Brotherton)

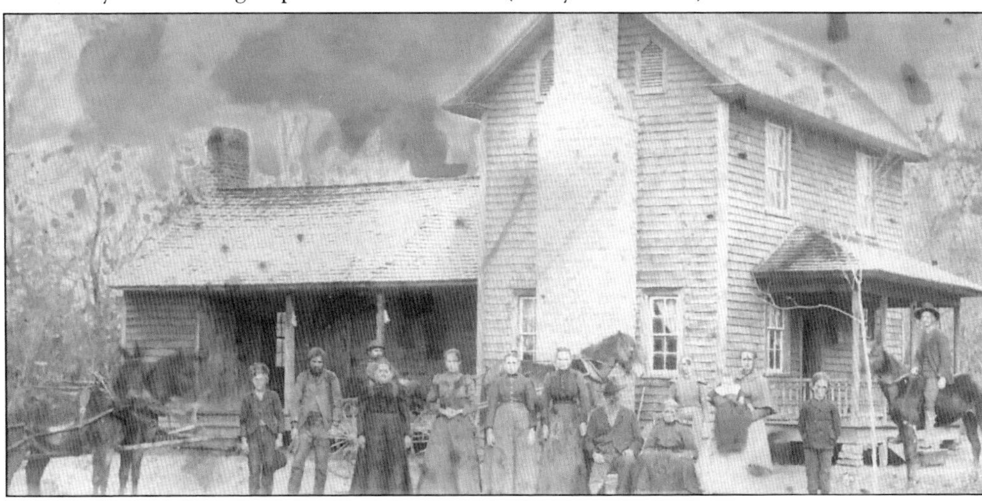

Sidney A. Sain built this house before the turn-of-the-century for his wife's parents, Robert and Mary Gilbert. Robert bears the mark from his service during the War between the States—his leg was amputated after being captured at Gettysburg. He enlisted in Iredell County on August 20, 1862, as a private in Company K, 23rd Regiment, NC Volunteers. Members of both families stand as the elder Gilberts take a seat for this photograph in western Lincoln County. They are, from left to right, as follows: Huston Clemmer, Uncle "Doc" Alexander Canipe, Sidney A. Sain, Mary Ann Sain, Maggie Gilbert, Jane Gilbert Canipe, Ila Mae Gilbert, "Grandpa" Robert Gilbert, Mary "Polly" Leonard Gilbert, unidentified baby, Josea Mary Jane Sain, Ida Catherine Gilbert Sain, Boyce Sidney Sain, and William D. Gilbert. (Patrick Houser.)

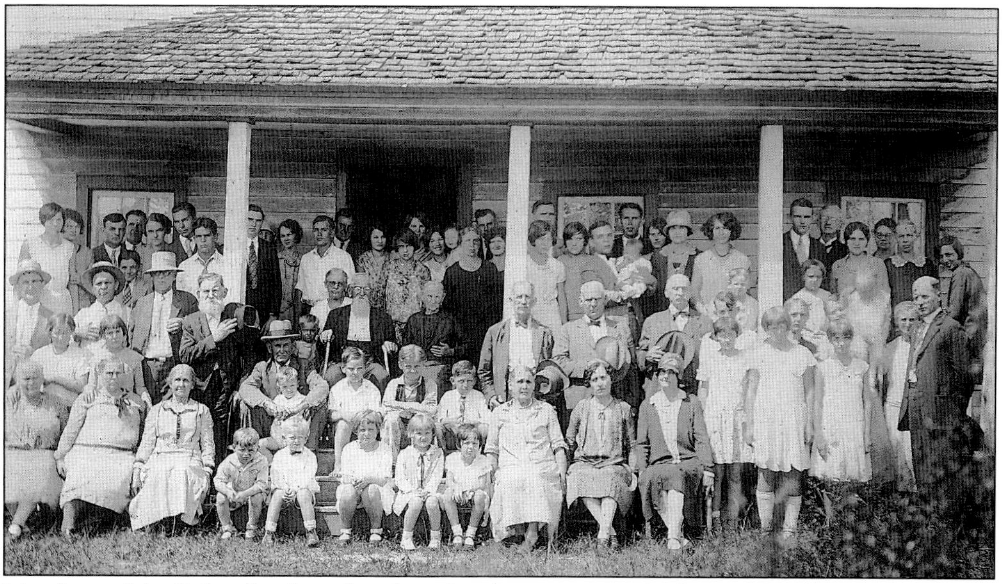

Members of the Baker family gather for a family reunion at the home of William L. Baker, off Hull's Grove Road in Vale. The house, built 1884–1885, holds the large group on its porch for this photograph taken around 1924. Lincoln County has purchased over 50 acres, on which this house sits, to be used as public recreational facilities, which may include picnic areas, hiking trails, natural areas, and sports facilities. (David C. Heavner.)

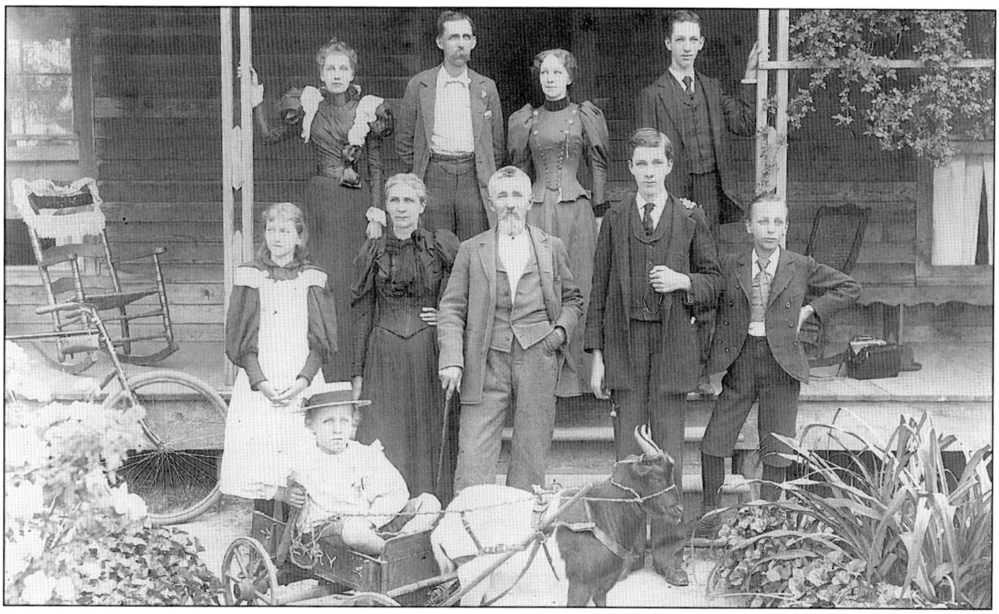

The Hauss family strikes a stately pose in front of their home near Hog Hill in western Lincoln County for this turn-of-the-century photograph. Hog Hill is so named because early settlers marked their hogs and let them roam there until fall when their owners took them home for the winter. Members of the family are, from left to right, as follows: (first row) Oscar Hauss (in wagon); (second row) Ada Hauss, Frances Hauss, William "Billie" Hauss, and Clarence Hauss; (third row) unidentified family members. Clarence started the Queen City Trailway Co. in Charlotte. (John Hauss.)

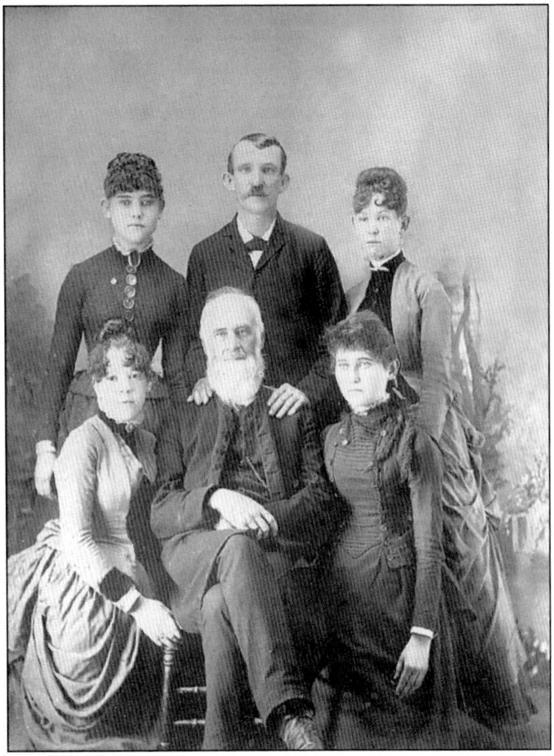

Captain W.R. Edwards (February 25, 1819–June 5, 1910) poses with his children in this photograph during the early years of the 20th century. Edwards served the county as a register of deeds from 1874 to 1884. His son, Robert Stuart Edwards (December 5, 1854–November 22, 1924), stands behind. (Ann Ford.)

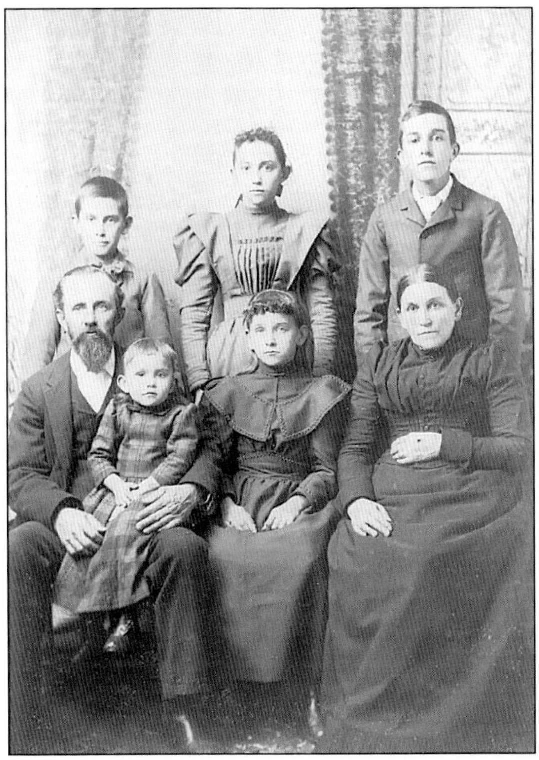

David Crooks Warlick (February 3, 1848–October 4, 1935) holds his young daughter, Mary Ethel, in this photograph from the 1890s. Warlick served in the War between the States from Lincoln County and years later was a member of the United Confederate Veterans, W.J. Hoke Camp No. 1596. The other members of the family are (front row) Cora Maggie and his wife, Mary Rhodes Warlick (September 11, 1845–December 8, 1916); (back row) Thomas Alfred Warlick, Lula Frances Warlick, and Solomon Rhodes Warlick. Their home stands 1 mile northwest of Daniels Church in Lincolnton, on the property that was part of the original land granted to Daniel Warlick. (Joe and Ruth Leonard.)

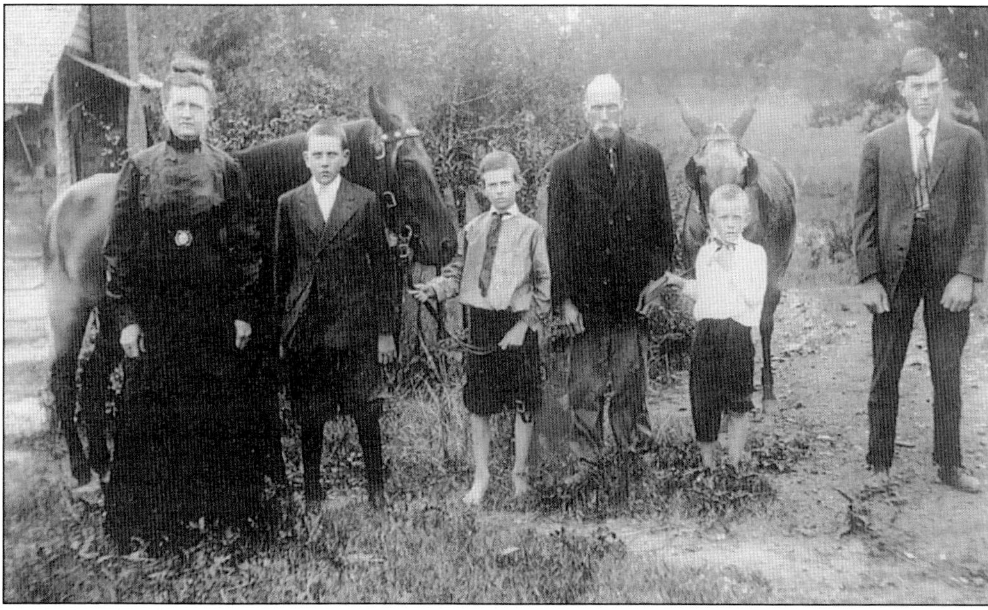

With the family steeds peering from behind, the Leatherman family stands on the grounds of the family farm in this c. 1911 photograph. They are, from left to right, as follows: Flora Lail (July 8, 1860– March 31, 1942), Richard (born May 10, 1898), Walter (born July 10, 1900), Noah Franklin (January 1, 1854–May 21, 1929), Ernest (born October 10, 1902), and Lawrence (born January 15, 1895). (Larry and Diane Leatherman.)

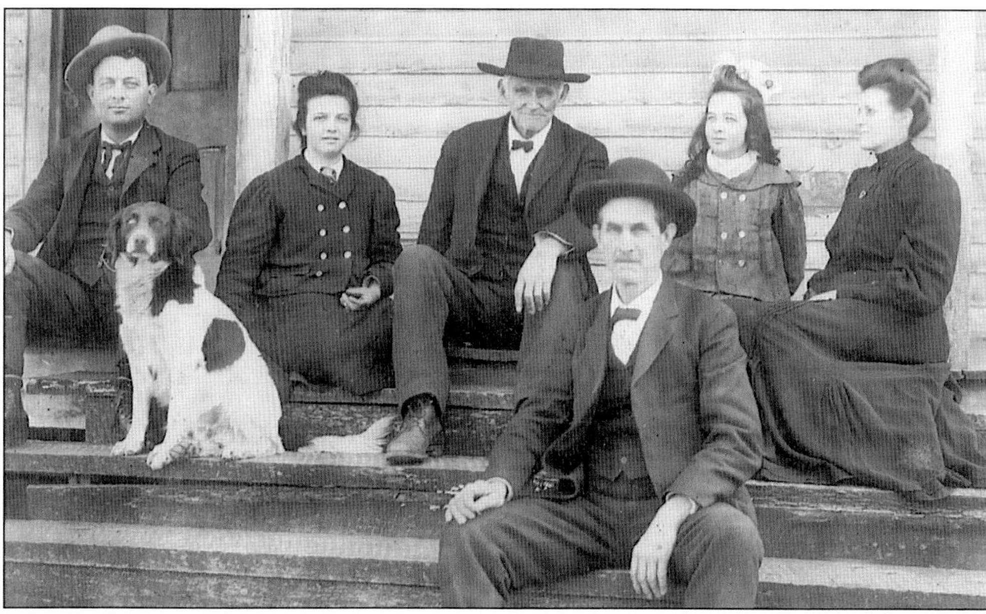

Sitting on the steps of the Mundy House, which stood on the present Will Proctor Road in eastern Lincoln County, members of the Proctor and Mundy families take a break with a faithful companion. They are, from left to right, as follows: (front row) W.C. Proctor, owner of Denver's first store; (back row) J.O. Mundy, owner of Denver's first drugstore in Denver; Clayton Mundy, daughter; Richard Proctor, an original trustee of Rock Springs Campground; Pinkie Mundy, daughter; and Lacy Mundy. (Terry Brotherton.)

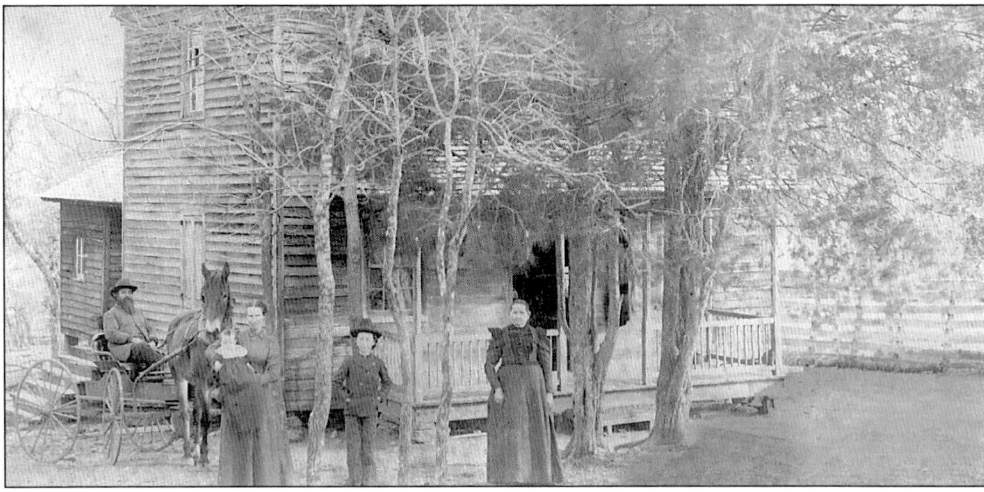

Patriarch Sidney Sain opts to remain in the family buggy with horse harnessed for this *c.* 1899 photograph. The Sain house was built of logs around 1840, off of present Grigg Road in western Lincoln County, by Abraham Sain (1809–1878) and occupied by he and his wife, Elizabeth Leonhardt Sain (1819–1892). The house burned in the 1940s, and the Sain family barn was relocated and rebuilt at the home of Robert and Ann Dellinger. Members of the family are, from right to left, as follows: Sydney Abraham Sain (1854–1903), Ida Gilbert Sain (1856–1942), Josie Sain Houser (1898–?), Boyce Sidney Sain (1890–?), and Mary Ann Sain (1844–1920). (Sidney Houser.)

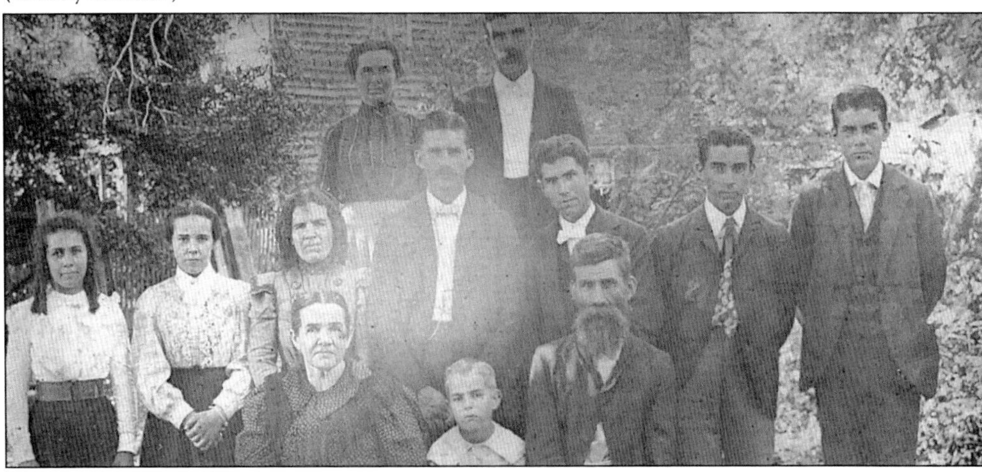

Confederate veteran John Franklin Haynes takes a seat on the front row with wife, Frances, and son, Samuel Harbin, for this *c.* 1899 family photograph. Haynes enlisted in the Confederate Army on April 24, 1862, and served as a private in Company K, 1st Regiment. Members of the family, from left to right, are as follows: (first row) Frances Barbara Julie Ann Hartzoe Haynes (September 7, 1850–February 3, 1930), Samuel Harbin Haynes (December 26, 1893–May 16, 1953), and John Franklin Haynes (January 10, 1842–April 22, 1918); (second row) Grace Edith Haynes (July 16, 1887–September 27, 1919), Lois Haynes (August 8, 1885–December 26, 1961), Mary "May" Haynes (April 15, 1877–November 23, 1945), Augustus "Gus" Haynes (September 25, 1869–June 11, 1928), Robert Elkana Haynes (April 5, 1879–August 13, 1935), John Henry Haynes (December 8, 1880–July 13, 1959), and Forney Haynes (December 10, 1882–February 3, 1966); (third row) Ella Haynes (July 21, 1867–August 8, 1925) and Calvin Haynes (September 12, 1874–July 28, 1941). (Paul Haynes.)

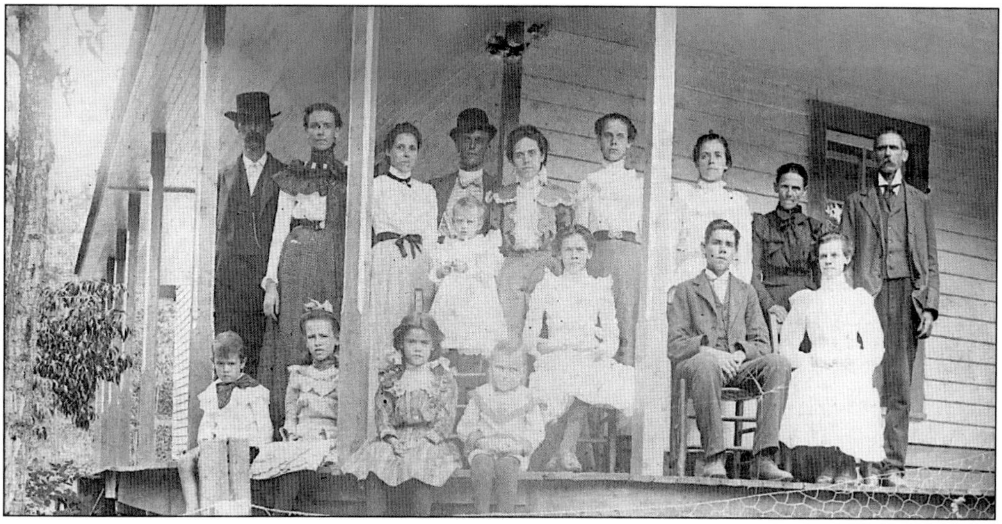

Members of the Huss family gathered for a group portrait on the porch of the family house. They are, from left to right, as follows: (children, seated) Wilburn Smith, Lena Smith Bell, Buena Smith Cauble, and Fred Connor; (middle row) Roxanna Connor Stone (daughter of Sally and Clarence Connor), Florence Huss Carpenter, Sylvanus Huss, and Cara Huss Wells; (back row) Lee Smith, Jenny Huss Smith, Sally Huss Connor, Clarence Connor, Alice Huss, Nora Huss Sigmon, Mary Nettie Huss Kelley, Roxanna Connor Huss, and Elias Calvin Huss. (Mary Ramsey.)

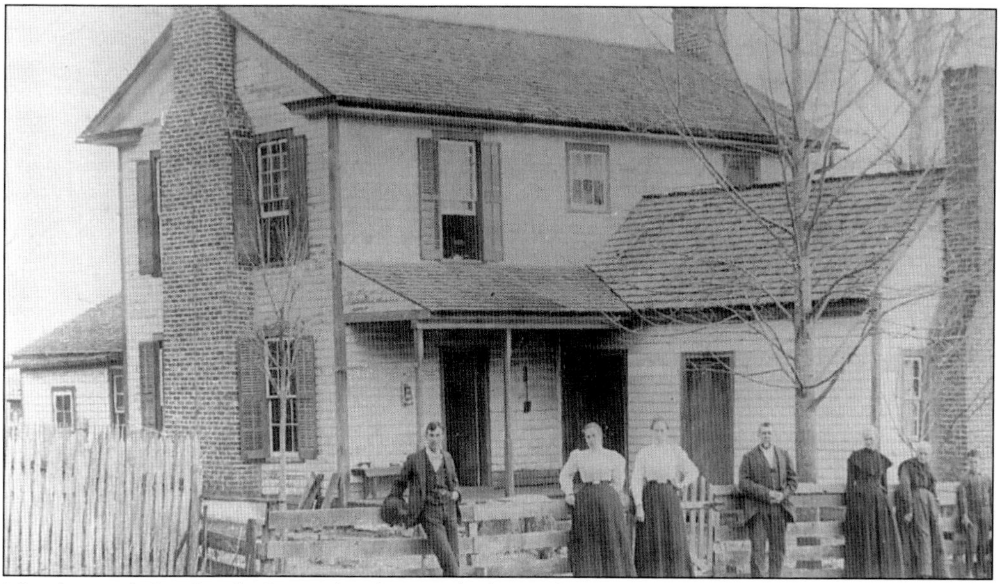

Members of the Jacob Saine family stand along the wood fence with their house in the background for this family photograph taken around 1900. The house is believed to have been built in 1887 from evidence painted on the floor joists under the house bearing the words "Jacob Saine 1887." Members are, from left to right, as follows: John Saine, Emma Saine Coon, Ola Saine, Jacob Saine Jr., Mary Jane Wood Saine (wife of Jacob Saine Jr.), "Aunt Mary," and Zeb Saine. Zeb Saine later lived in the house with his second wife, sister of Charles Raper Jonas. Gene Heavner undertook the restoration of the Saine house and currently resides here. (Gene Heavner.)

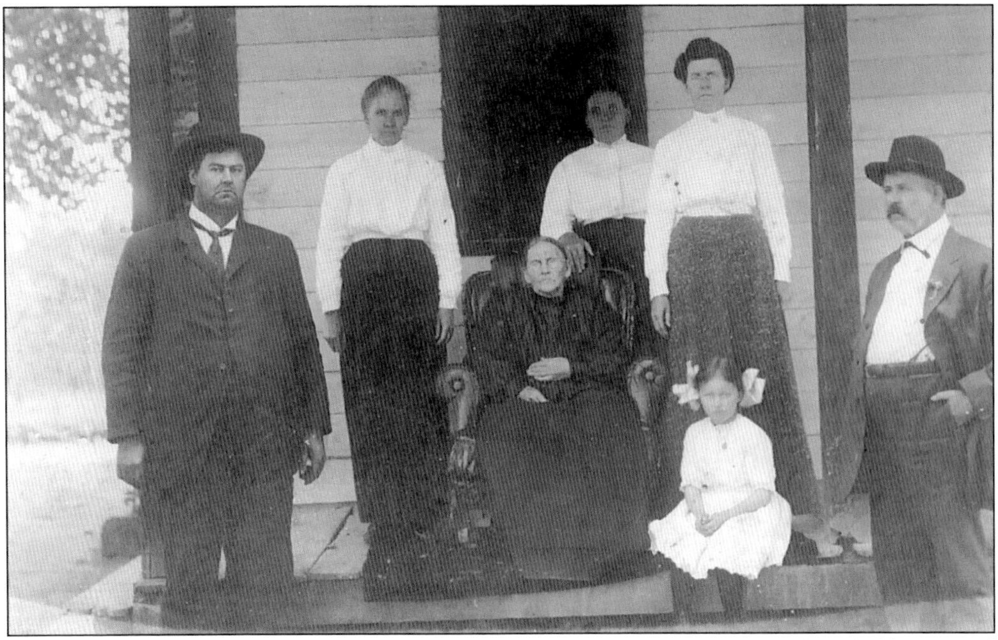

Matriarch Millie Womack Nixon rests in her comfortable leather chair as her children stand around her for this photograph from the early years of the 20th century in eastern Lincoln County. From left to right are Robert "Bob" Nixon, unidentified, Millie Womack Nixon, daughter Millie Nixon, Sally Nixon Cauble, unidentified, and Alfred Nixon. (Linda Graham.)

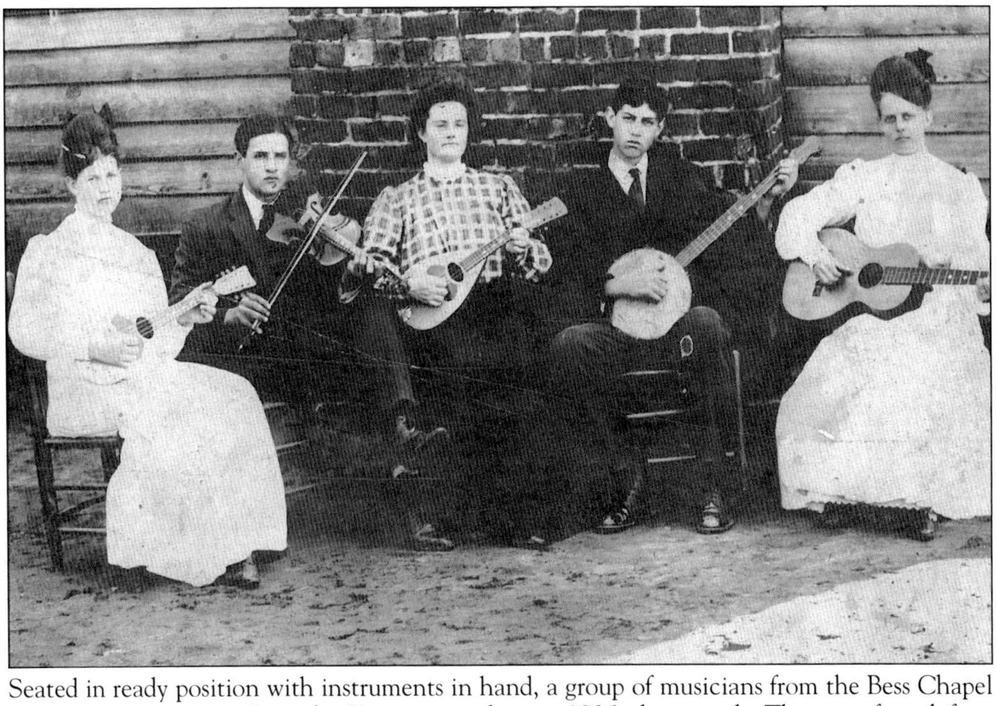

Seated in ready position with instruments in hand, a group of musicians from the Bess Chapel community in western Lincoln County pose for a c. 1906 photograph. They are, from left to right, as follows: Bryte Beam (1891–1966), Clifton "Clif" Jenks (1887–1962), Sally Bess (1882–1959), Lee Jenks (1889–1971), and Hattie Beam (1889–1917). (Bill Beam.)

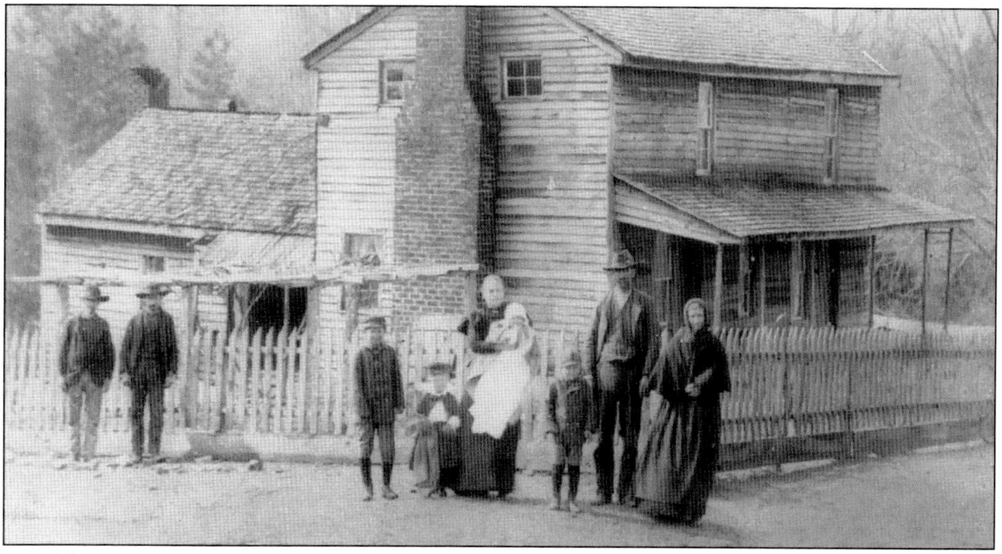

Adolph Reep (1760–1844) constructed this log house on 200 acres of land he purchased in 1795 on the headwaters of Leonard's Fork creek, now Reep Bros. Dairy Road in western Lincoln County. Jonas Reep razed the house in 1948 to make way for a home for he and his wife. Members of the Reep family include, from left to right, the following: ? Lingerfelt, unidentified, Jacob Alba Reep (1890–1970), Charley (1897–1909), Alice Ward Reep (1866–1957), Luther Jones Reep (1899–1971), Clarence Reep (1894–1963), Logan Jacob Reep (1858–1914), and Malinda "Linny" Speagle Reep (1824–1914). (Inez Reep Beam.)

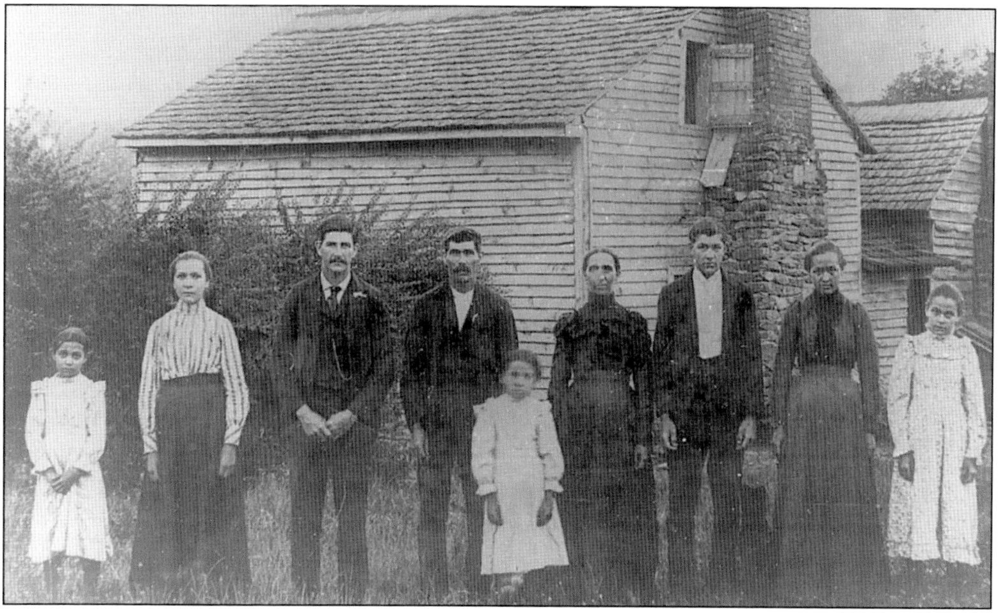

The John Adolphus and Mary Catherine Mosteller Seagle family stands in front of their home near the Mosteller homestead and Howard's Creek Mill in western Lincoln County prior to remodeling about 1901. Mary Seagle was a prolific weaver who was known for making old-fashioned wool coverlets. Pictured, from left to right, are Ida Sarah Seagle, Mary Grace Seagle, Thomas Frances Seagle, John Adolphus Seagle, Lula Ethel Seagle, Mary Mosteller Seagle, Doras Burton Seagle, Barbara Ellen Seagle, and Anna Rebecca Seagle. (Bill Beam.)

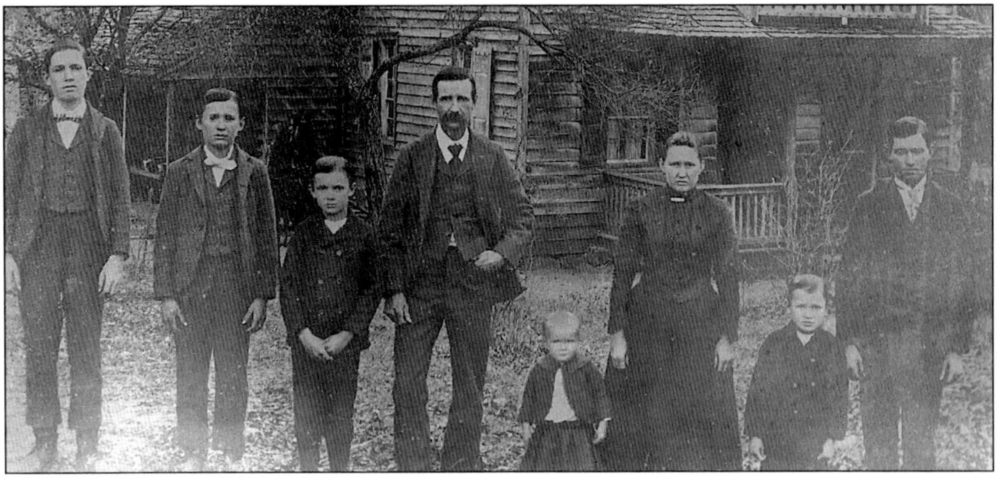

David Beam (1797–1852), grandson of Johann Dietrich Beam (1732–1807), acquired a 203-acre tract in 1819 which included "a mill and plantation house." In 1888, David "Dave" Beam (1861–1947), grandson of the owner, purchased the tract. Standing in front of the Beam house on the original tract, from left to right, are Lester Beam, Clete Beam, Clyde Beam, David Beam (father), Floyd Beam, Margaret Beam (mother), R.L. "Bub" Beam, and Frank Beam. (Bill Beam.)

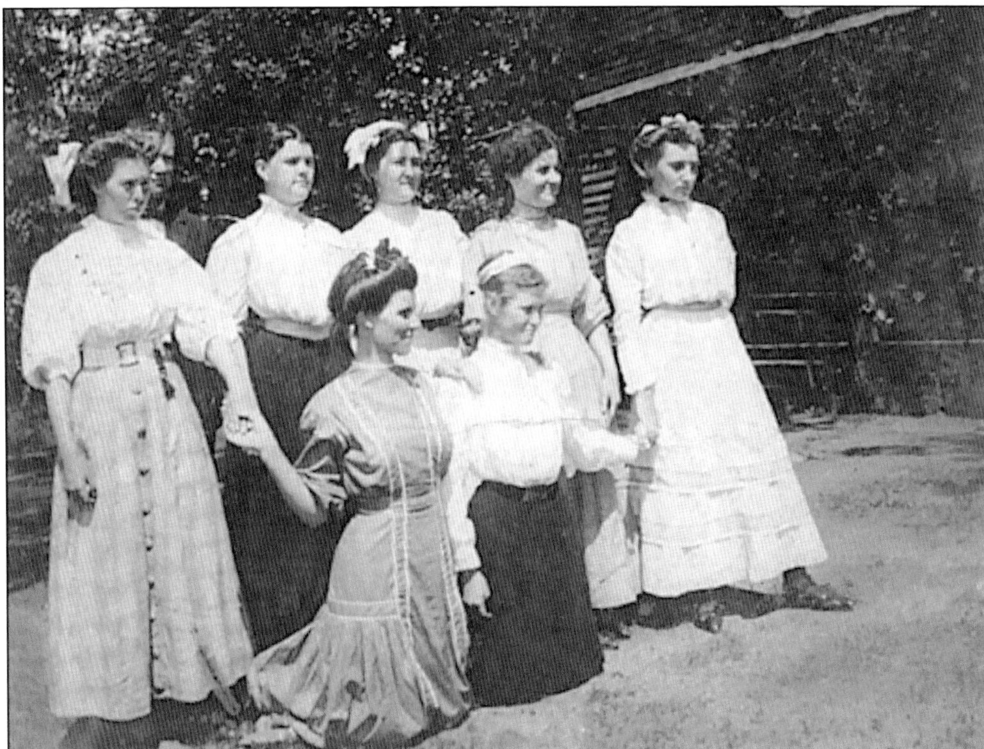

Hand-in-hand, a group of ladies waits for their image to be captured for this photograph taken in the eastern part of Lincoln County. Shown here, from left to right, are (front row) Willie Sifford Duckworth and Lava Carter Shy; (back row) Lelia Pryor Johnson, Lula Sifford Carter, Julia Sifford Williamson, Rena Sifford Killian, and Lucy Sifford Hager. (Frances Hampton.)

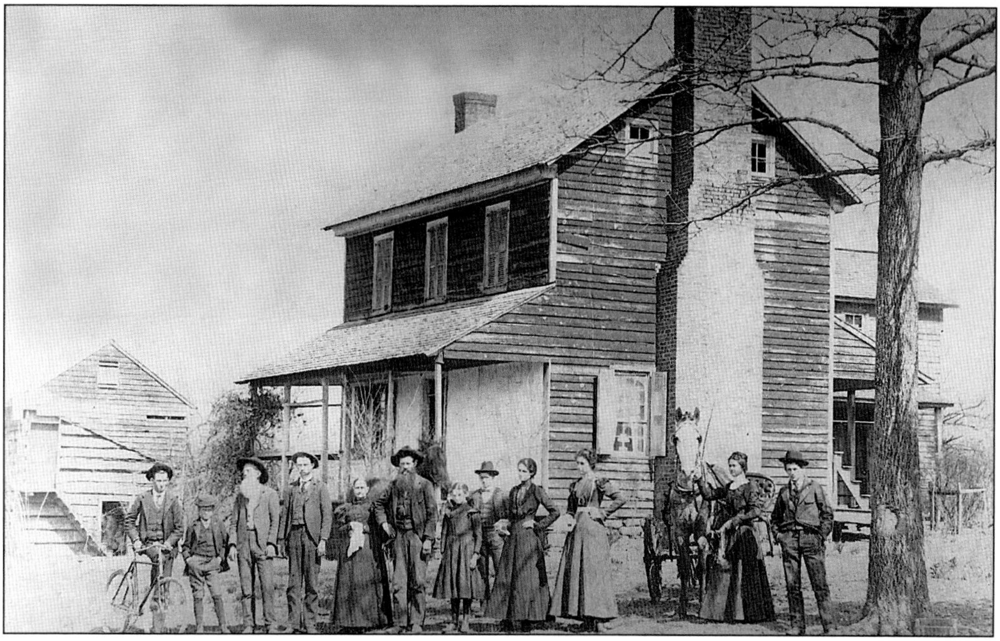

A few members of the Lutz family felt like including a bike and horses in their family photograph taken between 1890 and 1895. Odell Lutz stands tall in the middle of the group, eighth person from the left, with the family house, a frame dwelling built of logs and painted red, looming in the background with an outbuilding at the left of the group. (James Lutz.)

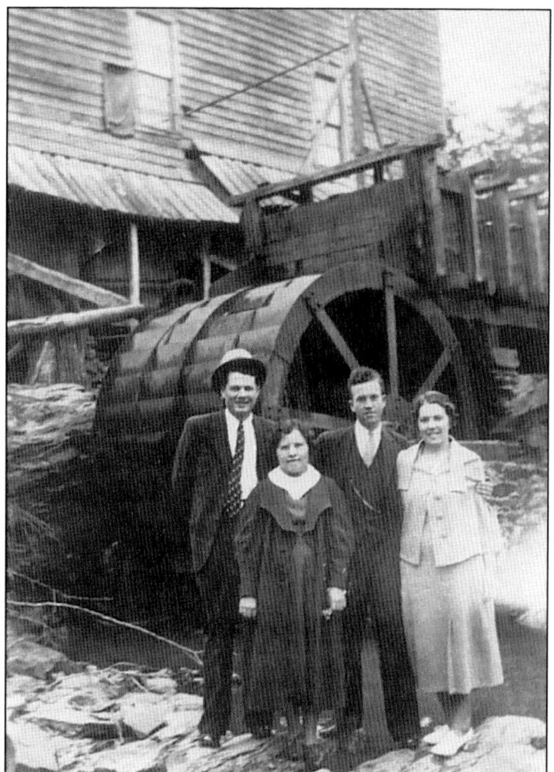

A group huddles at the base of the Howard's Creek mill on a large rock near the overshot waterwheel. Pictured, from left to right, are John D. Abernethy, operator of the mill; Florence Reep; Frank A. Flowers, brother-in-law of J.D. Abernethy; and Irene A. Flowers, sister of J.D. Abernethy. (Lincoln County Museum of History.)

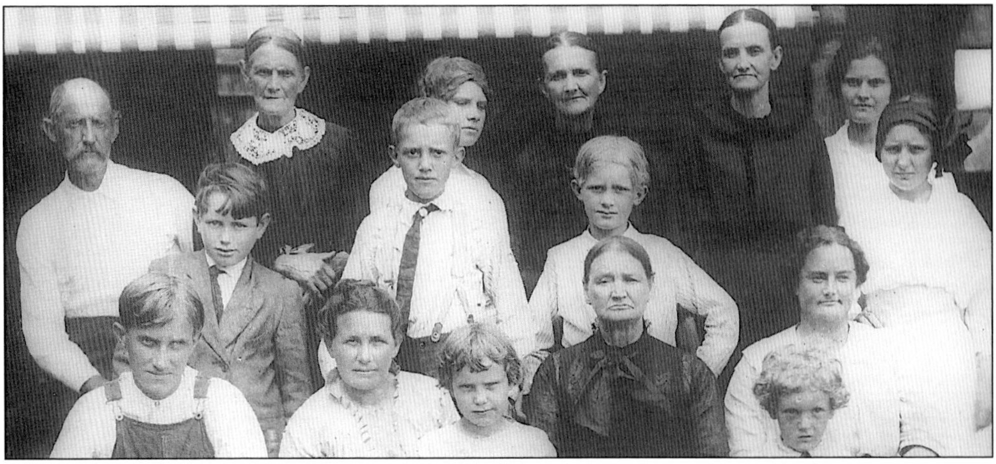

Both children and grandchildren of Peter and Sarah B. Bess gather together for a portrait around 1915. They are, from left to right, as follows: (front row) Grady L. Bess (October 5, 1895–January 19, 1922); Emma Cauble Bess (December 25, 1867–March 17, 1945); Hattie Bess; Euphemia Bess (March 18, 1845–July 28, 1924); Kenneth Scronce, son of Sallie Margaret Bess and John Conrad Scronce; and Sallie Margaret Bess (February 9, 1882–February 5, 1959); (second row) Charlie Scronce, son of John Conrad Scronce; David Boston Bess (July 6, 1901–December 11, 1967); John Frank Bess (December 10, 1903–April 6, 1964); and Prue Scronce, daughter of John Conrad Scronce; (third row) George Washington Bess; Elizabeth Catherine Candis Bess; Mary Ava Bess; Sarah Janie Bess; Cora Lee Bess; and Nannie Bess. (Bob Carpenter.)

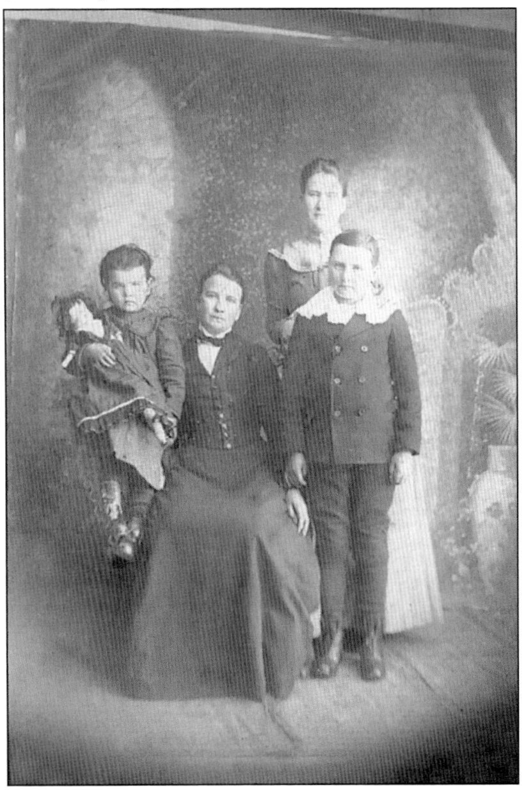

Members of the Cronland family present an unassuming gaze for this portrait taken from their Iron Station home on February 3, 1896. Mrs. Louella Cronland and son, Rickard Benjamin, stand, while Molly Killian and daughter, Alda, sit beside. The family later moved to their farm on Asbury Church Road in Lincolnton. (Jack and Estelle Cronland.)

Eight

'Round the County

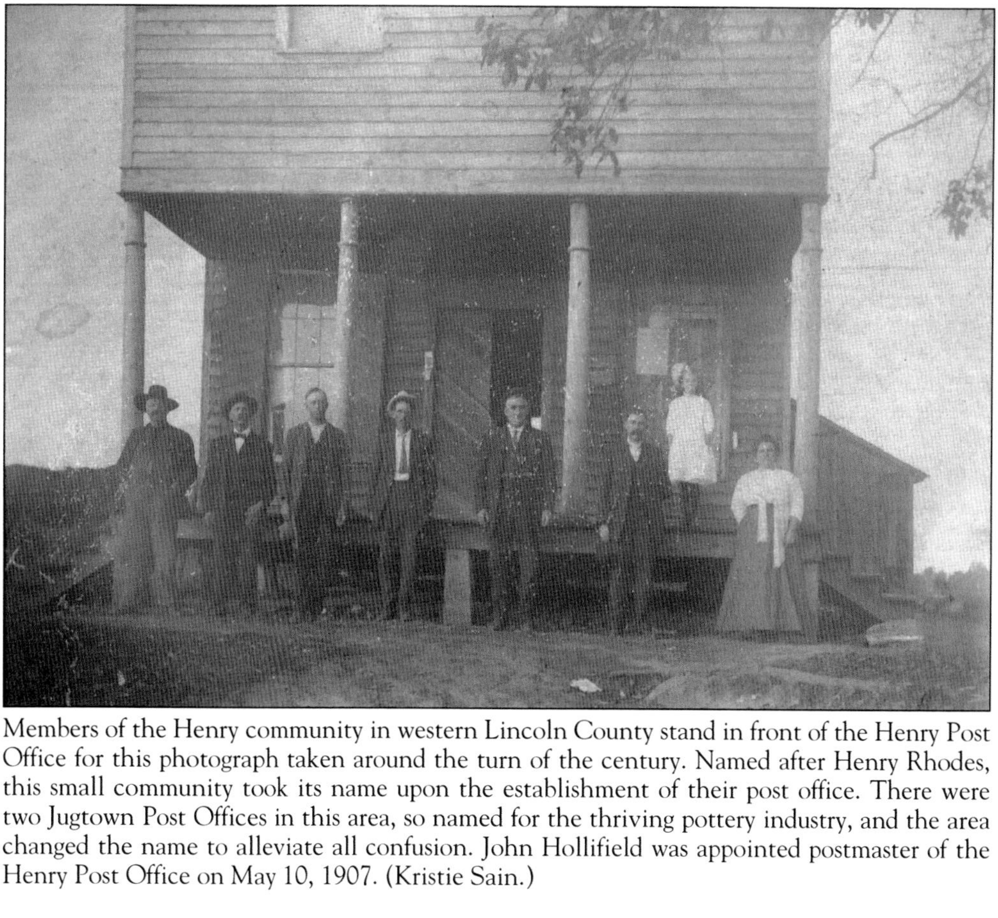

Members of the Henry community in western Lincoln County stand in front of the Henry Post Office for this photograph taken around the turn of the century. Named after Henry Rhodes, this small community took its name upon the establishment of their post office. There were two Jugtown Post Offices in this area, so named for the thriving pottery industry, and the area changed the name to alleviate all confusion. John Hollifield was appointed postmaster of the Henry Post Office on May 10, 1907. (Kristie Sain.)

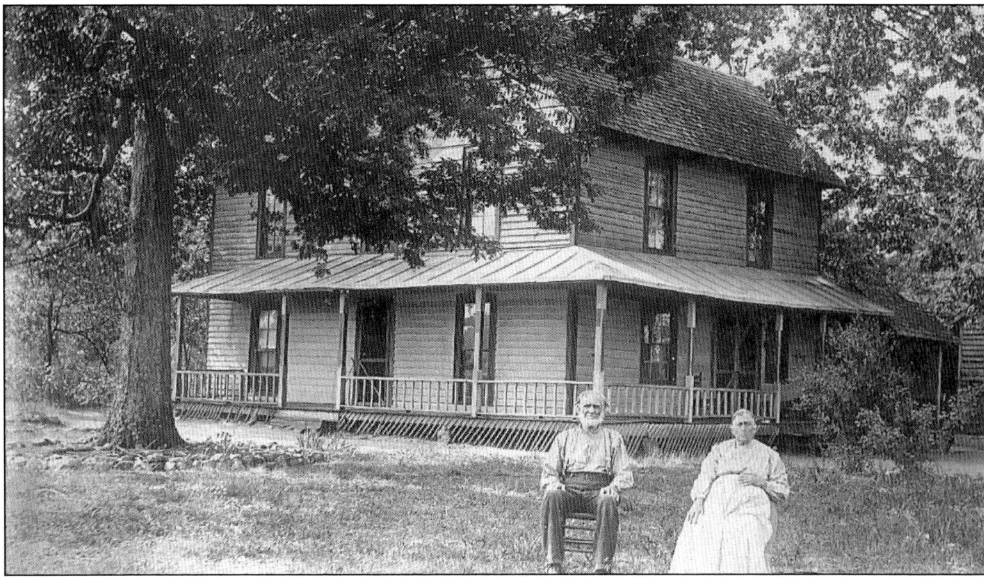

Henry and Mary Willis Cline have come out from under their wrap-around porch to enjoy the day outdoors. Located off of the present Reepsville Road in Lincoln County, this house retains a simple majesty that marks the county's rural and agricultural atmosphere during the turn of the century. Henry and Mary's daughter and son-in-law, Mary Lou and Julius Anthony, came to stay with their aging elders during the final years of their life and inherited the homeplace. The last occupants were Cline and Mary Eliz "Lizzie" Anthony. (David C. Heavner.)

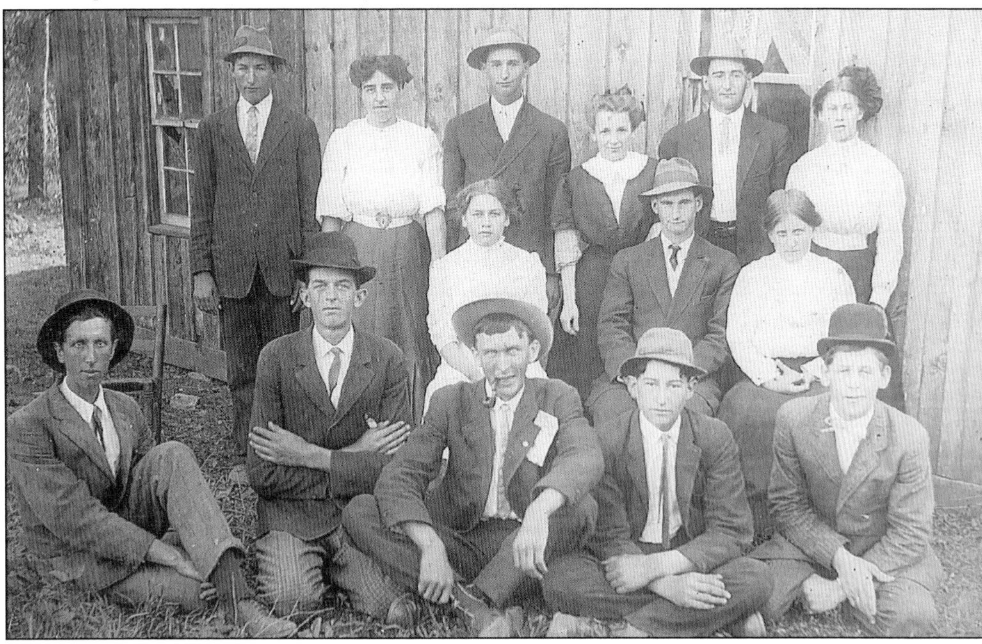

A group of young people from the Henry community in western Lincoln County gets together for this 1910s photograph. They are, from left to right, as follows: (front row) Wesley Houser, John Propst, unidentified (with pipe), Luther Reinhardt, and Ern Leonard; (middle row) Nannie Clyde Leonard, Neil Reinhardt, and Blanche Leonard; (back row) Hugh Reinhardt, Ada Rhoney, Ed Reinhardt, ? James, Ed Leonard, and Minnie Leonard. (Marie Whitener.)

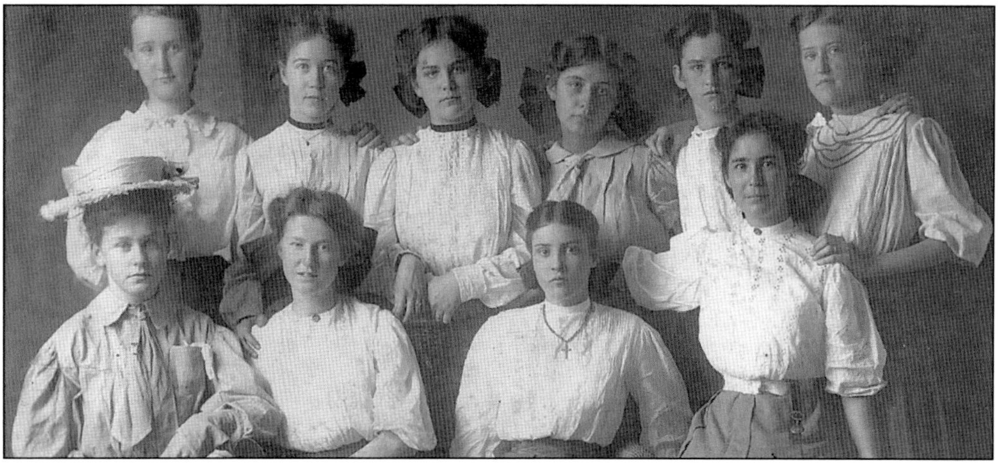

The bond of love and friendship is evident between a group of close-knit friends from Lincolnton in this late-1910s photograph. They are, from left to right, as follows: (front row) Peggy Nixon Costner, unidentified, Beatrice Bagley, and unidentified; (back row) Mattie Camp, Annie McKee Nixon, Mary Dellinger Fair, Rose Hinson Padgett, Stella Dellinger Tilson, and ? McKee. (Bobby Padgett Crowell.)

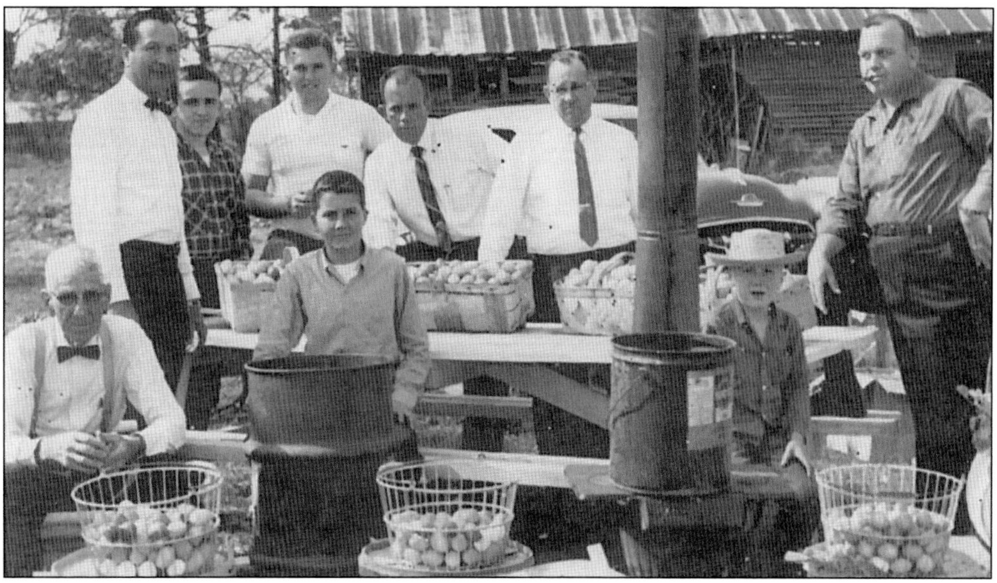

In the Sugar Hill community near the county line of southwestern Lincoln County and northern Cleveland County near Fallston, a tradition thought to be a Germanic origin occurs every Easter morning with several hundred people gathered along the side of the Sugar Hill road. "Egg Fighting" engages contestants in an Easter egg fight. Participants boil and dye between 1 and 20 dozen eggs for the contest. Contestants hold a single egg in their hand, exposing only the tip, and strike other contestants' eggs. A contestant is eliminated when his/her egg is cracked. The winner is determined when there is only one egg left unbroken. After the contest, participants and spectators leave to attend church.

This picture was taken about 1954 at Pete Howell's, on the site where his grandfather, Fox Craft, ran a store across from North Brook High School in western Lincoln County. Pictured are Dr. R.J. Morrison, Ed Chapman, Corky Howell, Bob Carpenter, Michael Quinn, Bob Foster, Grier Beam, David Anthony, and Peter Howell. (Bill Beam)

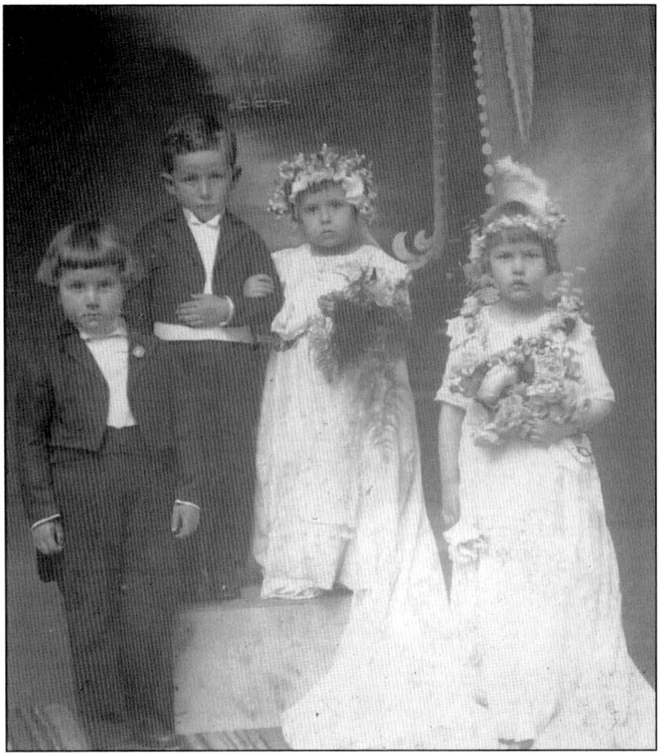

Dressed in wedding attire, the participants of the "Tom Thumb Wedding" stand patiently for this photograph taken around 1915. This traditional ceremony was conducted for children when they reached the age of four or five, usually put on by a kindergarten teacher at a school auditorium. Members of the wedding party are (from left to right) Jack Shuford, Randolph Shives, Elizabeth McLean, and Leila Self. (Jack and Ellen Shuford.)

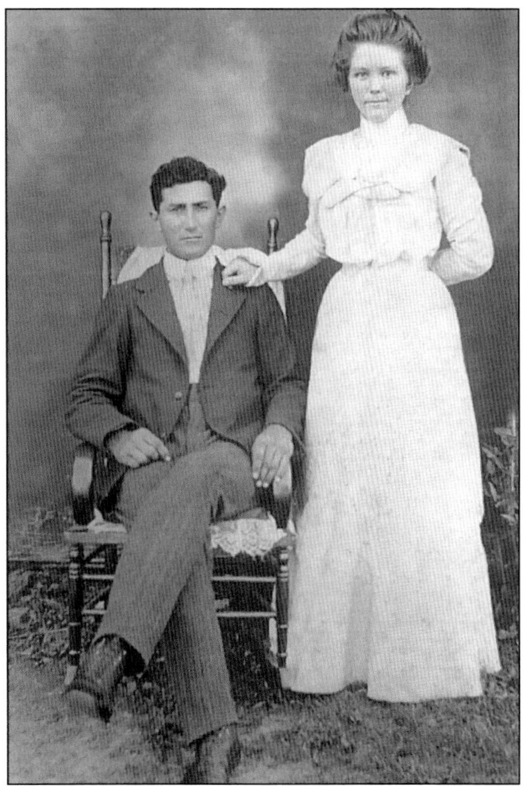

Taken at their home around the turn of the century, this photograph captures the usual visages of John E. (April 9, 1878–January 7, 1935) and Mattie Leona (April 15, 1880–November 16, 1926) Carpenter. The Carpenters lived beside John's father, "Old Tennessee" John Carpenter, and were lifetime members of Bethel Lutheran Church. The children born to this union include Mary Pauline, Raymond Andrew, Lewis Franklin, John E. Jr., Margaret D., Wade Lathan, Richard Everett, and Alvin M. (Sid Carpenter.)

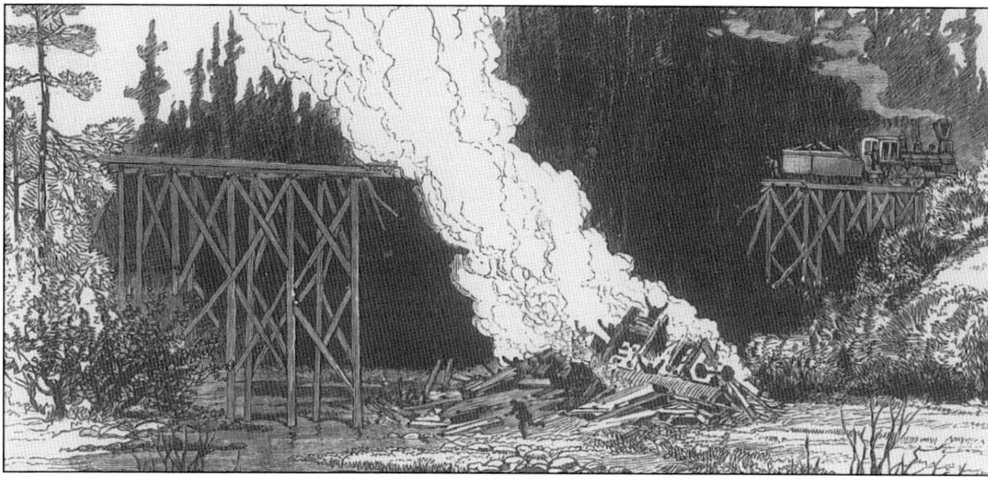

On Wednesday, December 22, 1880, an eastbound passenger train of North Carolina Central Railroad fell through the Indian Creek Trestle, 3 miles from Lincolnton. The trestle, measuring between 50 to 60 feet high and 150 feet long, crossed a deep ravine on Indian Creek. The train, composed of two passenger coaches and three boxcars, slowed as it reached the trestle. As the engine cleared the trestle, engineer John Hall heard a crash from the rear. The coupling connecting the train to the locomotive snapped and the entire train, except the engine, toppled into the ravine. The wrecked cars landed one on top of the other and almost instantly caught fire from the overturned stoves.

Among those killed on the train were the following: Samuel W. Goodson, a Statesville agent; F.W. Smith, a New York City salesman; John F. Bloom, mail agent of Charlotte; William McKenzie, a railroad brakeman of Lincolnton; and James Warlick, a railroad brakeman of Lincolnton. S.H. Griffin, a New York salesman, Richard Limerick, a foreman of a Cleveland County cotton factory, and the train's conductor, Harry Johnson, survived.

The remains of Samuel W. Goodson, F.W. Smith, and John F. Bloom were placed in a single coffin. Following a funeral service at St. Luke's Episcopal Church, the three men were interred in a common grave.

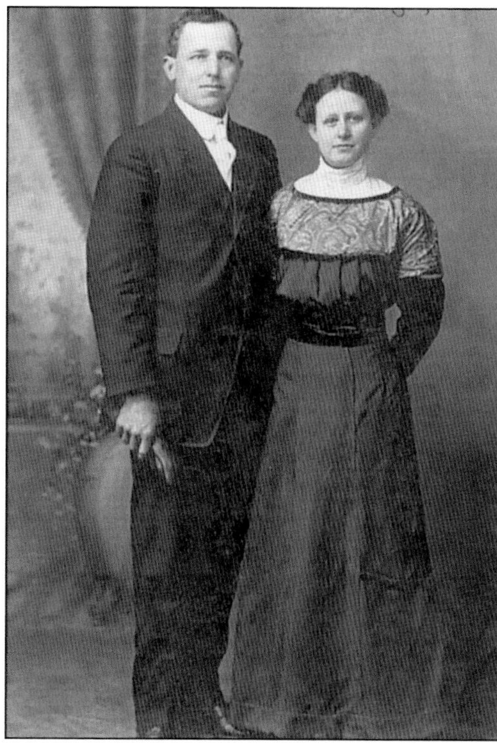

Robert (1870–1945) and Edith (1876–1960) McIntosh stand poised and ready for this photograph taken in January 1911 as a remembrance of their wedding on December 22, 1910. Robert and Edith lived and farmed at their home on Hager's Ferry Road in eastern Lincoln County. They had five children: John Alexander (1914–?), Edgar William (1915–1993), Henry Oliver (1916–1977), Katie Marie (1921–), and Robert Franklin (1924–1978). (Katie McIntosh Sigmon.)

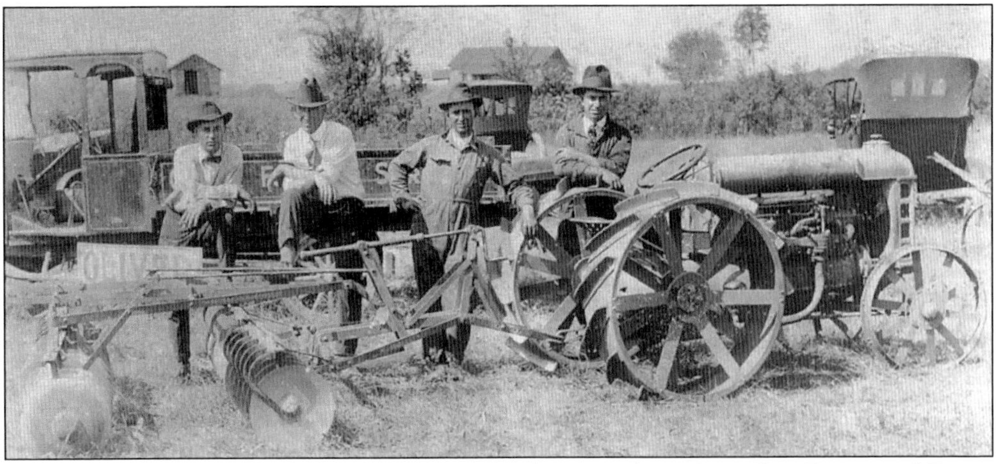

Dealer Guy E. Cline (second from left) and employees Bob Kistler, Clete Beam, and Boyce Sain take a break from the farm equipment demonstration on a Lincoln County farm. Featured in the demonstration is a Fordson tractor (manufactured by the Ford Motor Co.) and a disk manufactured by the Oliver Co. Cline sold both of these products and a wide range of farm equipment, along with Ford and Buick automobiles at his dealership in downtown Lincolnton. (Mike Cline.)

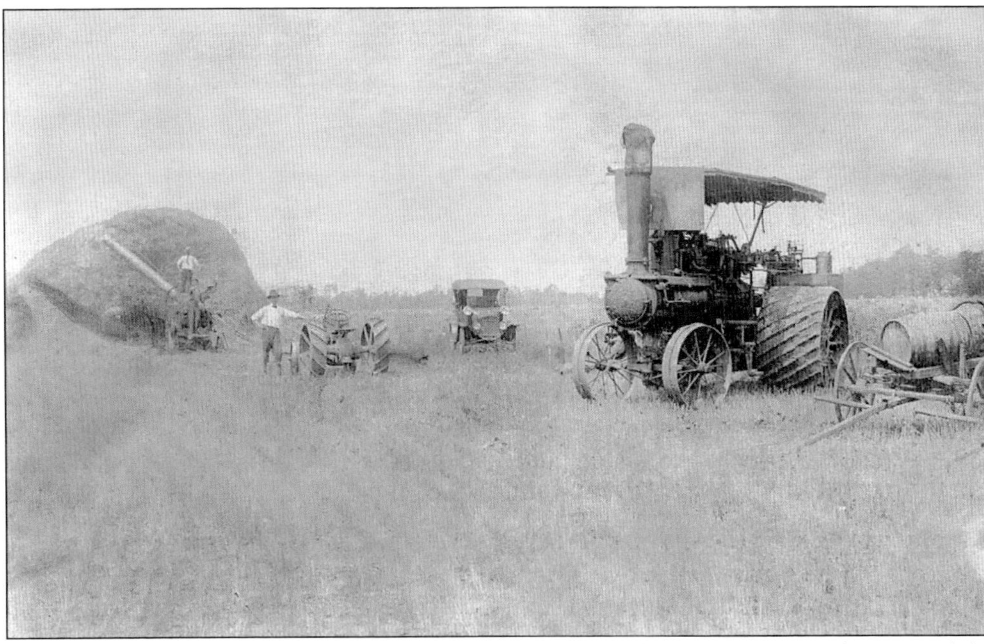

A large steam engine stands monumental against a group of machinery, an early automobile, and two men in this 1920s photograph. The turn of the century brought increased prosperity to North Carolina as well as Lincoln County, with agriculture remaining the primary arena of occupation, dominating the economy. The number of farms increased with a decrease in size, tenants worked a larger portion of the farms, and farmers produced a larger number of staple crops such as cotton and tobacco. Areas such as North Brook, Howard's Creek in western Lincoln County, and Ironton and Catawba Springs in the east experienced accelerated growth in agriculture with increased industrialization brought on by hydroelectric power, mining operations, and extended highways and railroads. (Mike Cline.)

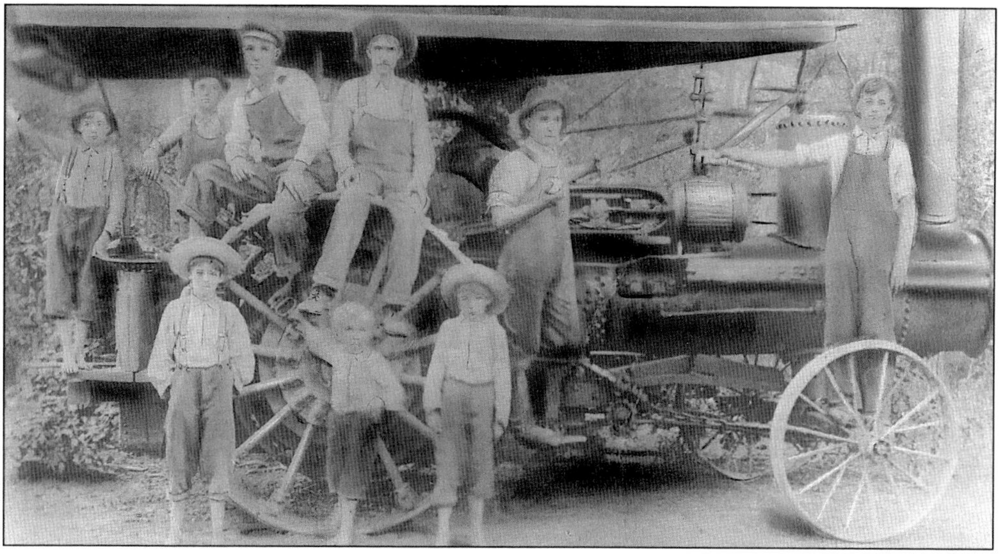

In Lincoln County, steam engines, like the one shown here, provided a significant improvement over horse- and waterpower-run cotton gins, sawmills, and threshing machines. Owned by John Elam Davis of the western Lincoln County community of North Brook, the Davis steam engine, photographed about 1915, holds the weight of men and boys ready to take on another day in the field. Pictured from left to right are (on engine) Jessie Davis, McKinley Davis, Haywood Hull, John Elam Davis, Pinckney Davis, and Carol Mitchem; (in front of the engine) Alvin Martin, Zeno Martin, and Lem Martin. (Guyann Johnson.)

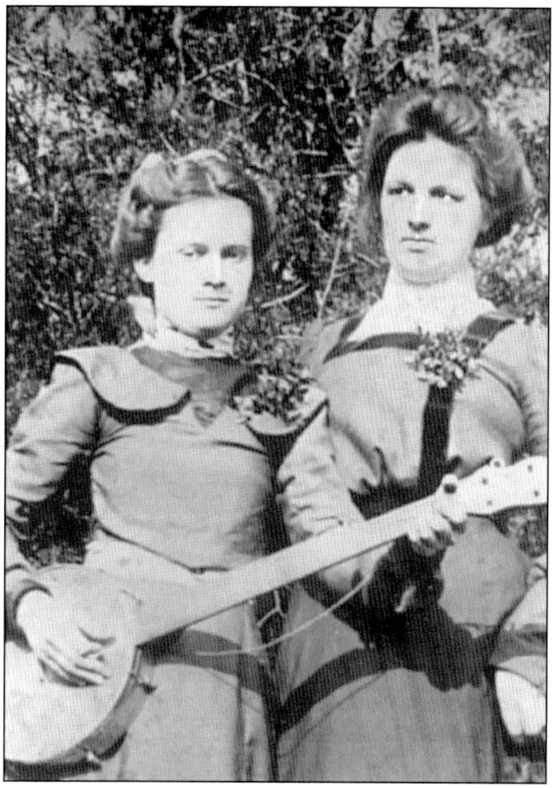

Sarah Yoder, with banjo in hand, stands with her friend and neighbor, Mallie Martin Taylor, in this photograph. (Sarah Yoder.)

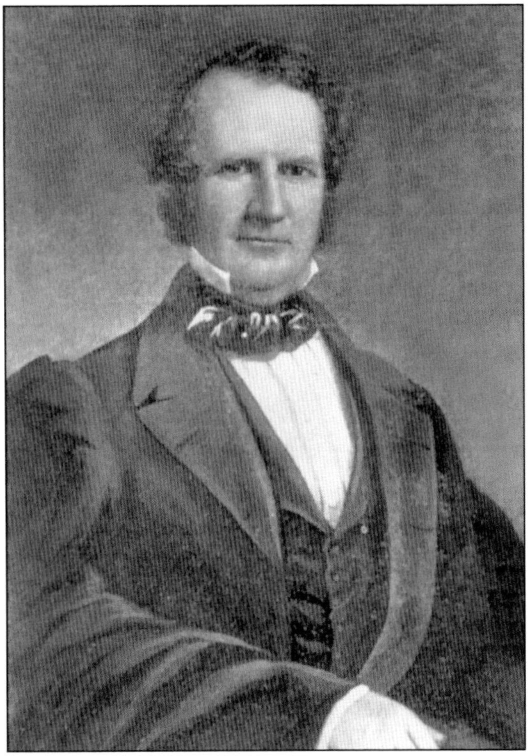

William A. Graham, son of General Joseph and Isabella Graham, was born at the Graham house, "Vesuvius," in eastern Lincoln County on September 4, 1804. He graduated from the University of North Carolina in 1824 and married Susan Washington of New Bern on June 8, 1836. He moved to Hillsborough as a young lawyer, served in the state legislature as a senator (1840–43), as governor of the state from 1845 to 1849, and as Secretary of the Navy in the Fillmore Cabinet from 1850 to 1853. Graham ran as a vice-presidential candidate on the Whig ticket in 1852 with General Winfield Scott. He was also a member of the Confederate States Senate and was one of the trustees for the Peabody Fund from 1867 to 1875. Graham died on August 11, 1875, and is buried in Hillsborough. (North Carolina Department of Archives and History, Raleigh.)

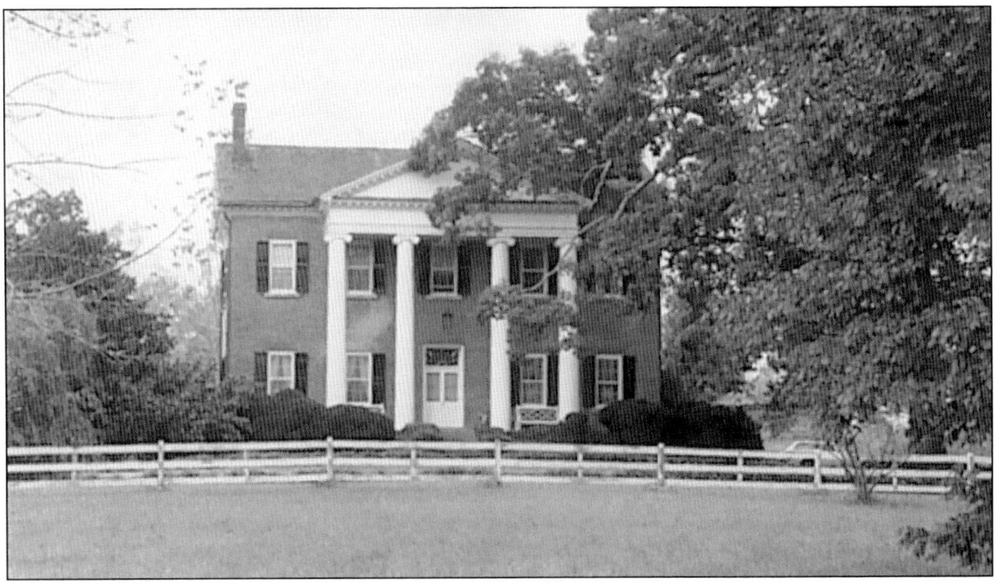

The beauty and elegance of this Federal-era residence stands as a testament to a time of grandeur and mystique that once existed in Lincoln County. Built for Daniel M. Forney about 1817 on the land of his father, General Peter Forney, "Ingleside" is the earliest example of a central-hall plan in the county. Attributed architecturally to Benjamin Latrobe, the house's pedimented portico and 30-foot-tall Ionic brick columns concede an overwhelming brilliance. Ingleside is listed on the National Register of Historic Places. (Lincoln County Museum of History.)

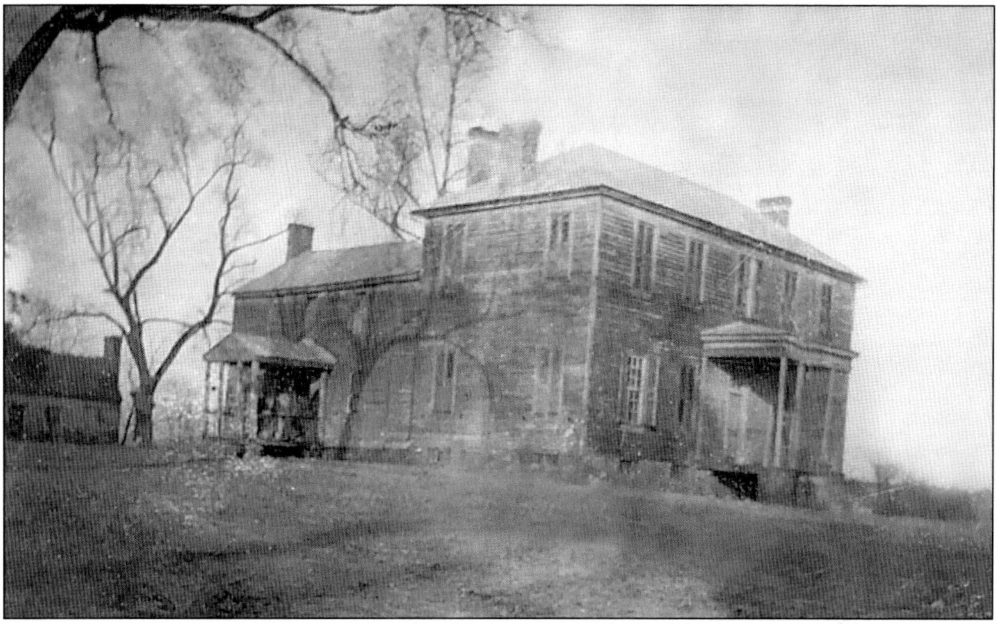

Built in 1811, the Burton Plantation sits atop a bluff in an area now part of Lake Norman known as Governors Island. Robert Burton, attorney and cousin of Governor Hutchins Burton (1824–27), owned the plantation. During the 1850s, Colonel John H. Wheeler, author of *Wheeler's History of North Carolina*, lived at the plantation. (Margaret Camelo.)

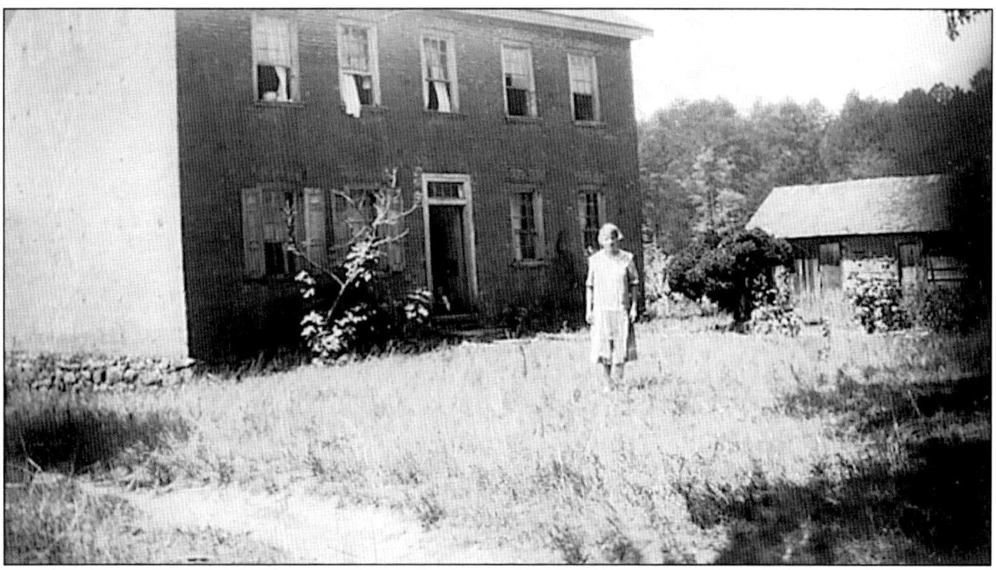

The daughter of David Logan, who purchased this property in 1926, stands on the front lawn of the Andrew Loretz house, Lincoln County's second oldest house, as the date "1793" looms from the east gable end. German minister Reverend Andrew Loretz (1762–1812) came to Lincoln County in 1788 and bought from Phillip Null a 125-acre tract of land. Five years later he erected this magnificent home. Loretz served the Daniels Lutheran and Reformed Churches, just to the north, until the time of his death. (Lincoln County Museum of History.)

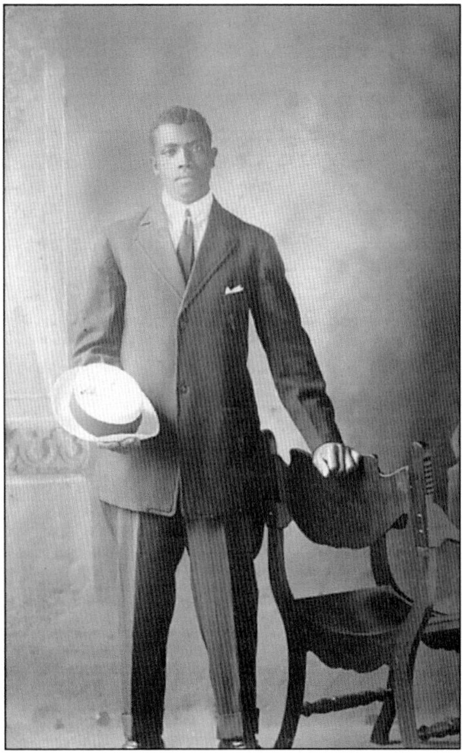

Mr. Nathan Foster, clothed in the high fashion attire of the time, takes off his hat for a photograph in the early 1900s. Foster, son of George and Amelia Foster, was born in Lincoln County and moved to Pinehurst in Moore County. Remembered as a civic-minded and religious gentleman, Foster promoted African Americans' attempts at building businesses and homes. He was active in establishing the Christ Memorial Missionary Baptist Church in Jackson Hamlet community in Pinehurst, and worked at the General Office Building in Pinehurst during the 1940s and 1950s. (Edith Lomax.)

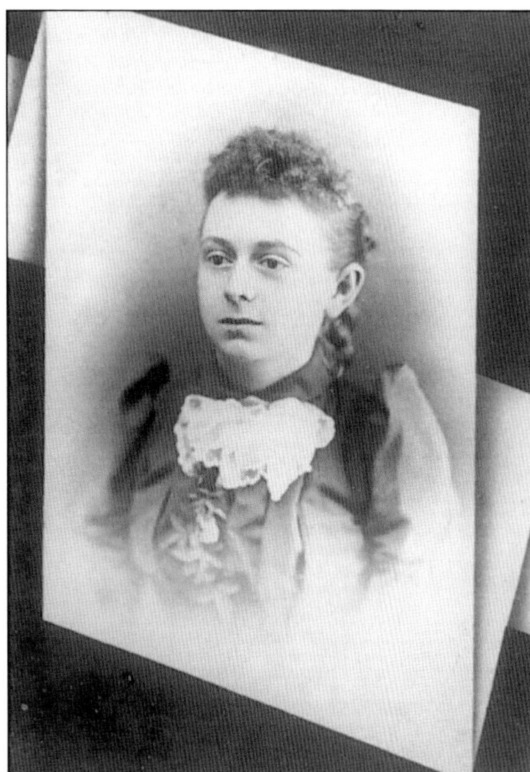

Carrie L. McLean, shown here in 1892 as a young woman of 18, was the daughter of James L. and Margaret Ann Smith McLean, and the sister of J.T. McLean Sr., stonecutter. Carrie graduated from Chowan College, Murfreesboro, North Carolina, taught school for one year, and went to Charlotte in 1894. While in Charlotte, she held a position in a business office for many years and was admitted to the North Carolina Bar in 1918. Some of McLean's further accomplishments include serving as a representative from Mecklenburg County in the legislature in 1927; public administrator for Mecklenburg County; and election to the North Carolina General Assembly in the 1930s. (Jack and Ellen Shuford.)

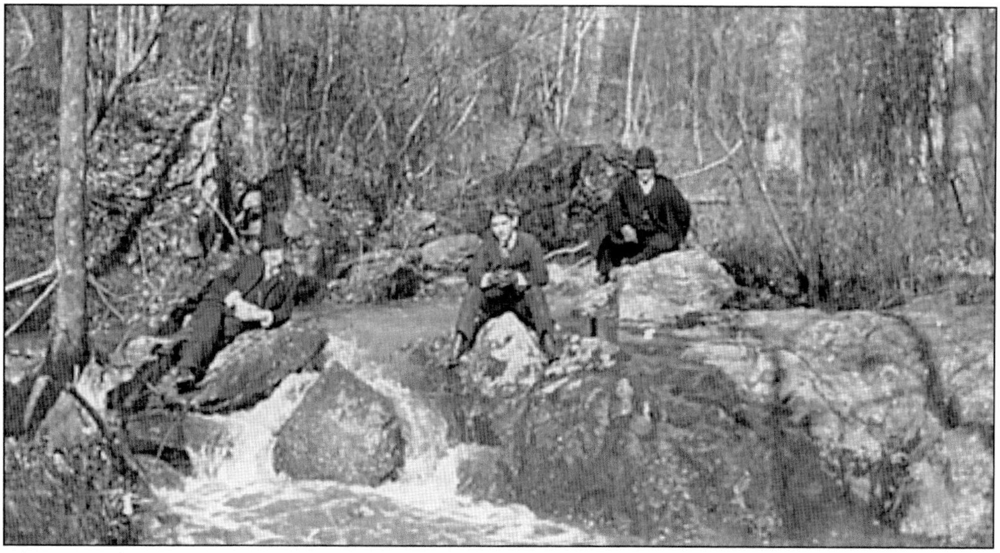

Three gentlemen dressed in their causal suits sit upon the rocks at McDaniels Springs enjoying an afternoon at a small waterfall along the stream in this turn-of-the-century photograph. Located near the site of the Schenck-Warlick Mill, built in 1813, the healing waters of the springs cured many ailments for both locals and visitors from other areas of North Carolina traveling to Lincolnton for a summer visit. While lodging at one of the area hotels or boarding houses, the visitors would take trips down to the spring to have a drink of the "miracle water." (Sue Ramseur.)

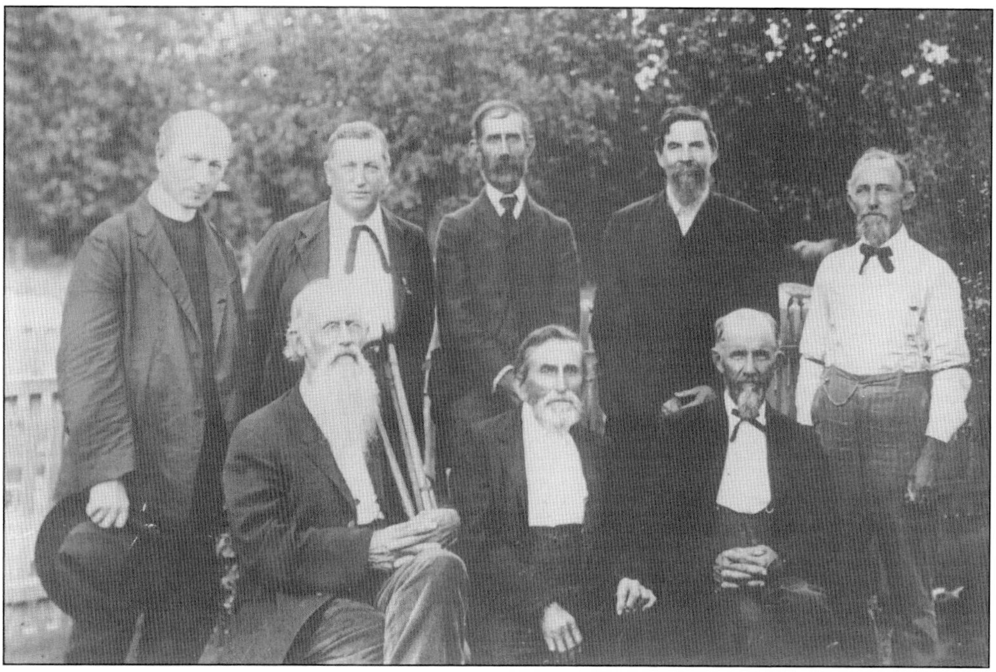

A group of gentlemen gather for this photograph; they are, from left to right, as follows: (front row) John Warlick, Titus Rhodes, and David Warlick; (back row) Reverend Heller, John Cline, Jacob Warlick, Jacob Crooks, and Billy Carpenter. (Lincoln County Museum of History.)

Family Name Index